D1572596

AGAINST THE ODDS

The Life of

GEORGE ALBERT SMITH

OTHER BOOKS, AUDIO BOOKS, AND TALKS ON TAPE

BY MARY JANE WOODGER

Women of Character

Doctrine and Covenants: A Pattern for Revelation

Women of Faith in the New Testament

For Single Saints

Of These Emblems (Essay)

He Hears You

D&C: Pattern for Revelation

David O. McKay: Beloved Prophet

Emma

AGAINST THE ODDS

The Life of

GEORGE ALBERT SMITH

MARY JANE WOODGER

Covenant Communications, Inc.

Cover image George Albert Smith Portrait by Lee Greene Richards © by Intellectual Reserve, Inc.
Courtesy of the Church History Museum.

Published by Covenant Communications, Inc.
American Fork, Utah

Printed in the United States of America
First Printing: October 2011

17 16 15 14 13 12 11 10 9 8 7 6 5 4 3 2 1

ISBN-13: 978-1-59811-809-4

For CSD,
whose love overcomes any odds.

ACKNOWLEDGMENTS

Any published book is the result of a collaboration of effort. I express heartfelt appreciation to Richard Bennett and the Religious Studies Center at Brigham Young University for research support. I wish to give thanks to the staff members of the University of Utah J. Willard Marriott Library Manuscripts Division, who are under the excellent supervision of Walter Jones, for their help. Kristin M. Giacoletto was especially helpful with photographs. I express gratitude for the meticulous work Glen R. Stubbs did on his 1974 dissertation for Brigham Young University, "A Biography of George Albert Smith, 1870 to 1951." This dissertation provided direction and guidance in my research of the George A. Smith Papers. I would also like to thank the staff at the LDS Church Archives for their service.

I am also grateful to my dear friends Nancy Ann Nielsen and Kristine Parker, who have included this project in their prayers and whose insights provided inspired direction in producing this book. I am thankful for several student assistants who have been involved in the large task of selecting, typing, and editing material included in this manuscript in varying degrees. Most especially, I express gratitude to my research assistants Melissa Caldwell, Amy Brennan, Eric Perkins, Teodora Hristova, Carolina Tilotson, Jennifer Porter, Emily Jane Rule, and Holly Baker, who were surely some of the most cheerful, dependable, and intelligent of assistants.

PREFACE

The epitaph of George Albert Smith states, "He understood and disseminated the teachings of Christ and was uncommonly successful in putting them into practice."[1] Though President Smith's generation knew, revered, and respected his life and teachings, he is relatively unknown among contemporary Latter-day Saints. The only George Albert Smith biography prior to this one—*George Albert Smith: Kind and Caring Christian, Prophet of God,* by Francis M. Gibbons—was published almost two decades ago and is now out of print. *Builders of the Kingdom,* by Merlo J. Pusey, published in 1981, contains biographical accounts of three men, including President George Albert Smith, and is also out of print.

This volume does not seek to replace these earlier works but to provide an outline of those incidents in the prophet's life that endeared him to the Church membership during his service. This is neither a history of his administration nor a fully chronological treatise of his life; rather, it is a homespun collection of the stories for which his life became known. It attempts to catch glimpses of his private life and, in so doing, make George Albert Smith a more personable figure. My hope is that this biography might be successful in portraying his private life within the framework of his public image so that the reader might come away as endeared to President Smith as I have become and be able to see his life in a harmonious, logical portrayal. This story is largely told in his own words, as found in his correspondence and journals from the University of Utah J. Willard Marriott Library's

1 George Albert Smith, *The Teachings of George Albert Smith: Eighth President of The Church of Jesus Christ of Latter-day Saints* (Salt Lake City, UT: Bookcraft, 1996), xv (hereafter cited as *Teachings*).

George A. Smith Papers. In addition, I have used the work of Francis M. Gibbons extensively. As a secretary to the First Presidency and General Authorities, he had access to materials that gave added insight into the life of this prophet. I also conducted interviews with descendants and friends of George Albert Smith, which gave added depth to an understanding of George Albert Smith's life.

In my research, I have found that the majority of George Albert Smith's life revolved around his relationship with a girl he met when he was just ten years old. That girl—Lucy Emily Woodruff, who later became his wife—is an integral ingredient in viewing the life of George Albert Smith. Therefore, readers will find that a large portion of this volume contains the recurring thread of love between Lucy Woodruff and George Albert Smith.

As I began to write this biography, I knew from the enormous amount of data I had collected that I could write several volumes about this man's life and still never fully tell his story. My greatest task was to decide what to include and what to omit. Readers of this finished work may be disappointed that I did not devote more attention to matters they would have liked to have seen more fully discussed. This portrait may be frustrating to those who would have liked a more critical treatise, but the complete story of George Albert Smith cannot possibly be told in these few pages, where warm and friendly thoughts take precedence. It is my hope that President Smith's well-known ability to love others will flow through these pages and into the hearts of readers.

TABLE OF CONTENTS

A Brief Timeline of the Life of President George Albert Smith

April 4, 1870	Born in Salt Lake City, Utah, to John Henry and Sarah Farr Smith.
June 6, 1878	Baptized in City Creek by James Moyle.
1878–1882	Attended common schools in Salt Lake City.
1882–1883	Attended Brigham Young Academy.
1883–1887	Worked for Grant–Odell Co. and ZCMI clothing factory.
1887–1888	Attended University of Utah.
1888–1891	Worked as a salesman for ZCMI.
1891	Served mission to Southern Utah in interest of the Young Men's Mutual Improvement Association.
May 25, 1892	Married Lucy Emily Woodruff.
1892–1894	Served couples mission in Southern States Mission.
1894–1898	Worked for ZCMI.
January 5, 1898	Appointed receiver of the US Land Office and Special Disbursing Agent for Utah; served two terms.
October 6, 1903	Sustained a member of the Quorum of the Twelve Apostles.
1916	Elected president of International Irrigation Congress.
1917	Elected president of International Dry Farm Congress.
1918	Elected president of International Farm Congress.
January 27, 1919	Called to preside over the European Mission.
1921	Returned to Salt Lake City.
1921	Appointed superintendent of the YMMIA.
1922	Elected vice-president of The National Society of the Sons of the American Revolution (SAR).
1930	Elected president of Utah Pioneer Trails and Landmarks Association.
1931	Elected member of the National Executive Board of the Boy Scouts of America.
1932	Received Silver Beaver Award from the Great Salt Lake Council of the Boy Scouts of America.

1934	Received Silver Buffalo Award from the National Council of the Boy Scouts of America.
1938	Made an extensive tour of the missions of the Church in the South Pacific.
July 1, 1943	Set apart as President of the Quorum of the Twelve Apostles.
May 21, 1945	Sustained as President of The Church of Jesus Christ of Latter-day Saints.
April 4, 1951	Passed away in Salt Lake City, Utah.

Adapted from George Albert Smith, *Sharing the Gospel with Others,* comp. Preston Nibley (Salt Lake City, UT: Deseret News Press, 1948).

Chapter 1
HUMILITY AND KINDNESS

George had attended other solemn assemblies in the Tabernacle on Temple Square, the last one having taken place at the 1919 general conference when Heber J. Grant had been sustained as prophet. What must George Albert have been feeling as he heard President J. Reuben Clark pronounce that the voting was unanimous in sustaining *him* as the eighth President of The Church of Jesus Christ of Latter-day Saints? Although he had been acting as President of the Quorum of the Twelve Apostles for two years, many new responsibilities and challenges would now be added to his role. Shortly before President Heber J. Grant died on May 13, 1945, George had gone to the Grant home to give the prophet a blessing before leaving for Chicago to organize a new stake. Nine days later, he had been informed that President Grant had passed away. The baton of leadership had been passed to him.[2]

Humbled by the turn of events, President Smith thanked conference-goers for their support, and after they sang "We Thank Thee, O God, for a Prophet," he reassured them that they had "extended these courtesies" not because of the man, "but because he represented the Lord as his humble servant."[3] The love and support of his fellow members of the Quorum of the Twelve were evidenced in the remarks of Richard L. Evans on that day: "I should like to echo also some of the things that have already been said concerning

2 George Albert Smith, Journal, 15 May 1945; in George A. Smith Family Papers, box 100, ms 46, 415; Western Americana Collection, Marriott Library Special Collections, University of Utah, Salt Lake City, UT (hereafter cited as George A. Smith Papers).

3 George Albert Smith, Conference Report (hereafter cited as CR), Oct. 1945, 23.

President George Albert Smith, borne out in my own experience as to his kindly consideration for all his brethren and all his fellow men. He is considerate and loving and kindly under all circumstances, and on all occasions in my experience."[4]

Perhaps his humility caused George to reflect on the memories of the past when fellow ward members who had known him as a boy described him as "the terror to the 17th ward." One former playmate asserted that had George remained a small boy, the Seventeenth Ward "would have been depopulated, the houses leveled, and the animals scattered far and near." He had been described as a "horrid boy" whom "poor frightened children needed protection from." It was said that back then, "any one of the girls would run blocks rather than meet him alone." And his school teacher "would breathe a sigh of relief if George were absent from school."[5]

Even family members were not immune to his bullying. When he was eleven years old, he became the proud owner of a banjo, and he "beat members of the household over their heads with the much prized instrument." It seemed that when George left the neighborhood for the first time, there was a general feeling of celebration: "Mothers no longer felt anxious when their infants were out for an airing, [and] the school children ceased to act as though they were afflicted . . . with fear." How many Latter-day Saints would be surprised to know that the man they would soon sustain as a prophet, seer, and revelator had once been "the worst boy [the townsfolk] ever knew"?[6] What were the odds that anyone who knew him while he was growing up would dub him as prophet material?

But here he was, the prophet of the Church, sustained at the 116th Semiannual General Conference at a time when world conditions were tenuous at best. President Heber J. Grant had passed away before World War II ended in August with the dropping of the atomic bomb, and this was the first general conference to be held since the fighting had stopped. There was much healing that needed to take place. President Smith was especially concerned about those who had no place

4 Richard L. Evans, CR, Oct. 1945, 43.

5 A Member of the Y.L.M.I.A., "A Brief Biography Written for the Present Occasion," George A. Smith Papers, box 151, fld 6, 1–7.

6 Ibid.

to stay after the war. During the priesthood session, he asked those who were less fortunate to raise their hands. He then requested that those with an extra bed take the less fortunate home so the homeless wouldn't "have to sit around the lobby of some hotel." He did "not want anybody to be left out."[7]

Perhaps the loss of his dear wife, Lucy Emily Woodruff, on November 5, 1937, helped George to further understand the plight of those who were lonely and in need. George had known Lucy from childhood. He always carried the gold locket she'd given him on their wedding day. In the locket, Lucy had included two photos cut to fit the tiny oval frames—one of the ten-year-old Lucy he had first met, her long braids streaming down her back, and the other of his bride as she had looked on their wedding day. He refused to ever be without this piece of jewelry, whether he was formally dressed to meet dignitaries, relaxing at home, or working outdoors. The locket, worn on his watch chain, was always close at hand.[8]

Shortly after being sustained, George spoke of his reverence for the women of the Church and of how important it was for the brethren to treat them well. In addressing the men of the Church, he said, "You are fortunate men if you have been blessed with a good wife, a daughter of God, to stand by your side." He continued to speak to each man in the audience about his relationship with his wife and declared, "God loves her just as much as he loves you," and "if you would have his blessings, you will treat her with love and kindness and tenderness and helpfulness." He said that if the priesthood holders would remember these things, each woman in the Church would "be able to carry on under the responsibilities that come to her to bring children into the world and nurture and care for them and teach them the plan of life and salvation." He concluded by pleading with the priesthood brethren to "let [their] homes be the abiding place[s] of love" and to realize that women "make their homes a heaven, when sometimes without them, the homes would be anything but heaven."[9]

---

7 George Albert Smith, CR, Oct. 1945, 94.

8 Martha Ray June Stewart Hatch (Socorro, NM), Phone Interview by Mary Jane Woodger, 16 Aug. 2007, transcription in possession of Mary Jane Woodger; and Edith Smith Elliott, Interview by Glen R. Stubbs, 6 Oct. 1973, cited in Glen R. Stubbs, "A Biography of George Albert Smith, 1870 to 1951," Ph.D. diss. (Provo, UT: Brigham Young University, 1974), 49 (hereafter cited as Stubbs).

9 George Albert Smith, CR, Oct. 1945, 23.

George Albert Smith had taken his first breath in "a little adobe house" just three hundred yards from the spot where he now sat.[10] Temple Square and the adjoining neighborhoods had served as the backdrop to every important event of his life. He had met every prophet who had filled the chair in which he now sat, starting with Brigham Young. When President Clark announced him as the next speaker, President Smith rose, walked to the pulpit, and began his first official address as President of The Church of Jesus Christ of Latter-day Saints:

> I wonder if anyone else here feels as weak and humble as the man who stands before you. I have been coming to this house since my infancy. I have seen all the Presidents of the Church since that time sustained by the congregation here, as their names have been presented from this stand. I have seen the Church continue to grow in numbers, and have realized throughout all my years that the Church of Jesus Christ is what its name implies.[11]

10 George Albert Smith, CR, Oct. 1946, 149–150.

11 George Albert Smith, CR, Oct. 1945, 18.

Chapter 2
BOYHOOD

George's lessons in kindness began when he was but a boy. Dressed in his Sunday finest, five-year-old George Albert crossed the street near his home, the street he usually crossed in his bare feet, feeling between his toes the three to four inches of dust that settled on the street every day.[12] His mother had dressed him for an important errand—to call on Brigham Young, then President of the Church, at his office on Temple Square.

But it was not because Brigham Young was President of the Church or even governor of the territory that George was sent to ask a favor of him on this particular day. Instead, George was going to see Brigham Young in his role as president of the Utah Central Railroad. Mother had called George in and asked him to hand-deliver a letter she had written to President Young requesting railroad passes to Ogden so the family could visit George's maternal grandfather. Lorin Farr—or "Grandpa Apples," as George called him—was also the mayor of Ogden and president of the Weber Stake. George called Grandpa Farr "Grandpa Apples" because of George's fondness for the fruit his grandpa grew in his orchard.[13]

George loved visiting Grandpa Apples so much that he once tried to go to Ogden on his own to see his beloved grandfather. On that day, George conned his friend Wilby Dougall into walking with him nearly half a mile to the railroad station. He and Wilby then

---

12 George Albert Smith, Life Sketch, unpublished manuscript, George A. Smith Papers, box 100, fld 2; and Stubbs, 11.

13 Merlo J. Pusey, *Builders of the Kingdom: George A. Smith, John Henry Smith, George Albert Smith* (Provo, UT: Brigham Young University Press, 1981), 83 (hereafter cited as Pusey).

climbed aboard a train on its way to Ogden. Luckily, the conductor spotted them and stopped the train before it was out of the station yard. He sent the two boys home, where they arrived to find their mothers frantically searching for them. It was then that George's mother promised him he could go visit Grandpa Apples some other day if President Young would give them the passes. And so, with the note tucked in his pocket, George Albert walked across the street to President Young's office.[14]

George was acquainted with President Young because his Grandfather Smith—or "Grandpa Nuts," as George liked to call him because of the pine nuts he brought home from his visits to the Native Americans—was President Young's Counselor in the First Presidency. George A. Smith—after whom George was named—was a familiar person in George's life because he lived next door.[15] One lesson Grandpa Nuts repeatedly taught young George was that "there is a well-defined line between the Lord's territory and the devil's. If you will stay on the Lord's side, the adversary cannot come there to tempt you. But if you cross onto the devil's side, you are on his territory, and you are in his power, and he will work on you to get you just as far from that line as he possibly can."[16] That lesson would become part of George Albert's own teachings later in life.

The elder George Albert Smith was born June 16, 1817, in Potsdam, New York. He was fifteen years old when he was baptized a member of The Church of Jesus Christ of Latter-day Saints in September 1832. The next year, he moved with his parents to Kirtland, Ohio, where he met his first cousin, Joseph Smith Jr., for the first time. At the age of twenty-one, George A. became the youngest person in the history of the Church to be ordained a member of the Quorum of the Twelve Apostles.[17]

After crossing the plains to reach the Salt Lake Valley, George Albert Smith led a group of immigrants to the southern part of the Territory of Utah to what was to become a settlement named after him—St.

---

14 Ibid.

15 Ibid.

16 George Albert Smith, CR, Sept.–Oct. 1949, 5–6.

17 "Fourth Generation: Leader's Ancestors Among Authorities," *Deseret News*, April 5, 1951, vol. 335, no. 5, 2.

George—and he became a favorite among the Native Americans.[18] Grandson and grandfather shared a particularly close relationship that began when, as a newborn baby, the future prophet was given his name and a blessing by his namesake.[19]

As George walked up to the gate in front of President Young's office, the watchman at the gate questioned George's motives for wanting to see the President of the Church. The gatekeeper didn't think President Young had time for the five-year-old. But just then, President Young happened to walk by. He invited George into the office, took him on his knee, put his arm around him, and asked, "What do you want of President Young?"[20]

George handed him the note and said, "My mother told me to give this to you." President Young opened the handwritten note and read it. In his biography of George Albert Smith, Pusey describes Brigham Young's reaction: "Eager to help the family of a missionary, Brigham Young rang a bell on his desk and instructed his secretary to provide the passes." President Young then asked George how he and his family were getting along since their father had been called on a mission to Europe. No one could have been kinder than President Young as he talked to the young boy, calling George's father and mother "wonderful" and admonishing George to always follow the example of his parents.[21] Leaving the office, George held passes to travel to Ogden on the Utah Central Railroad.

Walking back across West Temple Street was no problem for young George, for in those days Salt Lake City was still a village with no pavement on either the streets or sidewalks. Most of the time, people walked wherever they needed to go, but when the distance was too far, horses, mules, or oxen supplied the means of transportation. The growing town did not have electricity, either, and during George Albert's childhood, "tallow candles and kerosene lamps illuminated the houses . . . gas jets surmounting lamp posts, three or four to the block, furnished light for the pedestrian at night . . . [and] logs from

---

18 Pusey, 83.

19 Francis M. Gibbons, *George Albert Smith: Kind and Caring Christian, Prophet of God* (Salt Lake City, UT: Deseret Book, 1990), 1 (hereafter cited as Gibbons).

20 Arthur R. Bassett, "George Albert Smith: On Reaching Out to Others," *New Era*, Jan. 1972, 50 (hereafter cited as Bassett).

21 Pusey, 203–204.

the mountains furnished fuel for the fireplace and stove."[22] To add beauty to the simple living conditions, shade and fruit trees had been planted wherever possible in the twenty years since the valley had been settled.

Life was simple for the Smiths. In the 1870s, the Smiths retrieved their water from a ditch or gutter that ran along the edge of the sidewalk. Though City Creek was close to the Smiths' house, everyone in town depended on irrigation water during George's childhood. Most people had little gardens behind their houses, and neighbors—including the Smiths—took turns irrigating starting at three o' clock in the morning. George thought that the water from the ditch tasted even better than that from City Creek.[23]

George also loved to play in the gutter by the side of his house. Before George's father, Henry Smith, left on his mission, he told George, "I have never seen a child of God so deep in the gutter that I have not had the impulse to stoop down and lift him up and put him on his feet and start him again."[24] John Henry often did just that with his little son, lifting George up out of the gutter and sending him on his way. But George respected his father, and years later George would say of his upbringing that he "never knew anything wrong to happen in [his] father's home. There were always peace, happiness, and love; they observed the rules of the Church. . . . [He grew up] in one of the best moral and spiritual environments [to be] found."[25]

Later, George would ride one of the first bicycles ever to come to Salt Lake City and talk on one of the first telephones.[26] But since these were days before bicycles, telephones, streetcars, automobiles, or electric lights, George had no fear of being run over as he walked across West Temple that day.[27] Heading home, George entered a yard that was much like the others in the city. Brigham Young had divided

22 George Albert Smith, *Sharing the Gospel with Others*, comp. Preston Nibley (Salt Lake City, UT: Desert News Press, 1948), 155 (hereafter cited as *Sharing the Gospel*).

23 *Sharing the Gospel*, 155.

24 George Albert Smith, "President Smith's Leadership Address," *Church News*, *Deseret News*, 16 Feb. 1946, vol. 4, no. 8, 6.

25 George Albert Smith, CR, Oct. 1945, 173.

26 *Sharing the Gospel*, 40.

27 *Sharing the Gospel*, 155; and George Albert Smith, CR, Oct. 1946, 149–150.

the lots for homes, gardens, and orchards into ten-acre squares. Small homes were the general rule.

In the Smith home, George Albert was the second son of John Henry Smith and Sarah Farr Smith. John Henry had grown up in Provo, Utah, after crossing the plains when he was just a year old. He later met Sarah Farr, who had migrated with her family from Vermont, and the two were married in October 1866, when Sarah was just seventeen years old. In 1868, the couple's first son, John Henry Jr., died when he was only about seven months old.[28] John Henry was serving as the second counselor in the Fourth Ward bishopric in Salt Lake City and was keeping accounts for the Utah Central Railroad's freight department when his second son, George Albert, was born.[29]

Eventually, John Henry and Sarah would become the parents of eleven children—eight sons and three daughters, three of whom died in childhood. John Henry Smith later married Josephine Groesbeck as a plural wife, and their union resulted in more brothers and sisters for George. John Henry Smith would later become an Apostle and eventually a Counselor in the First Presidency to Joseph F. Smith.[30]

Half a block away from the Smith home, Apostle Wilford Woodruff lived at 23 North West Temple Street. The homes of President Brigham Young were two blocks east, and John Henry's second wife, Josephine Groesbeck, lived only two blocks north. George Albert also lived close to the homes of other Church leaders and family members, "practically all of which were graced with an abundance of growing, exuberant children."[31] Thus, George grew up in a home filled not only with the love of immediate family members but also with the influence of extended family.

One of George's favorite playmates was his second cousin Richard R. Lyman. As young boys, Richard and George liked to compete. Although George was always somewhat physically frail, his boldness made him a worthy opponent for Richard. There were times, however, when such courage got George into trouble. For instance,

28 George Albert Smith, unpublished talk, George A. Smith Papers, box 124, scrapbook 1, 11–12.

29 Pusey, 127–129.

30 Gibbons, 1, 3.

31 Gibbons, 3.

one day George decided he wanted to make his own lantern. He "crawled into the hayloft of the barn with a bucket, a candle, and a match. . . . Just as he struck the match, a hand reached up over the hay and grasped the young George Albert firmly and dragged him down from the haymow, which had only recently been filled."[32] The Smith's hired hand had seen and followed George to the haymow and had prevented George from accidentally setting the hay on fire.

George also enjoyed sledding in the streets during the cold season. It seemed "the steeper the hills and the smoother the ice that covered them, the greater the thrill . . . George got when coasting on his sled." On one particular occasion when George and Richard were out sledding, George was a little too daring. Coasting down a hill, he slammed headfirst into an iron lamppost, an accident that produced a long gash on the side of his forehead.[33] George's mother nursed his head, but the scar remained with him for the rest of his life.

George's mother, Sarah Farr, was ever a source of comfort and a shining example for the young boy. Before becoming a mother, Sarah was told in her patriarchal blessing that none in Israel would excel her posterity.[34] Sarah made sure she taught her young children the ways of the Lord, and from his mother George learned that he could pray to his Heavenly Father. When George was a toddler, Sarah took him by the hand and led him up the stairs and into the bedroom where his crib was. Sitting by his crib, Sarah knelt down, took both of George's little hands in hers, and taught him how to pray. After telling George that the Lord was his Father, Sarah had him recite these words:

> Now I lay me down to sleep
> I pray the Lord my soul to keep.
> If I should die before I wake,
> I pray the Lord my soul to take.[35]

---

32 Marba Josephson, "Humor—A Way of Life," *Improvement Era*, LIII, April 1950, 274.

33 Richard R. Lyman, "President George Albert Smith," *The Pioneer*, July 1951, 2-B.

34 Gibbons, 2.

35 George Albert Smith, "Mexican Mission Conference," holograph, 25 May 1946, George A. Smith Papers, box 100, 278.

Later, George's bed was moved from the bedroom to another small room. One night as the wind howled and the house swayed, George jumped into his bed only to remember that he had not yet prayed. Frightened, he got out of bed and asked the Lord to take care of him. When he got back into bed, the wind still howled, and the house still shook, but under the influence of the Spirit of the Lord, he went right to sleep. As young as George was, he had learned the power of prayer and realized the blessing of having a righteous mother.[36]

There was another time in George's boyhood when his faith in God and in the things he'd been taught became vitally important. One day George began to feel sick. Sarah put him in bed and called for a doctor. When the doctor came, he diagnosed George with typhoid fever. The doctor instructed George to stay in bed for at least three weeks, to eat no solid food, and to drink some coffee. When the doctor left, George told his mother he did not want any coffee. Having taught her son about the Word of Wisdom, Sarah wondered what to do—two of her three children had already died, and she felt anxious about her son's fever. George then suggested that his mother call their home teacher, Brother Hawkes.[37]

Brother Hawkes, who worked at the foundry, was poor and humble but had great faith. Brother Hawkes came, placed his hands on George's head, and blessed him that he would be healed. During the blessing, George promised his Heavenly Father that he would dedicate his life to serving Him if he would be healed. When the doctor came the next morning, he was surprised to find George playing outside with the other children. The fever was gone, and he seemed to be fully healed.[38]

Though George's bout with typhoid fever proved that George was spiritually alert, he was still a young, restless boy who got into a good deal of mischief as he teased the neighborhood children. There were times when George did not obey his mother, and she would spank him with a willow stick. On one such occasion when George had willfully disobeyed his mother, she took a willow stick and marched George into the kitchen. She was about to whip him with it when George took hold

---

36 Ibid.

37 *Teachings*, xvii.

38 Ibid.

of both of his mother's hands and would not let her proceed with the spanking. Sarah then said, "I'm not going to whip you, Son. If you're old enough to know you can stop me by holding my hands, then you're too old to be whipped." She never whipped him again.[39]

A strong bond developed between mother and son, especially after an incident when George was instrumental in saving Sarah's life. When a high cupboard fell on top of his mother, George heard the commotion and quickly ran to his mother's side. He found her lying unconscious on the floor and tried in vain to revive her. Then, remembering how his mother had taught him to pray, George asked the Lord to save her. He promised that if her life were spared, he would devote his life to the work of the Lord.[40] His mother did revive, and George learned once again that the Lord answered his prayers and was watching over him.

Along with learning how to pray, George also learned to be faithful in paying his tithing. When he started to earn a little money, he paid ten cents of tithing on each dollar he earned and soon found that his "income increased as [he] went along."[41]

Sarah also taught him other good habits. George thought it was "lots of fun to play ball and . . . other games," and a group of boys often invited George to play games on Sunday after Sunday School. But his mother thought there were better ways for George to spend his time on the Sabbath. Sarah didn't forbid George from playing games with other boys when the opportunity arose. She simply said, "Son, you will be happier if you do not do that. Let the boys go home and read a good book."[42]

George's parents encouraged him to read uplifting material. Although dime novels, the *Police Gazette*, and other cheap magazines were popular while George was growing up, John Henry and Sarah discouraged George from reading those kinds of materials; instead, they tried to surround George with good literature. One of the first books George came to love contained illustrated stories about biblical characters. The Smiths also owned small, illustrated books about

39 Luacine C. Fox, "Miniature from Life," *Relief Society Magazine*, vol. 33 (1946), 289.

40 Edith Smith Elliott, Interview by Glen R. Stubbs, 6 Oct. 1973, cited in Stubbs, 49.

41 George Albert Smith, CR, Priesthood Meeting, April 1947, 440.

42 George Albert Smith, CR, Oct. 1948, 188.

birds and animals, the *Juvenile Instructor, Poor Jack, Aesop's Fables, Life of Benjamin Franklin, Life of Napoleon Bonaparte, Captain Cook's Voyage, Pictorial History of England, Campfires of Napoleon, Arabian Nights,* and *Scottish Chiefs.*[43] Often, George felt it was as if he "had the companionship of some of the greatest and best people that lived upon the earth" as he read the things those authors "considered desirable to have printed and passed on for others to enjoy."[44]

Along with reading, George spent time playing with cap pistols, masks, and costumes with neighbor children Charles J. Dwyer, Wilby Dougall, and Lewis Peck. In the back of his family's barn, George and the boys staged theatricals, with George playing the Jew's harp and the harmonica. George was sure that neither Boothe nor Barrett (well-known actors of the day) ever felt any prouder of their performances than George and his friends did of theirs.[45] With his boyhood friends, George also enjoyed picnicking, dancing and singing, swimming in the Jordan River, and running to the hot springs and back as well as participating in other adventures in pioneer Utah.[46]

One such adventure took place in City Creek Canyon, where a natural bridge crossed into some green bushes. George and a group of friends had started toward a rock where Lewis Peck had previously killed some snakes. However, Lewis had missed one snake, and a rattler began to chase after another boy with them. The boy was making good time up the hill with the snake following him. But Lewis caught up to the snake, took his trusty walking stick, and cut the snake in two.[47]

Lewis Peck acquired a newspaper route and, as the best of friends, offered to let George help and receive half the profit. There was only one problem: George had no alarm clock to wake him. So the two friends developed a system. Each night, George tied a string around his big toe and hung the string out the window. In the morning

---

43 Stubbs, 23

44 Ibid.

45 George Albert Smith to Charles J. Dwyer, 11 Jan. 1937, George A. Smith Papers, box 60, fld 15.

46 Stubbs, 13–14.

47 George Albert Smith to Lewis Peck (Cove, OR), 31 March 1944, The Church of Jesus Christ of Latter-day Saints, Salt Lake City, UT (hereafter cited as Church Archives), ms 15591.

Lewis tugged on the string. Two or three pulls of the toe were usually enough to get George up and moving. George then got up and helped Lewis distribute the newspapers.[48]

Along with George's twenty-five brothers and sisters, George and Lewis attended the Brigham Young School on South Temple.[49] Soon after starting school, George's father bought George a desk and a chair. Once again, George's mischievous nature manifested itself in taunting the teacher:

> One day when the teacher left the room she said to the children, "Don't any of you leave your seats!" And as soon as she went out [George] picked his seat up and went all around the room. Some of the annoyed pupils, upon the teacher's return, protested that George had left his seat. The teacher said to [him], "Did you leave your seat, George?" [He] replied, "No, indeed I didn't." She said, "Well, all of the rest of the students say you left your seat." [George] said, "Oh no I didn't; I took it with me."[50]

It was at the old Brigham Young School that George first saw a United States president. When President Ulysses S. Grant visited the Territory of Utah, he called at the school in the Seventeenth Ward and spoke to the children there.[51]

On Sundays, George and his siblings worshipped in the Seventeenth Ward, "whose stately chapel, with its vaulted ceiling and beautiful stained-glass window, was just through the block."[52] George loved singing the hymns and even thought that singing "Haste to the Sunday School" made him fastidious about punctuality because he dared not go to class late.[53]

It was in the Seventeenth Ward during a testimony meeting that George learned an important truth. A member of the ward, Brother Folkers—an immigrant from Holland—did not speak English. Yet,

48 Emily Smith Stewart to T. Earl Pardoe, 12 May 1948, George A. Smith Papers, box 96, fld 1.

49 George A. Smith, Life Sketch, unpublished manuscript, George A. Smith Papers, box 102.

50 Emily Smith Stewart to T. Earl Pardoe, 12 May 1948, George A. Smith Papers, box 96, fld 1.

51 George Albert Smith, unpublished talk, George A. Smith Papers, box 124, scrapbook 1, 11–12.

52 Gibbons, 32.

53 George Albert Smith, "Tribute to Richard Ballantyne," *The Instructor*, vol. 81, no. 11, Nov. 1946, 503.

each Thursday Brother Folkers attended fast meetings to hear the testimonies, even though he could not understand what was being said. He and his wife would then get up and bear their testimonies in Dutch, which the congregation could not understand. One day after fast meeting, using many gestures, George managed to ask, "Why do you go to the English-speaking services? You cannot understand [what is said]." When Brother Folkers figured out what George had said, he replied, "It is not what you hear that makes you happy, nor what you see . . . ; it is what you feel [that makes you happy]."[54]

Though George had grown up hearing many testimonies like that of Brother Folkers, he did not bear his own testimony until he was eight years old, after he'd been baptized by James Moyle in City Creek. On that eventful day, George stood up and told the gathered congregation that he "was grateful before that [he] belonged to the true Church and [he] was just as sure then that [he] belonged to the Church of the Lamb of God as [he was] today."[55]

Two years later on a particular Sunday, George once again gave in to his mischievous side:

> He was a little late for Sunday school. He was drinking from the ditch when he noticed a shiny object on the bank in the grass. Curious, he reached down and picked it up. It was an empty 30-30 cartridge shell. Not sure what to do with it, he stuffed the shell into his pocket and hurried off to church. [George and the rest of] the children sat on the benches with their teachers. In that era the prayers were long; so were the talks and the songs. George Albert was pretty restless by the time they got to the sacrament. That's when he remembered the shell in his pocket and wondered what he could do with it, thinking maybe he could trade it for some marbles. The boy next to him suggested that he use it for a whistle, which he promptly did. Puffing up his cheeks, he blew as hard as he could. [56]

54 McIntosh, 76.

55 George Albert Smith, CR, April 1935, 43.

56 Heidi S. Swinton, *In the Company of Prophets: Personal Experiences of D. Arthur Haycock with George Albert Smith* (Salt Lake City, UT: Deseret Book, 1993), 21–22 (hereafter cited as Swinton).

The year George turned ten proved to be an important one. That year, 1880, his father was called to be a member of the Quorum of the Twelve by John Taylor, who was then President of the Church. George had another testimony-building experience when his father received his call:

> [John Henry] thought it likely . . . that President Taylor would ordain and set him apart. But because of the special relationship his father had enjoyed with Wilford Woodruff, he was anxious that Elder Woodruff ordain him [instead]. However, [George's father] was reluctant to express this desire openly [to the prophet] for fear that it would be misunderstood. [George watched his father pray] fervently in silence that his desire would be granted. . . . At the ordination ceremony, President Taylor first ordained Francis M. Lyman. Then, after hesitating, the Prophet, instead of doing it himself or calling on one of his counselors to do it as is customary, asked Wilford Woodruff, then the President of the Twelve, to ordain John Henry Smith.[57]

George Albert Smith was also ten years old when he became acquainted with a petite neighbor girl with long black braids—Lucy Emily Woodruff. Could George have understood at the tender age of ten what this young woman would someday become to him? Could he have even guessed what a vital role she would play in his life as he moved from youth into the responsibilities he shouldered as an adult?

57 Gibbons, 231.

Chapter 3

THE TERROR AND TORMENT OF HER LIFE

Life had not been easy for ten-year-old Lucy Emily Woodruff. Her life began in 1869 near the banks of the Muddy River in St. Thomas, Nevada, where her parents—Wilford Woodruff Jr. and Emily J. Smith Woodruff—had been sent two years earlier on a pioneering mission. The assignment to the Muddy had made their life replete with difficulty and hardship.[58]

The Brethren desired to establish a Latter-day Saint colony at the Muddy for two reasons. First, they hoped the fledgling cotton industry in Utah's Washington County and the surge of cotton prices from the Civil War would shift the market focus from the southern states to Utah. Cotton fiber could be grown in warm places near the Muddy River and near the lower reaches of the Virgin River valley, roughly fifty miles northeast of the future settlement of Las Vegas. Second, Church leadership wanted to secure a passage between Southern Utah and the Gulf of California for the transportation of merchandise and Mormon immigrants.[59] At the time, Mormon converts who arrived in New York from Europe either took the train to Iowa City or Nebraska, or they landed in New Orleans and followed the Mississippi River to St. Louis. At both Iowa City and St. Louis, these converts joined covered wagon trains that took them the rest of the way to Utah.[60] The Muddy Mission brought the Saints to a lonely, barren desert where they attempted to establish a community known as St. Thomas in Nevada's Moapa Valley.[61]

---

58 Clarissa A. Beesley, "Lucy Emily Woodruff," *The Young Woman's Journal* (Salt Lake City, UT: The Desert News, 1919), 347.

59 "Muddy Mission Settled a 'Forbidding Lonely' Area," *Church News*, 12 Jan. 1991, 11.

60 James G. Bleak, *Annals of the Southern Utah Mission* (Provo, UT: Brigham Young University, 1960), 35.

61 "Muddy Mission Settled a 'Forbidding Lonely' Area," *Church News*, 12 Jan. 1991.

At St. Thomas, food was scarce. Women made bread from coarse bran and used greens and roots for substance most of the time.[62] The Woodruffs and others nearly starved and were practically destitute.[63] Few settlers faced harsher circumstances than those of the Muddy Mission. It was "an ordeal beyond compare," as the forbidding landscape of nearly barren mountains and mesas provided scant fodder for livestock or wood for fuel and construction. Summer temperatures often reached 120 degrees Fahrenheit, and there was little rainfall. "'Oh, what a place it was!' wrote one settler. 'Nothing but deep sand and a burning sun.'"[64] It was under such circumstances that Lucy Emily Woodruff was born.

Even more doubtful than the chance of survival in the Muddy Mission was the likelihood of happiness in her parents' marriage, for they had come together under very strange circumstances, seemingly devoid of romance or sentiment. Lucy often heard the story of her parents' marriage repeated at various Woodruff family gatherings. In 1867, Lucy's father, Wilford Woodruff Jr., was a shy young man who was "literally pushed into marriage by a colonizing assignment." Wilford Jr. had gone to his father, who was serving as an Apostle, with "an insoluble problem" after receiving his call to go to Nevada. In the oft-repeated story, the following conversation took place:

> "President Young has called me to the Muddy River colonization mission," [Wilford, Jr.] said, "and I must be married before I can go."
>
> "That's fine," his father replied, "whom are you going to marry?"
>
> "I haven't any idea," the young man said. "I don't even know any girls."
>
> "Surely you know some," his father remonstrated.
>
> "Well," Wilford conceded, "I know *of* Emily Jane Smith, but I've never met her."
>
> "How would you like to marry her?" the father pressed.

62 Leon R. Hartshorn, comp., *Remarkable Stories from the Lives of Latter-day Saint Women*, vol. 1 (Salt Lake City, UT: Deseret Book, 1973), 118.

63 Henry B. Eyring, *To Draw Closer to God: A Collection of Discourses* (Salt Lake City, UT: Deseret Book, 1997), 74–75.

64 Susan Easton Black, "Courage—the Unfailing Beacon," *Ensign*, March 1997, 51.

"I guess it would be all right," was the uncertain reply.

"Come on," the Apostle said.

They put on their hats and walked over to Judge Smith's home even though it was still early morning.

"Have you come to breakfast?" the surprised judge asked.

"No," said Wilford senior, "We've come on more serious business. Wilford here has been called on a colonizing mission to the Muddy. He can't go until he has a wife, so he would like to marry one of your daughters."

"Which one?" asked the startled judge.

"He doesn't know any of them," the father of the red-faced young man admitted, "but he knows *of* Emily Jane."

Judge Smith summoned Emily Jane, then seventeen, and asked her if she knew Wilford Woodruff Jr.

"I know who he is," the girl said demurely, "but I don't think we've ever been introduced."

Her father explained young Wilford's problem and added: "He thinks he would like to marry you. Are you willing?"

"Is that what you wish me to do?" the girl asked in meek submission.

"Yes, Emily. I think Wilford would make you a wonderful husband."

"All right, father, I'll do anything you wish."[65]

With that terse beginning, Wilford Woodruff Jr. and Emily Jane Smith were married and then immediately left for St. Thomas.[66] Amid plagues of insects, desert heat, and renegade Native Americans, Wilford built a log cabin where his first daughter, Lucy Emily Woodruff, was born on January 10, 1869.

Another popular family story had its origins in the first months of Lucy's life, when a Native American came into the Woodruff cabin where Emily Jane and her daughter were alone and demanded food. When Emily told the Native American she had no food to give him, he took out a weapon and stared at the baby. Emily, who had been

65 Pusey, 205–206.

66 Pusey, 206.

ironing, tried to continue her work, but the man sat down with one leg on the table, blocking her way. Terrified, she thrust the hot iron against the Native American's bare leg, and he ran out of the cabin screaming.[67] Because Lucy was so young when this event occurred, years later she had the story validated:

> One day an Indian with an ugly scar on his leg came to a cottage in St. George, Utah, where Lucy Woodruff Smith was nursing a sick husband. As she turned and saw the man in her doorway, Lucy remembered the terror that had gripped her mother and the tale she had often heard.
>
> "You Emily Jane Woodruff's papoose?" the Indian asked.
>
> Lucy's heart almost stopped beating. She could only stammer, "Yes."
>
> "Your mother heap brave squaw," the scarred one said.
>
> Before Lucy could reply he was gone.[68]

Lucy's parents must have been relieved when "President Young, recognizing the extreme difficulties of the mission, advised the settlers to abandon the mission in 1870. The fact that the harshness of the environment forced the closure of this mission serves [and] remind[s] us of the faith and courage required to live there."[69] However, for the rest of Lucy's life, she would have a reminder of her infancy in the Muddy, for it was there that she contracted polio from the Native Americans. As a result, she ever after walked with a dropped foot.[70]

After leaving the mission, Lucy's family moved to Randolph, Utah, where three more children were born. The hardships of the Muddy Mission seemed to be a detriment to Emily Jane Woodruff's health, and when Lucy was just nine years old, Emily Jane died on

---

67 Ibid.

68 Ibid.

69 Susan Easton Black, "Courage—the Unfailing Beacon," *Ensign*, March 1997, 53; and Orson F. Whitney, *History of Utah*, vol. 4, 1893, 607.

70 Martha Ray June Stewart Hatch (Socorro, NM), Phone Interview by Mary Jane Woodger, 16 Aug. 2007, transcription in possession of Mary Jane Woodger; and Shauna Lucy Stewart Larsen (Orem, UT), Interview by Mary Jane Woodger, 23 Aug. 2007, transcription in possession of Mary Jane Woodger.

May 8, 1878, at the age of twenty-seven.[71] Her father then lived with another polygamous wife, and Lucy was sent to live with her mother's parents, Judge and Mrs. Elias A. Smith, just around the corner from the John Henry Smith home. Lucy found that her grandmother was a proper woman who did not "believe in hugging or kissing a child or telling a child that they'd done anything nicely."[72]

Lucy, too, had more than her share of illness. In January 1889, she recorded in her journal that she "felt sick nearly all day. Sometimes I think I will be sick forever . . . I hope some day I will enjoy health like other people."[73] Unfortunately, Lucy would not have this blessing. There were periods when she was well, but she suffered intermediately from arthritis, rheumatism, nerves, arterial sclerosis, and other minor ailments, and she underwent several operations.[74]

Besides health issues and the loss of her mother, Lucy had other sorrows in her youth. She "lost an eleven-year-old brother to whom she had been very close."[75] Another great loss was the death of her grandfather in 1888. Having lived with him and her grandmother since the death of her mother, Lucy's relationship with him had been close: "He had been like a father and a mother to her and was the only one who had been able to comfort her when she mourned the loss of her dear mother. She was at his side when he died."[76]

Lucy did not know how deeply becoming a motherless child at the age of nine would affect her. Often she was depressed nearly all day as she longed for her mother. Although she was fortunate to have the comfort of others, it did not make up for her mother's absence. It was especially difficult when she saw other little girls with their mothers. During those times, she felt a longing that never seemed to go away.[77] When she needed to make decisions or was upset about

---

71 Unpublished biographical sketch of Lucy Woodruff Smith, Sept. 1934, George A. Smith Papers, box 139, fld 1, cited in Stubbs, 37.

72 Martha Ray June Stewart Hatch (Socorro, NM), Phone Interview by Mary Jane Woodger, 16 Aug. 2007, transcription in possession of Mary Jane Woodger.

73 Lucy Woodruff, Journal, 13 Jan. 1889, George A. Smith Papers, box 138, book 2.

74 Stubbs, 39.

75 Lucy Woodruff, Journal, 30 March 1888, George A. Smith Papers, box 138, book 1.

76 Lucy Woodruff, Journal, 24 June 1888, George A. Smith Papers, box 138, book 1.

77 Lucy Woodruff, Journal, 4 Feb. 1888, George A. Smith Papers, box 138, book 1.

something, she would think, "O, if I only had a mother or someone I might ask what to do."[78]

Did she wish she could ask Mother what to do when she became the object of George Albert Smith's affections—especially when his affections manifested themselves in the form of teasing? The first time she laid eyes on George she was passing by his house carrying a pail of yeast to her grandmother. When George saw her, he chased her until the yeast was upset. The next day at school he dipped her braids in ink and then after school tied her to a tree by her braids. Lucy decided she would steer clear of George even if it meant walking an extra three blocks each day to avoid passing his house.[79]

At the age of ten, Lucy Emily Woodruff decided she would never have anything to do with George Albert Smith. The odds of the "terror of the 17th Ward" ever convincing Lucy Emily Woodruff to speak to him—let alone someday become his wife—were indeed low.[80]

---

78 Ibid.

79 Emily Smith Stewart to T. Earl Pardoe, 12 May 1948, George A. Smith Papers, box 96, fld 1.

80 A Member of the Y.L.M.I.A., "A Brief Biography Written for the Present Occasion," George A. Smith Papers, box 151, fld 6, 1–7.

Chapter 4
DON'T BE A SCRUB

Lucy lived just down the street from George. And as fate would have it, she was assigned the desk in front of George's in the Seventeenth Ward building. George constantly teased, tormented, and chased Lucy.[81] Though he was just ten years old, "the fact [was] that George Albert . . . loved Lucy and expected to marry her." And although she had shown little interest in him—and, in fact, had displayed a disdain for him and his boyish pranks—George persevered in spite of the odds.[82]

George was not a popular boy. He was not invited to the parties held by other youth in his neighborhood. The Smiths lived where "some of Salt Lake's well-to-do families lived, but George's family was not wealthy."[83] His father had two families to support, and with lots of children among which to spread his limited means, they lacked certain physical advantages that some other families had. In addition, John Henry was called to leave his family to serve as President of the European Mission.[84] In many ways, George had a lonesome childhood. He "wanted so much to be loved and accepted," but felt that he wasn't.[85] Perhaps because George wanted to be loved, his desire to impress Lucy became even more pronounced.

George decided that one of the reasons Lucy was not interested in him was the shabby appearance of his home. George hoped that

81 A Member of the Y.L.M.I.A., "A Brief Biography Written for the Present Occasion," George A. Smith Papers, box 151, fld 6, 1–7.

82 Gibbons, 9.

83 Vilate Raile, "When the Grass Grew," *Improvement Era*, XVIII, Dec. 1945, 748–749.

84 Andrew Jenson, "Smith, John Henry," *LDS Biographical Encyclopedia*, vol. 1 (Salt Lake City, UT: Deseret Book, 1901), 141.

85 Emily Smith Stewart to T. Earl Pardoe, 12 May 1948, George A. Smith Papers, box 96, fld 1.

by improving its appearance, he would increase his chances with Lucy. There were other young men in the neighborhood to whom she gave much more attention, "young men whose families stood much higher in the economic scale than the Smiths. These families, headed by men who had not been called to sacrifice their time and means for the Church to the extent George's father had, owned homes that were more pretentious than that of the Smiths, with more luxurious furnishings and well-manicured lawns."[86]

His mother attempted to soothe George by reminding him of his noble heritage. However, such intangibles could hardly compensate for an untidy yard in the mind of an adolescent trying to impress a girl. So his mother suggested he fix up the yard. This launched a Smith family project to plant a lawn around the home. George spearheaded the effort, which proved to be more difficult and time-consuming than he had expected. First, George and the rest of the Smith children earned dimes to buy grass seed and hauled rocks to make a path. Then they prepared the hard soil around the house for planting. Unfortunately, before the grass could take root, a huge thunderstorm washed out the seed, and George had to start over. He hauled water from the irrigation ditch every night. By degrees, and with constant watering and weeding, the lawn shaped up, creating a new image for the Smith family in the neighborhood. And George's labors were rewarded when "Lucy and her grandmother came and sat on the lawn, as George dreamed they would."[87]

George not only had a strong work ethic and a beautiful lawn going for him, but he was also quite musically talented. Would Lucy take note of that? In those days, people had to create music for themselves, and George manifested his musical ability at a very young age.[88] The Smiths didn't have an organ or a piano until he was grown, but he "did have a Jew's harp, a harmonica, banjo, and guitar; and [he] learned to play them."[89] George's love of music and funny stories led him to amateur show business. With Wilby Dougall

86 Gibbons, 9.

87 "Passing of a Saint," *Time*, 16 April 1951, 65; and Pusey, 210.

88 A Member of the Y.L.M.I.A., "A Brief Biography Written for the Present Occasion," George A. Smith Papers, box 151, fld 6, 1–7.

89 George Albert Smith, "Talk Given at Wasatch Seminary Graduation," George A. Smith Papers, box 124, scrapbook 1, 256.

and Lewis Tom Peck, he conducted minstrel shows in his backyard. Collecting a penny from everyone who attended, George became a musician and a businessman. Garbed in a homespun western shirt and a big western hat, he was so loud you could hear him down the road. George's gangly appearance caused people to go into "hysterics as soon as [he] would step on the stage with his guitar before he even uttered a note."[90] And if George's gawky appearance weren't enough, "with a few wry gestures and jokes, he could provoke a torrent of giggling."[91] But when he began to strum his guitar and play his theme song, people were even more enamored by George the entertainer. Accompanied by his guitar, he would launch into his theme song:

I'm not very handsome, I know that I'm not.
I'm as ugly as sin, and ought to be shot.
My mouth is a feature that can't be forgot—
If you travel east, west, north or south.
Chorus:
Shut it! Shut it! Don't open it quite so wide.
Shut it! O shut it! I don't want to get inside.[92]

Surely having so many people love and adore him as an entertainer would attract Lucy's attention. But that was not the case, and as the next couple of years rolled along, George continued to do all he could to get in Lucy's good graces.

When George turned twelve, his parents decided to send him to the Brigham Young Academy in Provo, Utah, where he would live with his grandmother's sister, Grace Smith (later Cheever), whose home was near the tiny campus.[93] As a going-away present, George received an autograph book with this inscription from his father:

My dear son,
Guard thine honor as thy life, be charitable, virtuous,

---

90 Emily Smith Stewart to T. Earl Pardoe, 12 May 1948, George A. Smith Papers, box 96, fld 1.

91 Pusey, 204–205.

92 George Albert Smith, "Theme Song," holograph, George A. Smith Papers, box 100.

93 George Albert Smith to Franklin S. Harris, 30 Oct. 1928, George A. Smith Papers, box 54, fld 22.

> just honest and truthful [sic] and life's stream will be a continuous scene of happiness and success.
> Your loving father,
> John Henry Smith[94]

After a few months away, George wrote home to his mother and declared, "I am going to school to the Brigham Young Academy . . . I am having a splendid time, I am not a bit homesick."[95]

While at the academy, George proved to be an excellent student. His English teacher "made the following comments concerning his written work: 'Spelling, I find no mistakes; Grammar, I find no mistakes; Penmanship, could be improved.'"[96] When George left for Christmas break, he wrote the following composition:

> Kind Teacher,
> I will endeavor to give an account of my holiday vacation. I left Provo to go to Salt Lake. The Friday afternoon before Christmas, on the Utah Central Railway I got there two hours and a half after I left Provo. The next day was Saturday and I worked in the store all day. The next day being Sunday, I went to Sunday School and I had a good time as it was [indecipherable word] day. The next day there was good coasting on several of the hills of Salt Lake. There was good skating on Hot Spring Lake . . .
> I remain as ever Your Noisy Student
> George Smith[97]

Though he was a good student, George continued his adventurous lifestyle at the academy. One day when his class was taking a tour of a

94 Pusey, 208–209.

95 George Albert Smith to Sarah Farr Smith, 11 December 1882, L. Tom Perry Special Collections, Harold B. Lee Library, Brigham Young University (Provo, UT), George Albert Smith Papers, "Letters," MSS SC 2037.

96 "Teacher's Critique of the School Themes of George Albert Smith," 1882, George A. Smith Papers, box 97, fld 3.

97 "Composition on My Holiday Vacation by George A. Smith BYA," 16 Jan. 1882, George A. Smith Papers, box 97, fld 3.

wool factory to inspect the manufacture of cloth, he fell into a tub of blue dye, which left his skin tinted blue for several days.[98]

Although he was part of a small student body at the academy, George, along with many of his friends, would later attain notoriety. Among these friends "were George Sutherland, a future United States Supreme Court Justice; Reed Smoot, who would become a member of the Twelve and a United States senator; Richard R. Lyman, another future member of the Twelve and a distinguished engineer; and Amy Brown Lyman, who became the general president of the Relief Society."[99]

George was affected more in classes taught by Karl G. Maeser than by any other experience at the academy. In 1928, George wrote: "I love the memory of Brother Maeser. I think I have spoken of him more than any other man perhaps among those who have contributed to my education."[100] Dr. Maeser was constantly saying, "Don't be a scrub."[101] It was at the age of thirteen, while George was attending one of Dr. Maeser's classes, that a lesson hit him as none had ever before. Dr. Maeser taught: "Not only will you be held accountable for things that you do, but you will be responsible for the very thoughts that you think."[102]

At first, George could not comprehend how he could be charged for his thoughts when he felt he couldn't control his thoughts, and that worried him. But Dr. Maeser's statement continued to "stick to him like a burr."[103] About two weeks later, George suddenly realized what Dr. Maeser had meant, and he later recounted:

> Why, of course, you will be held accountable for your thoughts because when your life is completed in mortality, it will be the sum of your thoughts. That one suggestion has been a great blessing to me all my life, and it has enabled me upon many occasions to avoid thinking

98 A Member of the Y.L.M.I.A., "A Brief Biography Written for the Present Occasion," George A. Smith Papers, box 151, fld 6, 1–7.

99 Gibbons, 5.

100 George Albert Smith to Franklin S. Harris, 30 Oct. 1928, George A. Smith Papers, box 54, fld 22.

101 Gibbons, 8.

102 McIntosh, xviii.

103 Ibid.

> improperly because I realize that I will be, when my life's labor is complete, the product of my thoughts.[104]

Though George had only been at Brigham Young Academy for less than a semester, a letter from his father took him back to Salt Lake City. John Henry, serving as the European Mission President, wrote George on May 31, 1883, telling him he "was needed at home to help support the family."[105]

Upon returning to Salt Lake City, George started job hunting and found himself at ZCMI (Zion's Cooperative Mercantile Institution) clothing factory, a Church-owned manufacturing plant and department store. When George applied for a job, the manager said he could not afford another employee.

> George reminded him that he had not asked for money, only for a job, adding, "I know that if I'm worth anything, I'll get paid." Such chutzpah earned him employment punching buttonholes in overalls at two dollars and fifty cents a week. Later he was 'promoted' to the cutting tables where, using a large, sharp knife, he cut fabrics according to patterns, guiding the knife along fissures in the table.[106]

Later, his father would write and counsel George about being a good employee: "My son, the way to gain approval of one's employer is to keep doing, looking very carefully after his interest and he will study the interest of those who labor for him. You want to do your best and not complain too much, for others don't see our afflictions as we see them ourselves."[107]

During the next year as George was working at ZCMI, he had an experience that would have great bearing on his life. On January 16, 1884, a visitor came to the Smith home and inquired after George. When the man found out George was there, he explained that "he

---

104 Hulme, 29.

105 Pusey, 209.

106 Gibbons, 8–9.

107 John Henry Smith to George Albert Smith, 22 June 1887, George A. Smith Papers, box 16, fld 3.

was Zebedee Coltrin, a patriarch in the Church, and that he had not been able to sleep or be at peace with himself for the past few days because of the feeling that he should come and give George a blessing." He then asked Sarah if she would mind if he did so. She replied that she wouldn't mind.[108] Then Brother Coltrin pronounced the following blessing upon George:

> Thou wast called and chosen of the Lord from before the foundation of the earth was laid to come forth in this dispensation to assist in building up the Zion of God upon the earth, and thou shalt be enabled to go forth to proclaim the gospel unto the inhabitants of the earth, and shall be enabled to bring many to a knowledge of the truth, for thy voice shall be as the voice of a trumpet in declaring the words of the Lord to the nobles of the earth, and many shall believe in thy words and embrace the gospel of the Son of God. . . . And thou shalt become a mighty prophet in the midst of the sons of Zion. And the angels of the Lord shall administer unto you. . . . And thou shalt be wrapped in the visions of the heavens and thou shalt be clothed with salvation as with a garment, for thou art destined to become a mighty man before the Lord, for thou shalt become a mighty Apostle in the Church and kingdom of God upon the earth, for none of thy father's family shall have more power with God than thou shalt have, for none shall excel thee, for thy reward shall be great in the heavens, for the blessing of thy father and of thy grandfather shall rest upon thee and thou shalt become a mighty man of faith before the Lord, even like unto that of the brother of Jared, and thou shalt remain upon the earth until thou art satisfied with life, and shall be numbered with the Lord's anointed and shall become a king and a priest unto the most High, for thou art of the pure blood of Jacob, and have a right to all the blessings of the house of Joseph.[109]

108 Emily Smith Stewart, Interview by Robert K. McIntosh, 12 Aug. 1972, cited in McIntosh, xviii.

109 "George Albert Smith Patriarchal Blessing Given by Zebedee Coltrin," 16 Jan. 1884, George A.

Sarah had been told in her own patriarchal blessing that her posterity would be numerous and mighty, and that none should excel them in Israel. As Brother Coltrin was leaving, he added one final promise to the young boy—that he would live as long as he chose to, and when he was ready to depart from this life, he would have that choice.[110]

As his youthful years progressed, the changes in George were noticed by others—most especially by Lucy Woodruff. George was no longer teasing or tormenting her: "One day after he had carried groceries home for her, tipping his hat as he left, Lucy, incredulous, said to her grandmother: 'I just met George Smith. He's home from school, and he's decent.'"[111] And so George and Lucy began to have a more congenial relationship.

By the age of fifteen, George was back in school attending the University of Deseret (later renamed the University of Utah), which was located on North Second West where Salt Lake City's West High School now stands. The University of Deseret was within the boundaries of the Seventeenth Ward, where the Smith family lived, and was within easy walking distance of their home. At the university, George Albert proved to be a good student.[112] He also continued to show his sharp wit:

> [He was a] member of Dr. John R. Park's class in arithmetic. . . . On one occasion Dr. Park assigned the class the problem of figuring out all the financial transactions involved in shipping a car load of potatoes. Various members of the class were called upon to report. After several had done so, each showing a modest profit, George Albert was called upon. His report included a very large profit.
>
> Dr. Park remarked, "But, Mr. Smith, you forgot to put in the cost of the potatoes." George Albert answered very promptly, "I raised my potatoes, Sir."[113]

Smith Papers, box 96, fld 13.

110 Shauna Lucy Stewart Larsen (Orem, UT), Interview by Mary Jane Woodger, 23 Aug. 2007, transcription in possession of Mary Jane Woodger; and Martha Ray June Stewart Hatch (Socorro, NM), Phone Interview by Mary Jane Woodger, 16 Aug. 2007, transcription in possession of Mary Jane Woodger.

111 Gibbons, 6.

112 Gibbons, 11.

113 Milton Bennion, "President George Albert Smith," *The Instructor,* LXXX, July 1945, 294.

While George was going to school, Lucy was also. After graduating from Salt Lake City public schools, she attended the University of Deseret for a year and a half. Lucy then received training in clerical work in the City and County Surveyor Office as well as in the County Recorder Office, and she soon became an expert at record keeping and mapmaking.[114]

George and Lucy saw each other regularly, and though Lucy was fond of George, theirs certainly was not an exclusive relationship.[115] One day in 1889, both George and Lucy had a memorable experience:

> George A and Lucy sat in the hammock on her grandmother's porch, looking toward Temple Square. They looked up and saw a hot air balloon floating overhead. All of a sudden George turned to Lucy and cried, 'I think it is going to hit the tabernacle roof,' and sure enough it did. As soon as it hit, the balloon burst into flames. George jumped up and ran to the nearest telephone to call the fire department, and then ran to the tabernacle grounds. When the fire department arrived they could not get their equipment inside the grounds because the night watchman did not have a key to the large gate. The fire chief motioned to George and about ten or twelve others who were nearby. He lined them up some distance away from the large wooden gate and told them to run toward the gate and jump as high as they could, striking the gate with their feet. At his signal, they did so, and thus the firemen were able to gain entrance to the tabernacle grounds. George was right behind one of the firemen as he scrambled up a ladder and through a trap door which opened directly into the space between the roof and the ceiling. Looking up he could see that the fire had already burned a hole in the roof, and the shingles were blazing. The fireman

114 Stubbs, 38–39.

115 "George Albert Smith: Eighth President of the Church," *Presidents of the Church: Student Manual, Religion 345* (Salt Lake City, UT: The Church of Jesus Christ of Latter-day Saints, 2003), 132.

> quickly sprayed water on the burning rooftop, and the fire was soon out after having burned a hole in the roof about six feet square. Speaking of the experience later, President Smith conjectured, "Another five minutes and I am afraid the whole roof and possibly the entire building would have been destroyed because it was of wood and dry as tinder."[116]

What were the odds that this building, which would play such an important part in the future life of George Albert Smith, would be saved by his own quick thinking? On the day George saved the Tabernacle he certainly had not been a scrub, but it would take more than this act of valor to win the heart of the girl who had sat in the hammock with him that day.

116 George Albert Smith, as related to William Odd, 26 Oct. 1949, unpublished manuscript, George A. Smith Papers, box 125, pasted in scrapbook 1. ("William Odd came to the office of President Smith for the purpose of having him relate the story. He was the man who had received at the fire station, the alarm phoned in by George Albert Smith." Stubbs, 19.)

Chapter 5
HOLDING SUBSERVIENT TWO HEARTS

George often took Lucy to dances and other events at the Seventeenth Ward, but Lucy was no wallflower and had many admirers. George was at somewhat of a disadvantage; his trousers were too short because of his quick growth, and he was no Adonis in looks.[117] In an effort to gain some kind of advantage, George often borrowed his father's buggy to take Lucy for rides, but John Henry's buggy did not measure up to that of one of her other boyfriends, who picked her up for dates "in his father's brand new Studebaker buggy with leather interior and red wheels."[118]

In January 1888, George and Lucy had some kind of misunderstanding. In trying to be nice to another suitor, she had slighted George. The misunderstanding was serious enough to cause Lucy to become quite unsettled about the prospect of any future with George. She spent the night of the argument "in wakefulness and sorrow" and suffered what she felt was "more real anguish than any other day of [her] life." She recorded in her journal, "Through a thoughtless, unintentional wrong I worry I have lost the respect, esteem, and regard of one whom I think more of than all else on earth." Over and over again Lucy wondered if "G.A.S. [would] ever believe or put confidence in [her] again."[119]

On February 5, not long after their argument, George forgave Lucy of the wrong. As Lucy knelt by her bed that night, she did so with a thankful heart for the forgiveness of "one of the best young

117 Pusey, 210.

118 Swinton, 24.

119 Lucy Woodruff, Journal, 5 Feb. 1888, George A. Smith Papers, box 138, book 1.

men that was ever placed on the earth," and she also prayed that the Lord would give her the strength to be more deserving of George's love. Tears came to her eyes as she thought of "the goodness and kindness" of the one she had hurt. As she lay down that night, she knew she would never forget that George had forgiven her after she had hurt him so.[120]

Perhaps wishing to give their relationship a bit more time to heal, George did not call on Lucy again until June 11.[121] During the intervening months, George was busy with school at the University of Deseret, and then he decided to earn some money by joining a surveying crew in the desert that was working on a line for the Denver and Rio Grande Railroad. He had taken a surveying class at the university and was prepared for his job of driving stakes and dragging chains.[122] What were the odds that this summer job would adversely affect the rest of George's life? But it was while he was working on the railroad that George suffered serious injury to both of his eyes. Because of the intense summer sun glaring off the desert sands, George's eyes were permanently damaged and had deteriorated so much before the summer's end that he was forced to return to Salt Lake.[123]

When George returned to Salt Lake City, he began seeing Lucy once again. The rest of 1888 brought more interaction between the young couple, and George asked Lucy for a date on October 7. But before long, the two had differences again, which lasted into the next year.[124]

In the meantime, George obtained a position with ZCMI as a traveling salesman. He set off for his first sales trip to southern Utah with fellow ZCMI employee James Poulton, who was a bit older than George. On the sales trip George took orders for groceries while Jim took orders for shoes.[125] Starting out for a small LDS community in Nevada called Panaca—about ninety miles northwest of St. George, Utah—Jim and George intended to cover all the towns between Salt

120 Lucy Woodruff, Journal, 5 Feb. 1888, George A. Smith Papers, box 138, book 1.

121 Lucy Woodruff, Journal, 24 Jan. to 7 Oct. 1888, George A. Smith Papers, box 138, book 1.

122 "Early Life Just Like that of Ordinary Boy," *Deseret News*, vol. 335, no. 8, 8 April 1951, LDS Archives (Salt Lake City, UT), ms 9163.

123 *Teachings*, xix.

124 Lucy Woodruff, Journal, 24 Jan. to 7 Oct. 1888, George A. Smith Papers, box 138, book 1.

125 Pusey, 211.

Lake City and Panaca on this trip.[126] The two salesmen traveled along the Mormon corridor in a covered wagon pulled by a team of horses. In the wagon, they carried their personal belongings, bedding, and a complete camping outfit in case they were stranded overnight in the wilderness. They also brought along their musical instruments: George had a guitar and a harmonica, and Jim brought his flute. George also carried a set of Indian clubs and dumbbells to keep his muscles toned.[127]

Many of George's days were occupied in the same way. He would rise at 6:30 AM and exercise with the dumbbells for thirty minutes and then with the Indian clubs for another thirty. He would then hitch up the wagon and visit one of the small outlying communities. After returning to the town, he and Jim would eat dinner, and then George would move their goods in for the night and he would write his mother or Lucy.[128] Sometimes George and Jim would end up sleeping in the wagon, and they spent much of their time trying to keep the wagon from becoming stuck in mud.[129] When beer was offered at the places they stayed, George would refuse and instead offer impromptu concerts—him on his guitar and harmonica, Jim on the flute, and the audience joining in song.[130] After their many concerts at local hotels, George gained a "reputation as a comedian by having his [hair] shingled close and wearing a fantastic tie pin."[131]

As a young salesman, George seldom failed to get an order, thanks to his gift of conversation and his genuine interest in people. He was far from the typical traveling salesman of the day, though; he refused to drink liquor, he went to church on Sundays (where he was frequently asked to speak), and instead of carousing, he kept busy exercising with his dumbbells. But Jim did not always show the same character. While traveling from Salt Lake City to American Fork, Jim let George know that he'd brought a jug of whiskey along so that they might offer some to their customers. George Albert was not happy

126 Preston Nibley, "George Albert Smith as a Salesman," *Improvement Era,* XLIX, Dec. 1946, 780–781.

127 Ibid.

128 George Albert Smith, Journal, 23 May 1890, George A. Smith Papers, box 73, book 1.

129 Pusey, 211.

130 George Albert Smith, Journal, 28 May 1890, George A. Smith Papers, box 73, book 1; and Preston Nibley, "George Albert Smith as a Salesman," *Improvement Era,* XLIX, Dec. 1946, 780–781.

131 Pusey, 211.

about this, and on the way to American Fork he decided he was going to somehow get rid of the whiskey. A few nights later, while Jim was away, George rummaged through the wagon, found the jug of whiskey, and gave it to a friend, asking him to empty the contents and to refill the jug with sulphur water. Jim did not discover that his whiskey was gone until a few days later.[132]

Without a doubt, the biggest disadvantage for George of being a traveling salesman was being away from Lucy. Often George would write of his hopes for a future with her. For instance, in May 1899, he wrote,

> I hope that God in his wisdom may return the past happy days to you and me . . . Lucy every dark cloud has a light behind it, and our father in heaven will not desert us when we are honest in the performance of our duty. . . . I feel that I have been too happy compared to some of my fellow travelers in life, and have been too much a lover of pleasure, and I take the present unhappy time as a trial of my integrity. I have almost idolized you, and have not realized that reverses in life are likely to come, but have thought only of our perpetual happiness. Our father in heaven has seen fit to check this happy dream, and with his assistance I shall strive to so direct my life that if in the wisdom of our father in heaven we are permitted to again enjoy ourselves as in the past, that I may be worthy of the society of one who has listened to the promptings of conscience. . . . May the blessings of heaven lighten up your life, and assist you at all times is my prayer.[133]

Sometimes George and Jim attended local dances, but because he had eyes only for Lucy, George seldom participated. When he compared them to Lucy, the other girls did not measure up. In one town he found the local girls "very good looking but a little too fresh."[134]

132 Preston Nibley, "George Albert Smith as a Salesman," *Improvement Era*, XLIX, Dec. 1946, 780–781.

133 George Albert Smith to Lucy Woodruff, 13 May 1889, George A. Smith Papers, box 135, fld 2.

134 Pusey, 211.

George often declined invitations to parties and other entertainments, preferring to write to Lucy. She was not very prompt in her letter writing to him, though—a fact that caused him quite a bit of pain. On December 8, 1889, he wrote, "I have looked for a letter from you, but I have not got a word. . . . Last trip your letters made me wish to get home. This trip I work hard to keep my mind employed, and wonder if I will enjoy myself when I get home."[135]

Christmas passed, and by January, George and Lucy's relationship was still uncertain. By March, George gave Lucy permission to go out with others while he was away on selling trips. He had debated whether to tell her to do so, but charity won out in the end, and George wrote one of the most selfless letters of his life:

> I felt in my heart to tell you to go out whenever you felt disposed, but something seemed to tell me no, and if I did, that we would be separated. I don't like the thought of you staying home all the time just because I am away. I have viewed the matter in almost every light possible, but come to the same conclusion every time. I don't feel right in being the obstacle, that is in the way of your going out when you are invited, when you feel like going, and you have said a number of things that have led me to believe that you sacrifice your feelings every time you refuse. You know I think too much of you to stand in the way of your happiness.[136]

In giving Lucy this freedom, however, George almost lost her. She dated a man a few years older named Jim, and she found she liked him more and more each time they went out. As Jim fell in love with Lucy and pressured her to end her relationship with George, she became more confused. On March 18, Jim wrote Lucy, "If you had only not made that promise with Mr. Smith but of course you knew what you wanted best and he can do so much more for you than I can. But he can't love and respect you more."[137]

---

135 George Albert Smith to Lucy Woodruff, 8 Dec. 1889, George A. Smith Papers, box 135, fld 2.

136 George Albert Smith to Lucy Woodruff, 3 March 1890, George A. Smith Papers, box 135, fld 3.

137 Jim to Lucy Woodruff, 18 March 1890, George A. Smith Papers, box 137, fld 26.

Two days after Lucy received this letter from Jim, she received one from George. He had heard about Jim and was concerned that she would end up hurting one of them in the end. He told her that she needed to make a choice. In conclusion, George added, "I have more confidence in you than any girl alive, and leave this matter entirely to you."[138] By April, Lucy had still not decided between Jim and George, and on George's twentieth birthday, he admonished Lucy, "I trust that you will be careful, for we all may be the cause of pain if we do not have a strict watch over ourselves. . . . I am Twenty today, and I feel great responsibility resting on my shoulders. If I live I hope that I will be as free from sin the next 20 years as I have been in the past."[139] Almost a month later, he revealed his state of mind during the stressful time:

> My love for you seems to get stronger instead of lessening and I trust you more and more. You have been [to me], the cause of most lasting pleasure and at other times the most exquisite pain. But it is a training, that has been for my benefit and I look back and thank our father in heaven that I have not acted unwisely, but have taken a course that has, [so far] I feel been for the best. Forgive me if I have said anything that has caused you to feel bad, for I have never intended to do so, but on the contrary I have tried to make your path one of sunshine. If I have failed it is not on account of my desires, but my own inability, and the combination of circumstances working against me.[140]

Part of what worked against George was that he was constantly out of town for his job. The remainder of 1890 passed by and the situation only worsened: "Lucy dated Jim occasionally and George Albert not at all. . . . The more time that passed, the more confused Lucy became [in making a choice]. She enjoyed Jim's company very much, and at times thought that he was the one she wanted, but

138 George Albert Smith to Lucy Woodruff, 20 March 1890, George A. Smith Papers, box 135, fld 3.

139 George Albert Smith to Lucy Woodruff, 4 April 1890, George A. Smith Papers, box 135, fld 3.

140 George Albert Smith to Lucy Woodruff, 28 April 1890, George A. Smith Papers, box 135, fld 3.

then she would see George Albert and the turmoil in her heart would begin again."[141]

By the early part of 1891, Lucy was still dating Jim, and George was avoiding her. In February she wrote in her diary: "I feel as though my life is a blank. I make everyone unhappy. My love has been my curse . . . I can stand no more."[142] Despite her sadness, Lucy's letters must have been encouraging to George. In the latter part of June, she wrote,

> Your words and opinions were perfectly just and timely. If it were not for you I don't know what would become of me. I need to be set to thinking and still at times my thoughts drive me nearly mad. You are the only one person on this earth that has enough control over me to persuade me to do anything. You must not let me sink. . . . I don't think I could stand alone without your help. Don't think I censure you when I stand in such great need of it myself. No one could realize to a greater extent than I do what little need there is to ever let a thought of the kind dwell long in the mind and hope I am forgiven for what I may have said to make you feel that way. O George I know we must both be happier some day and look at the past as trial given both from God. The burden of my heart and prayer continually is that the sunshine clouded by my actions in the unhappy past and I might say present sunshine again as it once did you know when no one but God could restore it.[143]

Lucy often expressed concern for George's health, telling George he was doing too much by "working day and night," and with each homecoming she expressed more pleasure at George's return than the

141 Lucy Woodruff, Journal, June to Dec. 1890, George A. Smith Papers, box 138, book 3, as cited in Stubbs, 44.

142 Lucy Woodruff, Journal, 5 Feb. 1891, George A. Smith Papers, box 138, book 4.

143 Lucy Woodruff to George Albert Smith, 23 June 1891, George A. Smith Papers, box 16, fld 5.

one before.[144] But still George did not ask Lucy out again. She was still dating Jim occasionally, but she maintained that the only bright spot of the summer for her was a night when she went to a party and George was there.[145]

Circumstances seemed to continue to work against George and Lucy's relationship when, in September, he was called by the First Presidency at the age of twenty-one to fulfill a short-term mission to the Juab, Millard, Beaver, and Parowan stakes in southern Utah. His mission was to labor among the young people for the Young Men's Mutual Improvement Association (YMMIA). George attended the temple to receive his endowment on September 3, 1891, and found that he "enjoyed [himself] very much." He only wished that his "friends would prepare themselves for the work to be done," too.[146]

After bidding Lucy good-bye, George departed by train for the mission field. He and his companion held meetings in various towns, organized Mutual Improvement Associations, and encouraged youth to live in accordance with Church principles. On one occasion while George was lecturing, a large fly flew into his mouth. George closed his mouth, removed the fly, and then said, "'That fly likes me better than I like him.' This set the audience in a roar."[147] Though he departed from one town feeling that it was a "spiritual graveyard," the net effect of his labors was to pump a good deal of energy into the YMMIA.[148] George wrote in his journal of what a typical day on his mission was like:

> Arose at 6-30 and took a ride on Bro. Park's Bicycle, enjoyed the ride but broke the Bicycle. Went to S. School and was called to address the School, only spoke a few words. Next was called to visit the Primary and had a nice time with the little ones. Told them the story of the Savior's Birth and Life and they told me

144 Lucy Woodruff to George Albert Smith, 2 July 1891, George A. Smith Papers, box 16, fld 6; and Lucy Woodruff to George Albert Smith, 4 July 1891, George A. Smith Papers, box 16, fld 6.

145 Lucy Woodruff, Journal, 30 July 1891, George A. Smith Papers, box 138, book 4.

146 George Albert Smith, Journal, 3 Sept. 1891 (Manti, UT), George A. Smith Papers, box 73, book 1.

147 George Albert Smith, Journal, 25 Oct. 1891, George A. Smith Papers, box 73, book 1.

148 Pusey, 212.

> who it was. Shortly after this I was surprised and much grateful to Bro. Dougall telling me that he had thought to lead in our labors together but that he felt to say to me that I was so much better qualified than him that he desired to follow me in all of our labors. . . . Held a meeting in the evening. Bro. Dougall spoke first for 25 minutes and I followed for 30 minutes. We both enjoyed the Spirit very well.[149]

Even though he enjoyed his mission, George's romantic drama continued. The emotional roller coaster he was experiencing can be observed in his brief journal entries:

> Sept. 19. Expected a letter from Lucy but did not get one. . . .
> Sept. 26. I received 5 very welcome letters from Lucy.
> Sept. 28. Wrote 20 pages to Lucy.
> Oct. 5. Went to the post office and again was very much disappointed.
> Oct. 7. Arose at 7:15 and took a short walk to the Post Office. But the same old cry of no mail greeted me.
> Oct. 20. . . . two splendid letters from Lucy.
> Oct. 30. Felt fine after reading a little while, but am puzzled about Lucy.[150]

His puzzlement about Lucy was somewhat due to the mixed messages she sent in her sporadic letters to George. Just a few weeks after George left on his mission, she expressed what seemed to be loving concern for him in addition to concern for her own health:

> My nerves and mind have been on such a strain and worked to such a pitch that I can hardly control myself at times. . . . Why must you do as you are doing that you can't have time to even rest yourself. I will do what you say. Don't say I always do just as I please no matter

149 George Albert Smith, Journal, 13 Sept. 1891, George A. Smith Papers, box 73, book 1.

150 Ibid.

> what you say. I won't take it any more if I can help it. I am very much better only in place of my heart I have such an aching. I feel like I must come to you and I can't hardly stand it. I beg of you with all the fervency of my heart to be careful and come home to me strong, strong enough for me [too] for I am very weak and you will find that my weakness is not all in my character. I cannot bear to think of you going night and day without time to hardly think. How foolish I am crying all over this letter until I guess I will spoil it.[151]

Yet, Lucy was still very confused regarding Jim and George. In October, right before George came home from a trip, she had decided to end her relationship with Jim once and for all, but a few days later she had given in to Jim's requests and went out riding with him again. That night she recorded in her diary, "I love him and I have loved someone else and I hope to do right. The spirit of God must guide me."[152] A few days later she added, "In the afternoon I was warned to marry whom I loved. Will love alone suffice?"[153] By mid-October Lucy's emotional state seemed to have deteriorated even more. She wrote in a letter to George that she was "incapable of uttering a prayer. The words would die with utterance and my senses would fail to control a sentence. You cannot imagine the condition I have been in at times and I might tell you things you would dislike but you will think I have the blues again and I haven't," she divulged.[154] She then closed her letter by making a promise: "With love of, your little wife—if God permits."[155] By October 28, just before George came home from his mission, she seemed to finally have found some peace, writing, "I have sometimes thought God almost unjust to send so many trials but my heart is at peace now more than it ever was before in my life."[156]

George must have become very puzzled after reading Lucy's

151 Lucy Woodruff to George Albert Smith, 24 Sept. 1891, George A. Smith Papers, box 16, fld 7. (There are actual tear stains on this letter.)

152 Lucy Woodruff, Journal, 30 Oct. 1891, George A. Smith Papers, box 138, book 4.

153 Lucy Woodruff, Journal, 3 Nov. 1891, George A. Smith Papers, box 138, book 4.

154 Lucy Woodruff to George Albert Smith, 16 Oct. 1891, George A. Smith Papers, box 16, fld 8.

155 Ibid.

156 Lucy Woodruff to George Albert Smith, 28 Oct. 1891, George A. Smith Papers, box 16, fld 9.

assertion that she was more at peace than ever before in her life when he learned through the grapevine that Lucy was making wedding preparations to be married to Jim! While visiting the town of Nephi, he wrote her a long letter in which he seemed almost resigned to losing her. Referring to her photo as a ten-year-old girl, which he always kept with him, he concluded:

> It recalled to me a time when I never knew what it was to be jealous, but it was a long time ago. I then thought that I could live for you and you for me and we would always be happy. But it seems that such a thing was not to be, and maybe it is better so. If you had not made me feel unhappy some times I would not have known what it was and consequently would not appreciate true happiness, when it was given to me. I do not mean to reprimand you for the things you may have done innocently, but I thank you for the confidence you have given me. My greatest blessing is my clear record. Be prayerful and humble, do not mistake the duty you owe to others. Your first duty is to yourself. I feel that you will be happy and my prayer is that you will.[157]

In November 1891, George was on his way home from his mission. He'd made sure there had been a change in his appearance before he saw Lucy again. At her insistence, he had shaved off the beard he had grown. As they headed into Salt Lake, George recorded, "the moon appeared over the hill and it was lovely. Everything [was covered] with snow; [and] seemed to be studded with diamonds from the moonlight."[158]

By the time George arrived home, it seemed that Lucy had ended her relationship with Jim. In reality, however, Lucy was still torn. She was brokenhearted, but George was home, and she began to see him on a regular basis. However, it was not long before she also began seeing Jim again. Finally, on the last day of 1891, Lucy decided to marry George, and she wrote a letter to Jim to inform him that their relationship was over. But her heart was still not at rest. Lucy didn't know how she

157 George Albert Smith, Journal, 13 Sept. 1891, George A. Smith Papers, box 73, book 1.

158 George Albert Smith, Journal, 14 Nov. 1891, George A. Smith Papers, box 73, book 1.

"refrained from the sorrow," and she described herself as feeling "scorched and burned" and like "this heavy feeling" would consume her.[159]

By the end of February, Lucy was near emotional breakdown, and George insisted that the trouble be resolved once and for all. While Lucy went to Brigham City to visit her Aunt Phoebe Woodruff Snow, George went on a ride with his rival. Imagine George's surprise when he learned that Lucy had assured Jim that all was well and that everything was over between her and George. After talking to Jim, George wrote a letter on March 18 letting Lucy know he was willing to sacrifice his happiness for her own:

> Dear Sister,
> . . . I feel to shoulder only part of the responsibility attached to our recent painful separation. I do not feel to reproach you, but your own disrupted condition of mind, and apparent fearfulness of results caused me to feel that all was not right. As my promised wife you failed in strength (and you were not to blame for that) to do as you seemed to desire. I desired you to be free, and [to] regain your lost strength, that in the vigor of your mind you might more carefully select the path to pursue. You ask me not again to encourage you, to bring disappointment to you. Lucy, will you never know me or am I devoid of language to express myself intelligibly? I will not encourage you any more, but will *wait* until you are strong again, and more able to realize the love that I bear you. When you, if ever, can come to me and tell me that you are not encouraging any one else, that all is over between you and them, I can then feel that I am free to hope for your love without doing any one on earth an injustice. . . .
>
> Let me entreat you to be careful, not to hold subservient two hearts. . . .[160]

159 Lucy Woodruff, Journal, 31 Dec. 1891, George A. Smith Papers, box 16, fld 9.

160 George Albert Smith to Lucy Woodruff, 2 May 1892, George A. Smith Papers, box 124, fld 8.

After receiving George's letter, she "prayed for strength and [then] felt much better."[161] Though George had suggested Lucy stay away for two months, she returned home in just sixteen days, prepared to marry George. However, when she got home, Jim insisted on seeing her again and she relented. Soon she was going out with Jim almost as frequently as she was going out with George, and as late as April 15, Lucy was still spending time with both young men.[162]

On May 2, George received a letter calling him to serve a full-time mission to the Southern States Mission. He would be gone for two years, and he felt that the matter must be resolved before he left. He felt his mission call could free both him and Lucy of the situation, and he realized that she'd probably be married to someone else before he returned. "I just wanted to say good-bye," he told her. Her reply surprised him: "George Albert Smith, if you think you're going to the Southern States without me, you're wrong. Let's get married and go together."[163] Lucy finally terminated her relationship with Jim and began to plan for her wedding in the Manti Temple on May 25, 1892. (The Salt Lake Temple was not yet open.) If she thought she would finally be at peace, she was wrong. As the date for the wedding approached, Jim begged and cajoled Lucy to reconsider, and finally asked that his gifts be returned. Jim eventually wrote Lucy, telling her he was leaving for Chicago and that he "hoped he would never return alive."[164] Jim's apparent threat of suicide left Lucy in a state of panic. Even until her wedding day, she was still in turmoil at the thought of him.[165]

George's parents and Lucy's Aunt Edith A. Smith accompanied twenty-two-year-old George Albert Smith and twenty-three-year-old Lucy Emily Woodruff as they left for their wedding early on May 24. Lucy's eyes were red and puffy. The next day, May 25—their wedding day—things did not improve. The temple was beautiful, but Lucy worried about Jim.[166] John Henry Smith performed the ceremony, sealing George and Lucy for time and all eternity. Wedding announcements were sent out, engraved with the following:

161 Lucy Woodruff, Journal, March 1892, George A. Smith Papers, box 73, book 4.

162 Stubbs, 47.

163 Swinton, 24.

164 Pusey, 214.

165 Lucy Woodruff, Journal, 23 May 1892, George A. Smith Papers, box 73, fld 1.

166 Lucy Woodruff Smith to George Albert Smith, 4 Sept. 1892, George A. Smith Papers, box 65, fld 2; and Pusey, 214–215.

Married
Wednesday May twenty fifth
Eighteen hundred and ninety two
Salt Lake City, Utah
George A. Smith
Lucy E. Woodruff

At home until
June 10th
23 N. West Temple[167]

Returning to the Smith home, Lucy found relatives and friends waiting to share her and George's joy as she presented George with the locket that contained her photographs. Her fears about Jim committing suicide never materialized. Years later, after Jim had married and started a family, he almost lost his home because the mortgage had been in default—but George, in a definitive act of charity, cosigned a loan with Jim and later paid the balance due on Jim's mortgage.[168] Much later, in regards to Jim, Lucy Woodruff Smith exclaimed again and again that she had "almost made a terrible mistake."[169]

For George, his wedding day marked the end of a twelve-year quest to make Lucy his. There was only one girl for him from childhood to death—and now, with the sealing ceremony completed, his childhood hopes were realized. Just a few weeks later, he explained his feelings to Lucy about their wedding and about the first prayer they had uttered as husband and wife:

> When in the sacred place we plighted our marriage vows and you were given to me by the servant of the Living God to Love and Cherish, a light seemed to break upon me, an opening in the darkness and a faint glimpse of

167 "Wedding Announcement of George Albert Smith and Emily Lucy Woodruff," LDS Archives (Salt Lake City, UT), ms 13155.

168 Pusey, 217.

169 Gibbons, 21.

> our pure childish days seemed to present itself. Then little by little the light seemed approaching and the Love and joy of our married life dawned upon me. I have ever since felt an increase of that holy feeling, that God given Light, that holy heavenly love coming upon me as if to say You never before knew the meaning of the word Love. I feel to acknowledge my Darling that our first prayer as Husband and Wife has been heard, and that we are learning the lesson of perfect Love and how sweet it is to me. Yes, my darling you can help me with my work.[170]

Though George felt secure after the ceremony, there were still rocky roads ahead for him and his bride.

170 George Albert Smith to Lucy Woodruff Smith, 9 July 1892, George A. Smith Papers, box 65, fld 9.

Chapter 6

I HOPE THEY CALL HER ON A MISSION

In the woods near a Mississippi farm, George attended his first missionary conference in the Southern States Mission. During the conference, George and the other elders balanced themselves on tree stumps or fallen logs or sat on the ground. Though the meeting had started right after breakfast, George found it unnecessary to eat anything more until evening. Much to his surprise, he was able to enjoy the blessings and "inspiration of the Almighty . . . notwithstanding the inconveniences and discomforts which surrounded [him]." George found that "the companionship of the spirit of the Lord is an antidote for weariness, for hunger, for fear, and all those things that sometimes overtake us in life."[171]

When George was set apart as a missionary to the Southern States on June 22, 1892, he was promised that the Spirit would guide him and that he would be "inspired to act in faith and understanding." He was also promised that he would be protected from "every evil both seen and unseen, from dangers upon the right and the left, from accidents, from storms, and tempests, temptations and devouring elements," that he would be preserved "from the hands of wicked men, from the ravages of disease and the power of the destroyer in every form and shape," and that he would return "home in safety and peace, after having gathered a harvest of experience."[172]

With these miraculous promises, it seemed nothing could possibly prevent George's missionary success. But right from the

171 CR, Oct. 1945, 115.

172 Setting apart of George Albert Smith to be a missionary in the Southern States Mission, George A. Smith Papers, box 100.

start, he encountered an enormous trial—his separation from his new bride. Although Lucy had hoped she would be able to accompany George on his mission, it was decided that Lucy should stay in Utah. When he departed for his mission on June 23, 1892, he had been married to Lucy for less than a month. The two and a half days it took for Lucy's first letter to arrive seemed to George like weeks, even months.[173] The letter, however, brought more worry than comfort. Lucy sounded almost hysterical. Her letter of June 28, written in response to a note George wrote on the train, read:

> If God in his mercy doesn't relieve me in a short time I cannot stand it. . . . Something is wrong, something is the matter that I neither comprehend or understand. I have done wrong. I have sought to repair that wrong and it seems my attempt only meets with repeated failure.
>
> Last night I wanted to write and I could not frame one sentence to express myself. I felt devoid of language of expression in any degree. . . . Would that I could paint before the eyes of every girl in flaming letters beware of my course, keep out of my footsteps.
>
> I don't know why I have written these words but my crazed brain feels relieved. . . . Please destroy this and if I have ever been cruel or unkind to you in any form whatever it was a fault of the pen or the tongue not the heart Good night."[174]

George attempted to comfort her in his reply: "Your long looked for and much expected letter came today and my eyes filled with tears. . . . I read it and read it and read it over and over. . . . I choked the tears back. . . . Your image is always near me."[175] What a struggle George must have had being away from his new bride, especially when he knew how she was suffering. The day after George departed, Lucy recorded in her diary, "How terrible I felt all night! God spare

173 George Albert Smith to Lucy Woodruff Smith, 30 June 1892, George A. Smith Papers, box 65, fld 9.

174 Lucy Woodruff Smith to George Albert Smith (Salt Lake City, UT), 28 June 1892, George A. Smith Papers, box 73, fld 2.

175 George Albert Smith to Lucy Woodruff Smith, 30 June 1892, George A. Smith Papers, box 65, fld 9.

me another such night."[176] Just two days later, Lucy's fears and loneliness were expressed in another poignant letter:

> You have been away from me only three days and yet it seems years to me. . . . I went to bed blew out the light and there my heart failed me entirely. I suffered all I could until I nearly fainted. I then went down stairs determined to call you[r] ma but was ashamed of my weakness and returned without doing so. I lit my lamp and went back to bed but it was of no use. I trembled [from] head to [foot] and had no control of myself. . . . I hope I never [have] to endure such a pang of separation again.[177]

Fortunately for George, Lucy had close friends and family to comfort her during his absence. The night she wrote the second letter, four of her friends serenaded her under her window, trying to comfort her with words such as "Bury your sorrow and look to Jesus for comfort." She reported to George that she was so touched by their kindness that she cried all night. However, the comfort was short-lived. The separation was too much for her, and she told anyone who would listen that she was suffering in deep agony. Lucy also complained of her weakness and delicate health. She called her suffering "terror" and complained to George that she could never again sleep well without his company. Closing her letter, she said, "If I soon know that I may again receive your loving embraces before this year is past how my heart will beat for joy."[178] Lucy's longing for her husband filled her nighttime hours. Perhaps the only thing that comforted her was the thought that she might be able to join him on his mission. She wrote:

> I dreamed again this morning you held me in your arms and was just pressing your lips to mine when I awoke and found it only a dream. I have felt so happy

176 Pusey, 216–217.

177 Lucy Woodruff Smith to George Albert Smith (Salt Lake City, UT), 26 June 1892, George A. Smith Papers, box 73, fld 2.

178 Lucy Woodruff Smith to George Albert Smith (Salt Lake City, UT), 26 June 1892, George A. Smith Papers, box 73, fld 2.

> to feel so convinced that I am alright and can come to you some time. I am so happy in your love and if you were only here with me it seems that I could dream of nothing more heavenly on Earth but I would not have you return to me on any consideration without first doing your duty to God and coming home honorably released; and I know your faithful heart echoes the same sentiments.[179]

Although Lucy was miserable during her husband's absence, she was also fearful about joining him in an unknown region. Her anxieties about George's absence, however, far outweighed her fears about their reunion. She wrote of her hope that the separation would be temporary in another letter:

> It seems so awfully hard to have just a little taste of happiness and then to have it snatched away from me but I am coming to you unless I find that by my coming it will lengthen your stay as has been suggested to me. If I thought such would be the case I should not come at all. . . . After the first letter I wrote you and I had overcome my outward grief I felt quite convinced that if my alarm had a foundation I must content myself and remain where I was but I feel so grateful that it was only an alarm for I feel quite convinced that I must have been mistaken; because now surely we won't be [separated] so long.[180]

Lucy was not only distressed about her own situation but fearful of what George was going through. On July 3, she wrote, "Yesterday I wondered all day where you were and what you were doing. If you were at meeting and if you were thinking of me. I wonder how you will spend today and if you are awakened with [cannons] and bombs." Along with her concerns she again expressed her love and the security she felt in George's faithfulness: "I am so confident of your

179 Lucy Woodruff Smith to George Albert Smith (Salt Lake City, UT), 2 July 1892, George A. Smith Papers, box 73, fld 2.

180 Lucy Woodruff Smith to George Albert Smith (Salt Lake City, UT), 3 July 1892, George A. Smith Papers, box 73, fld 2.

love and care I could stake my life against it and I hope it is not self conceit when I say you can trust your wife with utmost confidence wherever she is in your absence and I can trust my darling husband because I know he is true to me."[181]

Lucy constantly worried about George's well-being. On July 4 she responded to a letter from George, saying, "The feeling you describe about working yourself into a frenzy and an [aching] feeling tugging at your heart is just what I have been experiencing and it is just awful. . . . I fervently hope that before long I may be permitted to join you . . ."[182]

Letters back and forth between husband and wife continued to include a hope that they would soon be united in the mission field, but it seemed the odds were against that as time passed. And even though she tried to have confidence in her new husband, it seems their separation sometimes caused her to be anxious about the state of George's affections. Lucy wrote in one letter, "O my sweetheart don't ever love any one else but me."[183]

This anxiety may have been caused by letters that Lucy had begun receiving from another man less inclined to celebrate her marriage. Jim, her former suitor, had not killed himself and was still eager for Lucy's correspondence and company. One Sunday evening he walked her home from church, taking advantage of the opportunity to relieve her loneliness. Jim visited her at home a few times, apparently eager to break up the newlyweds.[184] George was in Tennessee when he received word that Jim was back in Lucy's life. As an overwhelming feeling of homesickness set in, he went to a secluded place and "knelt down and asked the Lord to rebuke the feeling." When he got up, he felt "sunshine in [his] soul" and never felt homesick again.[185]

Lucy did not have the same kind of experience. Jim's attentions frightened her, and Lucy's longing to be by George's side increased as time went on. On July 10, she wrote:

---

181 Ibid.

182 Lucy Woodruff Smith to George Albert Smith (Salt Lake City, UT), 5 July 1892, George A. Smith Papers, box 73 fld 3.

183 Lucy W. Smith to George Albert Smith (Salt Lake City, UT), July 8, 1892, George A. Smith Papers, box 73, fld. 2.

184 Pusey, 216.

185 George Albert Smith to Albert and Elsie Stevens (San Bernardino, CA), 13 March 1918, box 43, fld 26, 3.

> I cried myself to sleep. I felt perfectly alone in the world almost forsaken. It seemed so terrible to be married and no one near to protect me. I do hope the climate down there won't make me sick because I want to be with you so badly. . . . Tonight I feel just perfectly forsaken. I feel just as though I couldn't stand this solitude one minute longer and still this is wrong I was going to say why did you leave me but you are serving your God and I am only making your trial harder to bear but my heart feels tonight like bursting and I must not encourage this feeling. . . . My darling do you know that I felt somewhat anxious to-day over the way I felt least I should be prevented from coming to you. I think you will agree with me although I don't know how you are situated that you would have almost too much if I [came] to you and you had to nurse me but O tonight if I could only lie down in your arms but I must not talk like that or even think about [it] because I can't.[186]

It seemed George's letters were Lucy's lifeline—and when his letters were delayed for some reason, it caused her even greater anxiety.[187] George was doing his utmost to attain permission to bring his wife into the mission field, but things were not going as planned. Lucy would only be able to join George if he were stationed at the mission office. He wrote Lucy at one point that he would not be back in the office for two to three months, but then later he wrote and told her that he thought she could come in August. These letters left Lucy confused about when she would have the opportunity to join her husband.[188]

When J. Golden Kimball, President of the Southern States Mission and member of the First Council of the Seventy, returned to Salt Lake City in July on personal business, both Lucy and George hoped

186 Lucy Woodruff Smith to George Albert Smith (Salt Lake City, UT), 10 July 1892, George A. Smith Papers, box 73, fld 3.

187 Lucy Woodruff Smith to George Albert Smith (Salt Lake City, UT), 11 July 1892, George A. Smith Papers, box 73, fld 3.

188 Lucy Woodruff Smith to George Albert Smith (Salt Lake City, UT), 13 July 1892, George A. Smith Papers, box 73, fld 3.

that Lucy could travel back to the south with Elder Kimball when he returned. In fact, this seemed so likely that George arranged to rent a house and was trying to obtain furniture for it. President Kimball, however, did not agree with this plan and told Lucy in July that her husband would not continue to work in the office as they had been hoping. President Kimball felt George needed more experience in the field, and so their plans would have to be postponed.[189]

When J. Golden Kimball told Lucy of the postponement, she tried to compose herself as she wrote her husband on July 15: "Some might wonder and I sometimes do myself that I could compose myself but it is through Gods merciful kindness that I can. His mercies are so bountiful I pity those who cannot partake of his comfort. If you could go through life without tasting the bitter you nor I could appreciate the sweet."[190]

In August, however, the couple's faith was further tested when President Kimball delivered the news to both George and Lucy that she probably could not come to him at all.[191] The thought of Lucy not joining him put George into deep despair. Seeking solace, he read his wife's letters again and again. George knew he was "a little bit too anxious to see [his] wife," but knowing their separation might last for two years seemed unbearable. Upon receiving the bad news, George began to pray that the decision would be changed.[192]

A few days later, Lucy again began to feel somewhat insecure about George's affections, as is evidenced in the letter she wrote to George on August 10:

> I get along pretty well during the day but at night I am so lonesome I feel as though I were reaching and longing for something near and still so far away. Last night I lay on my bed and it seemed if I could only lie my head on your arm a few moments I would be so happy. . . . I lay here in the beautiful moonlight thinking and thinking

189 George Albert Smith to Lucy Woodruff Smith, 5 Aug. 1892, George A. Smith Papers, box 73, fld 3.

190 Lucy Woodruff Smith to George Albert Smith (Salt Lake City, UT), 15 July 1892, George A. Smith Papers, box 73, fld 3.

191 George Albert Smith to Lucy Woodruff Smith, 5 Aug. 1892, George A. Smith Papers, box 65, fld 9.

192 George Albert Smith, Journal, 20 Aug. to 29 Aug. 1892, George A. Smith Papers, box 67, book 1.

> of you and wondering if you knew me well enough yet to know you would be perfectly happy with me and not disappointed when I came to you. I hope I will be to you all that you expect because it would break my heart to be a disappointment to you.[193]

Though George continually tried to reassure Lucy by telling her that in his estimation she was superior to all other women, she still worried that his boundless confidence would prove to be unfounded. She wrote on August 11:

> My heart just thrills with joy to hear your loving words or rather to read them on paper because it seems to me such a long time to wait to hear you speak them. I sit and think and dream of you until I wonder if it is possible that we are married or that we will be again united. Will you forget my ways or think me queen when we meet again. I am glad if you think I manifest a patient spirit because it seems to me I am very impatient because I feel sometimes so uneasy that I could fly. If my letters are any comfort to you I am very much pleased because to me they don't seem to contain very much comfort. . . . You need not imagine for one minute that I want you to come in contact with all the filth in Tennessee because I sometimes imagine George will be disappointed in me or some of my ways but I will try hard to please you; so I don't want you to go through anything you don't have to but some of your experiences I thought might make it more easy for you to endure my imperfections.[194]

Though her grief was poignant, Lucy tried to reconcile herself to the conditions in which she found herself and showed faith that things might change in the future. She wrote George on August 21:

193 Lucy Woodruff Smith to George Albert Smith (Salt Lake City, UT), 10 Aug. 1892, George A. Smith Papers, box 73, fld 3.

194 Lucy Woodruff Smith to George Albert Smith (Salt Lake City, UT), 11 Aug. 1892, George A. Smith Papers, box 73, fld 3.

> Even though I have been feeling badly I can't help but feel grateful to God for [not permitting] me to join you without being a great care to you at the present. . . . After my grief was calmed so that I had control of myself after you left, I just felt resigned and thought I will acknowledge the goodness of my Father in Heaven let my condition be what it may but my Darling my mind was fully made up that had it been otherwise my place was here and that I would not burden you should have patiently waited your return. . . . My only desire in life is to be a true woman worthy [of] the love and respect of my husband and [the] friendship of all my brothers and sisters. I feel that I have very much to learn and you can help me, that when if God permits I shall have become the noblest instrument or attain in my opinion to the most important part of woman's life that of—mother—I may have the joy of hearing some one's lips whisper that they love me for my goodness I shall be so happy! I feel that I need so much preparing not only in that direction but in so many ways that I know our little stay in the South will be a school for both. I need it badly. . . . I know I am weak but hope I will have strength to overcome my temptations. If I were to fall in your estimation I would [feel] very badly indeed.[195]

Just as George and Lucy seemed resigned to the cancellation of their reunion, President J. Golden Kimball reversed his decision. The change was probably sparked by the influence of George's father, John Henry Smith, who "was keenly aware of Lucy's loneliness and suspicious of [her former suitor's] intentions." John Henry arranged to have Lucy called on a mission to the Southern States with her husband. When George heard Lucy was to join him, he wrote to her in great anticipation: "My own darling wife, You will never know how I have longed for you the last few days. I can

195 Lucy Woodruff Smith to George Albert Smith (Salt Lake City, UT), 21 Aug. 1892, George A. Smith Papers, box 73, fld 3.

hardly wait for you to come. . . . You are the dearest, sweetest wife in the whole world. I am until the morrow yours in dreamland."[196]

Still, the couple worried over the decision. On September 18, George wrote Lucy that he was uneasy concerning something President Kimball had said to him. Lucy wrote immediately back: "Please tell me what you mean."[197] Despite her worries, as the time drew nearer Lucy began to express more excitement at the prospect of seeing George once again:

> When I think of the possibility of coming to you I can't hardly contain my self I am so overjoyed. . . . My Darling my all I can't find words to express myself on paper to you I love you so dearly. . . . Don't think I will ever be dissatisfied with you I love you too dearly. With you I think I could be strong enough to bear anything or go through any trials. Darling I hope I don't go crazy with joy over the prospect of joining you. There is no attraction for me here without you.[198]

By October Lucy's feelings of inadequacy resurfaced, and she became concerned that their separation may have caused a change in George. She wondered if he would be the same husband with whom she had spent such a brief few weeks. She wrote George:

> If Bro Geo A Smith gets to be an unapproachable minister I shall almost be afraid of him. He may tower way above poor little me. You don't know how terrible it makes me feel to read of your exploits in caves and some of the terrible places you get into . . . What did you mean when you said I could come and pay you a long visit? Darling can't I stay with you when I come I don't think I could leave you again. The morning you left me I felt almost as though the whole world had passed away and I never could be happy again.[199]

---

196 Gibbons, 216.

197 Lucy Woodruff Smith to George Albert Smith (Salt Lake City, UT), 18 Sept. and 21 Sept. 1892, George A. Smith Papers, box 73, fld 3.

198 Lucy Woodruff Smith to George Albert Smith (Salt Lake City, UT), 27 Sept. 1892, George A. Smith Papers, box 73, fld 3.

199 Lucy Woodruff Smith to George Albert Smith (Salt Lake City, UT), 7 Oct. 1892, George A. Smith

Finally, after a painful five-month separation, George and Lucy were reunited when Lucy arrived sometime in November. Despite their expectation of being together, George was often traveling, and so the couple was, again, frequently apart. Furthermore, Lucy had a difficult time adjusting to life in the South. She missed her home, her familiar environment, and her friends. Due to so many physical adjustments and the emotional upheaval, Lucy's health wavered. In response to her ailments, a doctor prescribed morphine and bromide.[200]

Lucy's letters to George while he was away from the mission home were full of both cries of loneliness and gushes of affection. For instance, in one letter, Lucy wrote, "I have been so blue since you left but am alright now. . . . I can't live without you. . . . I am the richest woman in the US because I have such a jewel of a husband. Every thing is alright. Did you ever have such a jangling letter but [this] is the way I felt. Imagine yourself kissed nearly to death with my arms around your neck."[201] George's frequent trips produced more of Lucy's complaints and fears. On one journey away from the mission home, George had a dream that may have served as an admonition to Lucy to become more of a helpmeet to her husband on his mission:

> I had a very funny dream about you night before last. I thought I was going somewhere in a boat but you was [sic] afraid to go with me. It seemed as if the journey was right out on the ocean in a little row boat, and did appear dangerous. It was as though I had to have a female companion before I could perform this very important mission. You were delaying all the time for fear. All at once a lady stepped into the boat and as I rowed away the people on the bank cheered us, for it seemed to be a dangerous yet necessary trip, and they were pleased to find someone willing to do the work. The journey was not a very pleasant one for me, although the other occupant of the boat seemed to be enjoying it very well, and tried to be

---

Papers, box 73, fld 3.

200 Lucy Woodruff Smith to George Albert Smith, 29 Sept. 1893, George A. Smith Papers, box 73, fld 3.

201 Lucy Woodruff Smith to George Albert Smith, 2 Nov. 1893, George A. Smith Papers, box 73, fld 3.

> very agreeable. I kept wishing you had trusted me more and had tried to forget home and friends. I didn't pay much attention to my companion until we appeared to be nearing a beautiful Island where it seemed we were to land. Everything seemed so inviting yet very strange. I was wondering what I would do with my company, when the boat touched the shore and it seemed as if the dangerous journey was completed without any trouble, which was very strange to me. I jumped out and turned to help the stranger when to my surprise you sprang from the boat into my arms. No one can tell how happy I was. The person in the boat had been you in disguise. We went up on top of a hill and feasted on all kinds of luscious fruit. I awoke and have thought of my dream several times since.[202]

As time went on, Lucy seemed to settle into her work at the mission home, though she was still concerned about what might be happening to her husband. And Lucy's fears about her husband's safety were not unfounded. From the very start of his mission, George needed his promised blessings of protection. The work of the gospel had to move forward amongst intense hatred and violence. At the time of his arrival in the mission field, missionaries there had already undergone persecution. The following note was found on the rostrum of a college building where two missionaries were scheduled to speak:

> To the Mormons:
> We Citizens of Montgomery respectfully notify you that you will not be allowed to propagate your nefarious Mormonistic doctrines in this part of the country. And in order for you to be safe will allow you only 3 days to make good your escape otherwise you will be dealt with in a manner that may prove very unpleasant for you. We have not forgotten some of the depredations committed upon some of the citizens of the U.S. by some of your sect and we call your attention to the fate of your leader,

202 George Albert Smith to Lucy Woodruff Smith, 30 Nov. 1892, George A. Smith Papers, box 65, fld 9.

> Joseph Smith, and think that a hint to the wise should be sufficient.[203]

One hot summer day, George and his companion came to a small house at the bottom of a hill where they found some friendly people who invited them to supper. After the meal, they invited George and his companion to "go outside in the cool of the afternoon shade" on an open porch between two rooms and to sing some hymns. Though the people were not members of the Church, they enjoyed Latter-day Saint hymns. While the missionaries had been having dinner, a man who had previously threatened the missionaries learned that George and his companion had arrived. This man "sent word to his associates, who saddled their horses and took their guns, and rode to the top of the hill overlooking the little house." As George and his companion sat and sang hymns, they were unaware of the armed horsemen nearby. One hymn that the two missionaries sang was "Do What Is Right," which "seemed to have been prepared for the occasion." George, with his beautiful tenor voice, sang into the afternoon air, loud enough for the mob to hear. George later recalled, "They had only sung one verse when the leader of the mob took off his hat. They sang another verse, and he got off his horse, and the others got off their horses, and by the time the last verse had been sung," the mob's leader advised the rest of the horsemen to "[ride] away without making their presence known." George later learned that the leader was so impressed with what he had heard the missionaries sing, he said to his associates, "We made a mistake. . . . They must be servants of the Lord." Later, the mob's leader was converted to the Church and baptized.[204]

As George came back and shared such experiences with his sweetheart, her heart began to soften, and she began to fulfill her role as a mission wife without much complaint or fear. George continued to experience the protection of the Spirit as he found himself in precarious situations.

For instance, on one pitch-black night, George and his companion, Elder Stout, were walking along a high, narrow precipice on their way to a home where they expected to find shelter. On one side was the wall of the mountain, and the Caney Fork River ran below on the

203 Copy in George Albert Smith's handwriting of notice posted on rostrum of a college building in Montgomery County, Tennessee, George A. Smith Papers, box 135, fld 11.

204 George Albert Smith, CR, Oct. 1945, 116.

other side. The missionaries groped their way along the ledge with one hand extended toward the wall of the mountain. Elder Stout was ahead of George as they walked along, but at one point, George had taken a few steps away from the wall. He immediately felt impressed to stop. George called out to Elder Stout and found that the direction from which his voice came indicated that George had wandered off the trail, so he backed up until he reached the wall of the mountain again and then proceeded forward. Elder Stout was now just a few steps in front of him. As George reached him, they came to a fence piling. They explored the piling with their hands and feet to see whether it would be safe for them to climb over and then proceeded to do so. While George was on top of the big pile of logs, his suitcase popped open and its contents were scattered about. George felt around and gathered his belongings, and he believed he had recovered everything he had lost. George and Elder Stout arrived safely at their destination later that night, but George soon discovered the next morning that he had lost his comb and brush.

George and Elder Stout returned to the scene. After recovering George's comb and brush, the curious missionaries retraced George's tracks where they left the trail by the mountain wall. They discovered that in the darkness George had wandered to the edge of a deep precipice. If he had taken one more step, George would have fallen into the river. George later wrote, "I felt very ill when I realized how close I had come to death . . . and was very grateful to my Heavenly Father for protecting me."[205]

Another frightening experience occurred on November 5, 1893, in southern Alabama when George, J. Golden Kimball, and four other missionaries had retired to some investigators' log cabin, located in a wooded rural area. Their preaching in the neighborhood had apparently aroused bitter opposition. Consisting of only two rooms and a log lean-to, the little house was filled to capacity. During the night, George and his companions were awakened by a terrible shouting from outside. According to George, "A man pounded on the door and used filthy language, ordering the Mormons to come out [and saying] that they

205 George Albert Smith, "How My Life was Preserved," *A Story to Tell*, General Board of the Primary Association and Deseret Sunday School Union Board (Salt Lake City, UT: Deseret Book, 1959), 157–158.

were going to shoot them. President Kimball asked me if I wasn't going to get up and dress and I told him no, I was going to stay in bed, that I was sure the Lord would take care of us." Soon the mob, having divided into four groups, shot at each corner of the house, sending splinters in every direction. Though perhaps "experiencing one of the most horrible events of [his] life," George was calm. He knew that "as long as [he] was preaching the word of God and following his teachings that the Lord would protect [him], and he did." Finally, the mob became discouraged and left. The next morning when the missionaries opened the door, they found a large bundle of the heavy hickory sticks that mobs often used to beat missionaries in the South. George kept some of the splinters that had fallen on his bed as a reminder of the miraculous experience.[206]

As their missions progressed, the friendship and mutual respect between George and J. Golden Kimball grew. President Kimball had left the mission field in the middle of November 1892 and had not returned until the end of August 1893. He was only back for about two and a half months when he found that he had to again return to Utah, where he remained until May 1894. During President Kimball's absence, George—at only twenty-two years of age—was given charge over the one hundred missionaries scattered throughout the Southern States Mission. The only guidance George received during this time was through occasional letters from President Kimball. He learned to love J. Golden "for his courage and kindness [and found that] his sense of humor drew men to him." George and the other missionaries found much inspiration in President Kimball's testimony of the gospel.[207] The respect between the correspondents was reciprocal. J. Golden found that George exhibited a commendable work ethic and predicted that if George would continue in his faithfulness, he would become a great man.[208]

As had been promised when he was set apart, George was blessed with a "harvest of experience" that helped him grow. While on his mission, George developed many praiseworthy traits, including his great ability to trust in the Lord. He also developed a speaking style

206 George Albert Smith, "How My Life Was Preserved," *A Story to Tell*, General Board of the Primary Association and Deseret Sunday School Union Board (Salt Lake City, UT: Deseret Book, 1959), 156.

207 Claude Richards, *J. Golden Kimball* (Salt Lake City, UT: Bookcraft, 1966), 114.

208 J. Golden Kimball to George Albert Smith (Salt Lake City, UT), 29 Dec. 1893, George A. Smith Papers, box 66, fld 14; and Stubbs, 65.

that became a trademark for his future ministry. George's speaking "style [was] marked by natural eloquence, vigor, and adaptability to the demands of the moment. [He] was a superb extemporaneous speaker. Only seldom did he prepare a talk. But he always filled his mind with ideas, scriptures, and apt stories."[209]

A diligent missionary, George often found opportunities to speak to people about the gospel on the train trips he took. On one such trip, George's train passed a little Native American settlement by the side of the track. George recorded:

> I boarded the train and started home, and we passed a little Indian settlement at the side of the track. I saw evidence that there were quite a number of Indians there, so I reached over and touched the man who was sitting in the seat in front of me, and I said, "Do you know what Indians these are?"
>
> He said, "They are the Catawbas." . . .
>
> I asked, "Do you know where they come from?"
>
> He said, "Do you mean the Catawbas?"
>
> I replied, "Any Indians."
>
> He said, "Nobody knows where the Indians came from."
>
> "Oh," I said, "yes, they do." I was talking then to a man about forty-five or fifty years old, and I was twenty-one.
>
> He questioned, "Well, where did they come from?"
>
> I answered, "They came from Jerusalem six hundred years before the birth of Christ."
>
> "Where did you get that information?" he asked.
>
> I told him, "From the history of the Indians."
>
> "Why," he said, "I didn't know there was any history of the Indians."
>
> I said, "Yes, there is a history of the Indians. It tells all about them." Then he looked at me as much as to say: My, you are trying to put one over on me.
>
> But he said, "Where is this history?"

209 Gibbons, 26.

"Would you like to see one?" I asked. And he said that he certainly would. I reached down under the seat in my little log-cabin grip and took out a Book of Mormon and handed it to him.

He exclaimed, "My goodness, what is this?"

I replied, "That is the history of the ancestry of the American Indian."

He said, "I never heard of it before. May I see it?"

I said, "Yes," and after he had looked at it a few minutes, he turned around to me and asked, "Won't you sell me this book? I don't want to lose the privilege of reading it through."

"Well," I said, "I will be on the train for three hours. You can read it for that long, and it won't cost you anything." I found that he was getting off farther on, but I had to get off in three hours.

In a little while he turned around again and said, "I don't want to give up this book. I've never seen anything like this before."

I could see that he apparently was a refined and well-educated man. I didn't tell him I really wanted him to read the book, but I said, "Well, I can't sell it to you. It is the only one I have." (I didn't tell him I could get as many more as I wanted.)

He said, "I think you ought to sell it to me."

I replied, "No, I'll tell you what I'll do. You keep it for three weeks, and at the end of that time you send it to me at Chattanooga," and I gave him my card with my address on, secretary of the mission.

So we bade one another good-bye, and in about two weeks he wrote me a letter saying, "I don't want to give this book up. I am sure you can get another, and I will pay you any price you want for it."

Then I had my opportunity. I wrote back, "If you really enjoy the book and have an idea it is truly worth

> while, accept it with my compliments." I received a letter of thanks back from him.[210]

Many years later when George was visiting the Southern States Mission, he ran into this man once again:

> [The man] said, "I want to tell you something. I read that book, and I was so impressed with it that I made up my mind I would like to take a trip down into Central America and South America, and I took that book with me in my bag when I went down there. As a result of reading it, I knew more about those people than they knew about themselves.
>
> "I lost your address; I didn't know how to find you, and all these years I wanted to see you, and today after you registered downstairs I happened to be looking at the hotel register and I saw your name. That is how I found you.
>
> "I am a representative of the Associated Press for this part of the United States. I understand you are here in the interest of your people."
>
> And [George] answered, "Yes, Mr. Roberts and I both are here for that purpose."
>
> And he said, "If there is anything I can do for you while you are here, if you want anything put in the press, give it to me and it won't cost you a cent. But," he continued, "I want to tell you one other thing, I have kept your missionaries out of jail; I have got them free from mobs; I have helped them every way I could; but have never been able to get your address until now."[211]

George had opportunities to meet all kinds of people, but not all of them were "golden investigators" and helpful friends like the man in this story. For instance, one man George tried to teach was ill and bedridden. When George suggested that the man take a bath to feel a little better and get out of bed, "the patient replied in boastful tones

210 "President Smith Relates a Mission Field Experience," *Improvement Era*, LIII, May 1950, 363.

211 George Albert Smith, CR, April 1950, 144.

that he had never taken a bath in his life and insisted that one of his friends had died from taking a bath." George disagreed, saying, "No one ever suffered from bathing. Why, I take a bath everyday."

"You do?" was the skeptical comeback. "Well, I reckon you must be the dirtiest person I ever saw."[212]

The final blessing George had received when he was set apart—that he would return home safely—was fulfilled when George and Lucy were given an honorable release from their missionary responsibilities in June 1894. Lucy had served well, making a worthwhile contribution in the mission home as a secretary, and George "had shouldered responsibilities beyond the experiences of most missionaries. He had shown himself to be a leader among men" and was prepared for further service in the work of the Lord.[213]

212 Pusey, 218.

213 Stubbs, 67.

Chapter 7
HIS HEART WAS RIGHT

After being honorably released from their missions, George and Lucy decided to take the long way home on a much-postponed honeymoon to Niagara Falls. But even their honeymoon was fraught with adventure. The couple was traveling by way of Chicago during the Pullman strike and "had to lie on the floor while the train was moving through the city to escape the firing of snipers."[214]

Upon returning to Salt Lake, George and Lucy rented a house at 125 North Temple in the neighborhood in which they had grown up. By this time, Lucy's grandfather, Wilford Woodruff, was President of the Church. While serving as the prophet, President Woodruff continued to own a home on West Temple, and John Henry Smith still lived with his two families in close proximity. Soon after the couple's return, Lucy's father moved in with them.[215] After being gone for two years, George and Lucy relished their close associations with family. A few years later, George and Lucy built their own home on a lot John Henry gave them, right next to his own, at 21 North West Temple.[216]

George immediately tried to secure employment at ZCMI. A man named Thomas G. Webber told him that the only job available was a position accompanying a salesman to St. George to drive and take care of the horses. Mr. Webber was sure it was a job George would not do, but George decided to take the job nobody else wanted. On the way home from the sales trip, George washed the wagon in Provo

---

214 Pusey, 219.

215 Gibbons, 32.

216 Pusey, 219.

and cleaned the horses again in Sandy. When he brought the horses and wagon back in such excellent condition, ZCMI made a place for him in its packing-box shop. There, George set a goal to make more boxes per day than the average worker did. He made a hundred boxes while the others made only sixty. Soon he became a wholesale grocery salesman and was put in charge of all grocery sales for Salt Lake City.[217] Though the nation experienced an economic slump during the 1890s, beginning with the panic of 1893, George did quite well providing for his family. In fact, he was doing so well that at one point, his own father came to him and borrowed $586 to pay his taxes.[218]

George also became involved in other activities that gave him valuable experience. In the late 1890s, he became secretary of the Kanab Cattle Company.[219] He also enlisted in the Utah National Guard, where he served as a first sergeant in Troop C, First Cavalry.[220] George had a fine horse "and made a good showing in the practice charges on Arsenal Hill." One of George's friends, noticing his performance, "advanced his name for an important office in the guard, but a jealous associate circulated false charges about him. The result was a landslide [vote] in favor of his rival." George was deeply hurt when he learned that lies had been told about him. In an uncharacteristic flair of temper, George vowed to "'beat the life out of the rumormonger' if he got a chance." The next Sunday George was still angry and did not partake of the sacrament. Soon, however, George began to feel that the "hate was cankering his soul," and after praying, he decided to turn the other cheek. The story ends as follows:

> He crossed the street to his enemy's office. As George walked in, the fellow put up his arm as if to shield himself. But George's voice was mellow with contrition. "My brother," he said, "I want you to forgive me for despising you the way I have for the last three or four weeks."

217 "Early Life Just Like That of an Ordinary Boy," *Deseret News*, vol. 335, no. 8, 8 April 1951, LDS Archives (Salt Lake City, UT), ms 9163.

218 Pusey, 221.

219 George Albert Smith, George A. Smith Papers, *Letterpress Book #1*, 53.

220 Bryant S. Hinckley, "Superintendent George Albert Smith," *Improvement Era*, XXV, March 1932, 270; and George Albert Smith, George A. Smith Papers, *Letterpress Book #1*, 53.

> "Brother Smith," the rumormonger replied, "I don't need to forgive you; you need to forgive me. If you will do so, I will try to make it right."
>
> The result was a lasting friendship between the two men.[221]

Wanting to further his career, George began a legal course from the Sprague Correspondence School of Law in 1898. George completed two out of the four books for the course but, unfortunately, his eyes gave him too much trouble and he had to drop out.[222]

During this time, George and Lucy experienced another disappointment. After four years of marriage, they still did not have children. One day in the fall of 1894, Lucy's grandfather, Wilford Woodruff, was visiting Lucy and asked her if she had any children. When she replied no, she burst into tears and said, "Much as we would like to have some we haven't any." Her grandfather then told her to sit down. He laid his hands on her head and promised her that she would have children.

About one year later, on November 19, 1895, Lucy gave birth to a daughter. John Henry blessed his granddaughter, giving her the name of Emily. Four years later, George and Lucy had another daughter, Edith, on November 10, 1899.[223]

Interestingly, George and Lucy's daughters "were a study in contrasts. The elder girl, Emily, was so active and filled with self-confidence it was said of her later that had she been a boy, she surely would have risen to the presidency of General Motors or some other major enterprise. Edith, on the other hand, was quiet, shy, demure, and retiring."[224]

George's journal entries often noted the differences between his two daughters. He wrote on November 19, 1907: "It is Emily's birthday. She is twelve years old. She is such an active, strong-willed child. I pray that the Lord will protect her and make her a woman of strength and ability. She has a keen intellect and makes splendid progress in school."

221 Pusey, 219–220.

222 George Albert Smith to Sprague Correspondence School of Law, April 1899, George A. Smith Papers, box 74, fld 6.

223 Pusey, 220.

224 Gibbons, 34–35.

A year later, on November 10, 1908, after Edith's ninth birthday party, George wrote, "Edith was very happy and seemed much pleased with several little presents she received. Edith is a quiet, lovable child and is very solicitous for her mother."[225]

The Smith family was complete on September 10, 1905, when Lucy gave birth to their only son, her husband's namesake, George Albert. George was grateful to his Heavenly Father for the birth of his son and that Lucy had survived the difficult birth.[226] The recovery time for Lucy was prolonged, and George secured a nurse to help her with the baby.[227] Even a month later, Lucy was still not feeling well, and she struggled with her health for the next several years.[228] But even with her poor health, she was grateful to have her son: "My boy is certainly a gift from God. He is just about as perfect as his father."[229] George loved and enjoyed his son as well, and as the boy grew, he and his father became hiking and camping companions.[230]

As George's family grew, George decided to look for more lucrative employment. John Henry—who, with George, was very active in the Republican Party—suggested that George become postmaster for Salt Lake City. John Henry and George wrote to various persons in political positions, seeking endorsements.[231] Service to the party in power was the first qualification for federal office in those days, and George had earned this reward by vigorously campaigning for President William McKinley in 1896. Utah had just received statehood, and George and John Henry were anxious to take an active role in the state's future. While seeking the appointment of postmaster, George received an interesting visitor. The caller said that the President of the United States wanted to know if George would accept another position instead of the postmaster position. George agreed that he would accept another appointment if the position

225 George Albert Smith, Journal, 19 Nov. 1907 and 10 Nov. 1908, George A. Smith Papers box 73, book 5, journal 4; and Gibbons, 34–35.

226 George Albert Smith, Journal, 10 Sept. 1905, George A. Smith Papers, box 73, book 3.

227 George Albert Smith, Journal No. 2, 1 Oct. 1905, George A. Smith Papers, box 73, book 3,

228 George Albert Smith, Journal No. 2, 9 Oct. 1905, George A. Smith Papers, box 73, book 3, 127.

229 Lucy Woodruff Smith to George Albert Smith, 1912, cited in Gibbons, 35.

230 Gibbons, 35–36.

231 George Albert Smith Correspondence, 1897, George. A. Smith Papers, box 17, fld 14–15.

of postmaster were "tied up."[232] Not long after this visit from the President's representative, George received a letter from Department of the Interior Secretary Cornelius Newton Bliss, offering George the position of receiver of the land office. Governor Arthur L. Thomas (not a member of the Church) had been appointed postmaster. In January 1898, George was officially appointed receiver of public monies and disbursing agent for Utah at a salary of $3,000 a year.[233] He started this new job at the age of twenty-seven and became one of the first Latter-day Saints to hold a federal office by appointment of the President after Utah achieved statehood.[234]

In his government position, George witnessed several important political events. In September 1901, George traveled to the Pan American Exposition in Buffalo, New York, and while he was sitting outside the Music Hall, he heard the shot that took the life of President William McKinley. Shortly after, when Theodore Roosevelt arrived in Buffalo, George spent the afternoon with him in the home of Anthony Wilcox on Delaware Avenue the day before Roosevelt was sworn in as the new President.[235] In 1902, *The Deseret Evening News* commented on George's work in his government position:

> He has applied himself with great care and diligence to the duties of his office, with the result that when Binger Herman, commissioner of the general land office, was here, he declared that Mr. Smith's record was not surpassed by that of any receiver in the country. . . . He retained his position without an effort.[236]

George was reappointed for a second term by President Theodore Roosevelt and served in the land office until April 1906, when he requested a release.

Between 1898 and 1902, George also served as Republican chairman of the 28th voting district, as a delegate from his State

232 George Albert Smith to Senator Francis E. Warren, 16 Dec. 1897, George A. Smith Papers, *Letterpress Book #2.*

233 George Albert Smith, George A. Smith Papers, *Letterpress Book #2,* 112–131; and Stubbs, 71.

234 Pusey, 221.

235 Pusey, 223.

236 "Reappointment of George A. Smith," *Deseret Evening News,* Salt Lake City, 18 Feb. 1902, no. 76, 8.

League to the 12th National Republican League, as secretary of the Republican County Commission, and as one of the speakers in the 1900 campaign for the Republican State Central Committee.[237]

Along with being active in the Republican Party and with the land office, George was busy with Church service. Having been ordained a Seventy before leaving for his mission to the Southern States, upon his return he was assigned to the presiding council of the Third Quorum of Seventy. He also became in succession a librarian, a teacher, the assistant superintendent, and the superintendent of the Sunday School in the Seventeenth Ward.[238]

Serving in Church leadership positions, George was concerned that others would perceive his attainment of these roles as the result of nepotism. He often joked about the proliferation of Smiths. "There was a time," he would say, "when we were all Smiths, but some lost their status through iniquity."[239] Or he would tease, "In the beginning, Adam's last name was Smith. Whenever anybody in his family did anything wrong they had to change their last name."[240] Though he joked about the situation, he was sincerely concerned about favoritism toward the Smiths and voiced that concern in 1902 while attending a Salt Lake City Stake conference where several Smiths were being presented for a sustaining vote. Sitting in the meeting, "George whispered uneasily to the Smith next to him that if one more Smith were named, he intended to walk out. It was then that his own name was presented as the new superintendent of the Salt Lake Stake YMMIA."[241]

Prior to this call, George had served as the second counselor to Superintendent Richard R. Lyman. Joseph F. Merrill served as the other assistant superintendent, and these three creative young men introduced innovations in the YMMIA that were ultimately adopted throughout the Church.[242] George was an excellent motivator of leaders and young men alike. Years later, Richard R. Lyman said of his service, "You very wisely allow men with fine ideas freedom to

237 George Albert Smith Correspondence, 1902, George A. Smith Papers, boxes 14–18.

238 Pusey, 219–220.

239 Pusey, 222–223.

240 Martha Ray June Stewart Hatch (Socorro, NM), Phone Interview by Mary Jane Woodger, 16 Aug. 2007, transcription in possession of Mary Jane Woodger.

241 Gibbons, 42–43.

242 Gibbons, 41.

put them into operation. Any leader who tries to manage all the details himself is sure to preside over an institution whose growth and development will be slow."[243]

In the spring of 1903, George found himself in charge of a missionary training program in the Salt Lake Stake that proved to be highly successful. At the MIA conference in the spring of 1903, the corps of 110 missionaries over which George presided led all the rest, and he was warmly commended by the First Presidency.[244]

These were busy years for the Smiths, but "there were many diversions for the young couple—parties, dances, picnics in the summertime, and especially the theater. Lucy and George saw nearly every production that came to the Salt Lake Theater. When no baby sitter was available, they took Emily with them, and she slept in her carriage in their box."[245]

Whenever the couple was separated, they wrote voluminously, though because of George's weak eyes, "he often had to rest after writing a single page."[246] Though it was difficult, George persisted in writing his wife, and she appreciated his letters. One time she told him, "I couldn't help but think it was almost worth being away from you to get such a sweet letter. In fact all my letters from you are just lovely. You are an ideal correspondent husband and sweetheart."[247] Lucy often reminded George to take care of himself because she needed him "for many years yet to come."[248]

As the years edged on, George and Lucy's love deepened and matured. When they were apart, they could not wait to be reunited. Lucy wrote to George on September 8, 1901, "When you come home I will talk you to death. I have been so lonely today without you."[249]

---

243 Richard R. Lyman to George Albert Smith, 26 Nov. 1932, LDS Church Archives, cho, box 1, as cited in Stubbs, 216.

244 Pusey, 223.

245 Pusey, 222.

246 Ibid.

247 Lucy Woodruff Smith to George Albert Smith, 29 April 1902, George A. Smith Papers, box 22, fld 11.

248 Lucy Woodruff Smith to George Albert Smith (Ocean Park, CA), 31 March 1902, George A. Smith Papers, box 22, fld 11.

249 Lucy Woodruff Smith to George Albert Smith (Salt Lake City, UT), 8 Sept. 1901, George A. Smith Papers, box 21, fld 14.

In 1902, on George's thirty-second birthday, the couple was apart on the anniversary of his birth for the first time in many years. While on a vacation with the children in Ocean Park, California, Lucy reminisced,

> I shall not be with you on your birthday for the first time in many years but you shall be in my thoughts every hour of the day and my prayers shall be that you shall live long and have health and happiness. . . . You have been so patient with me and if I don't always seem to appreciate it I want you to know now that I do and my heart is all yours. My desire[s] are all for your welfare. It makes me shudder all over when I think I might have lost you once in my life.[250]

And on the actual day of George's thirty-second birthday, April 4, 1902, Lucy wrote:

> This is the day that gave you an introduction to this world thirty two years ago . . . almost ten years ago you promised to love and cherish me how well you have done so surely my face and condition in life plainly tell. Every year since our union life has been brighter to me and my love has increased so many fold that it has assumed enormous proportions but not large enough yet to want to migrate from its original location.[251]

Even though George was constantly busy with civic and Church duties, he was ever concerned for the welfare of his own family. His letters were full of advice to his wife. "Don't get out of patience with the baby," he wrote once. In another letter he advised, "Do try to prevent them [the children] from getting too much sweet." Probably recognizing the amount of advice he delivered, in one letter he admonished, presumably tongue-in-cheek, "Please watch the children's teeth to see that they grow straight."[252]

---

250 Lucy Woodruff Smith (Ocean Park, CA) to George Albert Smith, 1 April 1902, George A. Smith Papers, box 22, fld 12, 8.

251 Lucy Woodruff Smith (Ocean Park, CA) to George Albert Smith, 4 April 1902, George A. Smith Papers, box 22, fld 12, 1.

252 Pusey, 221–222.

One letter Lucy sent reveals that George considered running for US senator, a plan he later decided against. On April 18, 1902, Lucy wrote, "Who wanted you to run for Congress and how could you refuse such an offer? Now I know you refused for the best and I only asked the question in fun."[253] But George was quite active in politics. In fact, both George and John Henry were among the sixteen men who first organized the Republican Party in Utah.[254] George believed that the men and women associated with the party would do what was right.[255] He was of the opinion that his father had done "more to establish the Republican Party in Utah than any other man," and George also did all he could in "going out on the stump," referencing the political tradition popular in the nineteenth century of standing on a tree stump to deliver a campaign speech.[256] John Henry had run for senator in 1898, and two years after his defeat he suggested to George, "Lay your plans to get to Congress after a time." He explained, "If a good live Republican Mormon Monogamist can be elected it will do more to restore quiet than anything else."[257]

For these reasons, many thought George was in a key position to run for the US Congress, but he decided against it out of a deep loyalty for his friend Reed Smoot. His position was made clear in a letter to Henry Welsh on December 2, 1902:

> I deplore the fight that is being made on him [Smoot] as he is an honorable man, and much as I might desire to be considered as a senatorial aspirant, I would not do anything that might smack of unfriendliness to him. Of course if anything happens to prevent his candidacy being pushed to the point of election, I will enter the field.[258]

---

253 Lucy Woodruff Smith (Ocean Park, CA) to George Albert Smith, 18 April 1902, George A. Smith Papers, box 22, fld. 13, 3.

254 George Albert Smith to H. Clay Evans, 6 March 1897, George A. Smith Papers, *Letterpress Book #1.*

255 Inter-Mountain Republican, "How George Albert Smith Points to the Only Way," 24 Feb. 1909, LDS Archives (Salt Lake City, UT), ms 00234.

256 George Albert Smith to H. Clay Evans, 6 March 1897, George A. Smith Papers, *Letterpress Book #2.*

257 John Henry Smith to George Albert Smith, 30 Jan. 1900 and 1 Feb. 1900, George A. Smith Papers, box 17, fld 32.

258 George Albert Smith to Henry Welsh, 2 Dec. 1902, George A. Smith Papers, box 23, fld 16.

Even when party members wanted to draft his name, George refused. After the election was over, a fellow Utah politician wrote that if George had "not thrown his strength behind Mr. Smoot in 1902 for the United States Senatorship, it would have been Senator Smith instead of Senator Smoot" in the US Congress.[259] In hindsight, it is apparent that the Lord had other things in mind for George Albert Smith.

On October 6, 1903, George left the land office early because he had promised his daughters he would take them to the Utah State Fair. On the way home, he tried to catch the last few minutes of a general conference session, but the Tabernacle was too crowded, so he continued home. When he arrived home, he found that he had some enthusiastic visitors waiting for him. Instead of being met at the door by his girls, he was met by Nellie Colbrook Taylor, who began to offer earnest congratulations to George. George was very confused at her behavior:

> "What is this all about?" he asked.
>
> "Don't you know?" she countered, incredulously.
>
> "Don't I know what?"
>
> "Why, you've been appointed and sustained to succeed Brigham Young, Jr. as a member of the Quorum of the Twelve Apostles," exclaimed his eager informant.
>
> "That couldn't be right," he said. "There must be some mistake."
>
> "I heard it myself," Mrs. Taylor insisted.
>
> "It must have been some other Smith," he persisted. "Not a word has been said to me about it, and I can't believe it is true."
>
> Mrs. Taylor felt confused, crushed, and rather doubtful of her own hearing. Could she have made a dreadful mistake? Tearfully she apologized for having so upset the Smith household.
>
> "Don't apologize," he said. "I'm glad for the error, but please don't frighten me like that again."
>
> Nellie Taylor hurried back to the Tabernacle to get the story straight. There she was assured that she had

259 C. P. Overfield to Major W. I. Lincoln Adams, 25 March 1929, George A. Smith Papers, box 57, fld 2.

> indeed heard the announcement correctly. The new apostle was none other than George Albert Smith. Mrs. Taylor hastened back to the Smith home determined to make the young man eat his words. She was followed by others intent on offering congratulations. George could no longer doubt the accuracy of their reports.
>
> With all doubt cleared away, George felt "completely dumbfounded and could hardly believe it possible."[260]

Seeing that the stream of people coming from the Tabernacle was delaying their father from taking them to the fair, Emily and Edith said to their father that they "thought that being an apostle must be the worst thing that could possibly happen to you." But even amidst the crowd of well-wishers, George "picked his children out of the crowd and took them to the fair anyway—although he did not see much of it. He spent the whole time with his back to the wall talking to people."[261]

Even though his patriarchal blessing indicated that he would become an Apostle, George "sometimes wondered if it ever could be fulfilled; but not having read it for a number of years it had become but a vague impression in [his] mind."[262] At best he had thought it would happen sometime later in his life. George was only thirty-three years old, and the thought of having a Smith father and son in the Quorum of the Twelve at the same time left him feeling unsettled.

The first time George saw his father after learning of the call, John Henry was quick to assure George that he'd had nothing to do with it. In October 1903, Joseph F. Smith was the President; John Henry Smith and Hyrum Mack Smith were members of the Twelve; and John Smith was the Patriarch. John Henry must have known that George would be concerned about nepotism, because he tried to soothe his son's worries. President Joseph F. Smith had approached John Henry two days before the conference, saying that the mind of the Spirit was that George Albert should fill the vacancy in the Quorum of the Twelve Apostles. John Henry replied that if it were a

260 George Albert Smith, Journal, George A. Smith Papers, box 67, book 2, cited in Pusey, 224–225.

261 "Pres. Smith Mementos at Y," Church News, *Deseret News* (Salt Lake City, UT), 14 Oct. 1967, 6–7.

262 Copy of instructions given to George Albert Smith at the first council meeting of the Twelve that he attended, Oct. 1903, unpublished manuscript, George A. Smith Papers, box 96, fld 23.

political office, he would advise against it, but he could not stand in the way of suggestions from the Spirit to the prophet.[263] John Henry later added, "Well, he's not healthy. He won't last long."[264]

George's fears about nepotism continued, but, strangely enough, it was a conversation overheard between two drunks that gave George some solace:

> As [George] had walked down the street one night, he had overheard two drunks discussing the appointment as they leaned against a lamppost.
>
> "You zee," said one of the drunks, "zhey put in another Smith—more relation than revelation, if you ask me. I don't think the Lord wants George Albert for an apostle."
>
> "Now Bill," his companion answered, "did ya ever stop to think that the Lord doesn't [care] what you think?"[265]

George decided that if this man was not concerned about idle gossip, then he wouldn't be either.

As George attended his first meeting with the Quorum of the Twelve, he prayed that the person who had nominated him to his position might ordain him. In answer to that prayer, his ordination was performed by President Joseph F. Smith,[266] who later informed George that he had initiated the appointment. John Henry, however, delivered the traditional "apostolic charge" to his son:

> In the exercise of the duties of the apostleship I would have you remember that you are now wedded with a tie stronger than life or death to the Priesthood of the Son of God. . . . My son, I feel very much honored in this call which has come to you, and I fully sense the spirit that might be shown by some of our people from

263 George Albert Smith to Nicholas G. Smith (South African Mission), 6 July 1914, George A. Smith Papers, box 42, fld 10.

264 John Henry Smith, Journal, George A. Smith Papers, box 14, book 25, 710.

265 Pusey, 226.

266 Gibbons, 90.

> the fact that you are my son, and from the fact that at no time in the history of our Church has our blood been represented by so many apostles. But the call of the Almighty has been to our race, and all men have received the priesthood as the result of the choice of the Lord manifesting itself in the calling and raising up of the Prophet Joseph Smith.[267]

John Henry also told George that the Lord wanted him to continue to work in the land office, to live an exemplary life, and to honor the office of Apostle as his grandfather had before him. John Henry also challenged his son that if it were required, he should even be willing to lay down his life in the line of duty.[268] After the charge, the Brethren expressed their love and support. In humility, George told his fellow Apostles that he felt weak and lacking in judgment compared with those who were older, but he assured them that his heart was right and that he desired to help the work of the Lord progress.[269]

---

267 Copy of instructions given to George Albert Smith at the first council meeting of the Twelve that he attended, Oct. 1903, unpublished manuscript, George A. Smith Papers, box 96, fld 23.

268 Ibid.

269 Ibid.

Chapter 8
THE ART OF APOSTLESHIP

As a young boy, Boyd K. Packer was sitting in a stake conference in Brigham City, Utah, when George Albert Smith, an Apostle of the Lord, took the stand. President Packer later described the powerful witness he received as he watched Elder George Albert Smith: "I do not remember what he said, whether he was talking about the Word of Wisdom, or about repentance, or about baptism. But somehow while he was speaking it was fixed in my little-boy mind that there stood a servant of the Lord. I have never lost that testimony or that feeling. In my mind I came to know that he was an apostle of the Lord Jesus Christ."[270]

Like future Apostle Boyd K. Packer, most people who heard George speak felt the great love he had for the people to whom he spoke. Whether he "spoke or sang there was an intimacy about it. He did not have a stentorian voice. It was tender, and it had a great influence on the people who surrounded him."[271]

During the early years of his calling, George learned that being an Apostle involved much more than speaking. His one-on-one interactions with people helped him learn the art of apostleship.

George took an active interest in the lives of individual Latter-day Saints. Just four months after his call, A. M. Cyrus wrote in appreciation of the Apostle's efforts, "You don't know with what force your response to my feeling out for you in the dark space about me has touched me. I put out my hand in search of you and your touch

270 Boyd K. Packer, "Behold Your Little Ones," *Ensign*, July 1973, 51.

271 Truman G. Madsen, *The Presidents of the Church* (Salt Lake City, UT: Deseret Book, 2004), 230 (hereafter cited as Madsen).

in return is magnetic. It is this magnetism that has made your success in life so complete."[272] Similarly, Leo Woodruff thanked George for his genuine concern: "You gave me some good advice which I have been thinking over and have concluded that I am in need of some advice of this kind."[273]

George also spent time with Church members in more informal settings. On one particular assignment, he went fishing with Stake President Daniel Heiner. George was so delighted when he caught a trout weighing five and three-eighths pounds that "he had the brethren who were with him sign a certificate telling of his catch so it would not be just another fish story."[274]

During the first three years of his service in the Twelve, George received assignments that kept him close to home so that he could work at the land office during the week. In May 1905, he was given his first assignment to reorganize a stake as a senior Apostle, with Charles W. Penrose as the junior Apostle. As the two Apostles interviewed various candidates, they narrowed the choice for stake president down to two men. Leaving the decision until the next morning, George "awoke feeling the assurance Oleen Stohl is the man for president" and was not surprised when Elder Penrose had received the same answer.[275]

Another happy experience George had during his early Apostleship was attending the dedication of the Joseph Smith Birthplace Memorial on December 23, 1905—the one-hundredth birthday of the Prophet. The Church had purchased about eighty acres of the land surrounding the birthplace of the Prophet Joseph Smith, including the orchard, the old cellar, and the hearthstone of the home in which the Prophet was born. The task of building the monument had been immense, and George described its construction and transport in a later conference address, also offering his commendations for Brother Junius F. Wells's dedication as overseer on the construction:

---

272 Cyrus A. M. (Des Moines, IA) to George Albert Smith (Salt Lake City, UT), 22 Jan. 1904, George A. Smith Papers, box 25, fld 6.

273 Leo Woodruff (Germany) to George Albert Smith, 25 Jan. 1904, George A. Smith Papers, box 25, fld 6.

274 "Diary Records Story of Catching First Fish," *Deseret News*, 5 April 1951, LDS Archives (Salt Lake City, UT), ms 00303.

275 George Albert Smith, Journal, 29 May 1905, box 25, fld. 7; and Gibbons, 48.

> The shaft itself weighs somewhere near forty-three tons . . . and had to be carried five and a half miles from the railroad upon a specially prepared wagon, the wagon weighing eight tons, the tires of the wheels being twenty inches wide. The country road could not bear the great weight of the immense blocks of stone of which the monument is constructed, and a track of oak planks was laid upon the ground and the big wagon was rolled upon that. When the first effort was made to haul it, twenty of the best horses in that country could not move the wagon. Afterwards, by means of block and tackle, it was successfully moved, although sometimes only a few yards, or a few rods a day, until the monument was gradually taken to its destination. The people of that country said to Brother Wells, "You will not be able to get it into position because of storms and snow; the roads will be so slippery that you cannot haul it." Brother Wells said to them (evidencing the faith of his lineage), "We will get there, the Lord will open the way." So the storms held off until the monument was in place, the cottage roofed, and the doors and windows roughed in, then it began to snow. The people of that country refer to this two months of pleasant weather, at a time when ordinarily they have snow, as Wells' weather, in compliment to the man who had faith in our Heavenly Father in carrying out the purpose undertaken.[276]

Upon arriving in Vermont, Elder George Albert Smith and twenty-nine other Latter-day Saints were greeted by Elder Wells. The blessing of fair weather that had facilitated the placing of the monument continued for the dedicatory services. The few inches of snow that had fallen just before the party arrived had thawed the night before. When George entered the home that had been built on the site of the Prophet's birth, the Spirit came over him and tears filled his eyes. He knew that the Lord had prepared the way for the monument to

276 George Albert Smith, CR, April 1906, 53–55.

be erected, and he expressed gratitude for having the opportunity to witness a miracle.

Not all of George's experiences during those early years, however, were quite as uplifting. When he was called to the Quorum of the Twelve, anti-Mormon sentiment was rampant, the Church was in debt, and objections were being raised to the election of Apostle Reed Smoot as a senator from Utah. George not only had to deal with such opposition from outside the Church but also with dissension from within. As 1905 began, there was controversy in the Quorum of the Twelve over two Apostles who refused to accept the manifesto that ended plural marriage. Elders Matthias Cowley and John W. Taylor continued to practice plural marriage despite the prophet's declaration.

George wrote to his father—who was in Washington, DC, in February of that year—of the problems facing the Quorum: "I feel certain that our only danger lies in the fact we have not cut Cowley and Taylor right off of the church. These men demand that we do something heroic. They say that if we can't and won't act they will finish the matter completely by our disfranchisement."[277] That same month George wrote fellow Apostle Heber J. Grant, who was then President of the European Mission: "The Devil is still after us and is making it very unpleasant for the whole people. The unwise position taken by some of the Brethren has put us in a most unpleasant corner, and the whole people are made to feel uncomfortable as a result of their personal actions."[278] On March 1, President Joseph F. Smith called a meeting of the Twelve to determine what to do about Apostles Taylor's and Cowley's violations of the manifesto. As a result of the meeting, both men resigned from the Quorum.

More than five years later, both Elder Cowley and Elder Taylor were still causing problems for the Church. The Quorum of the Twelve took further action by excommunicating Elder Taylor and suspending Elder Cowley's priesthood. This incident was a "source of deep sorrow" for George, having "to deal with men who were at one time so faithful and true." Though George did not attend all of the meetings involved with these cases, the experience disturbed him so much that he could hardly

277 John Henry Smith (Washington, DC) to George Albert Smith, 9 Feb. 1906, George A. Smith Papers, box 28, fld 4.

278 George Albert Smith to Heber J. Grant, 5 Feb., 1905, as cited in Pusey, 233.

keep himself out of bed. In a letter to Apostle Rudger Clawson, who was serving as President of the European Mission, George wrote that "being weak . . . my feelings . . . and my sympathy are very much to my own detriment." He knew, however, that "their judgment [had] been approved by the Lord."[279]

Amongst so much drama and dissent, George still had to balance the responsibilities of his home life. Lucy missed spending time with him. In August 1906, when George was away on assignment, she wrote, "I can't tell you how I long to have you home again with me. I have dreamed of you almost every night and I am getting so I need you more all the time. I feel like we must have a long talk and second honey moon when you come home. I wish we could have a little time by ourselves once again. I must have you some way."[280] In October, though she recognized the good George accomplished while away, Lucy wrote:

> How shall I stand all these winter days without you. I guess the same way others do without their husbands but you are so much to me. I love you more every year we are together and wonder when we can be with one another for a good visit. When you went away even at the depot someone was there to talk with you. I want you to do all the good you can in this world but I must have you to.[281]

The next month she expressed her loneliness once more but also let him know that she knew he would be with her if he could: "When I go out and see other women with their husbands it makes me feel very lonesome indeed and I wonder if you will ever have the health and time to go out with me once in a while like you used to do. Sometimes I get so hungry for personal attention from you," but she then added, "I do console myself with the knowledge that you give me all you possibly can it is not due to neglect on your part."[282]

---

279 George Albert Smith (Salt Lake City, UT) to Rudger Clawson (Liverpool, England), 15 May 1911, George A. Smith Papers, box 35, fld 6.

280 Lucy Woodruff Smith (Salt Lake City, UT) to George Albert Smith, 21 Aug. 1906, George A. Smith Papers, box 28, fld 16.

281 Lucy Woodruff Smith (Salt Lake City, UT) to George Albert Smith, 16 Oct. 1906, George A. Smith Papers, box 28, fld 17.

282 Lucy Woodruff Smith (Salt Lake City, UT) to George Albert Smith, 15 Nov. 1906, George A. Smith Papers, box 28, fld 21.

George tried to relieve some of the burden Lucy felt by hiring a housekeeper, and he pitched in when he was at home. One day when the housekeeper was gone and Lucy was sick, George did the washing. Before all the clothes were clean, George was sick to his stomach from the task. So he went to ZCMI and asked for a washing machine with an electric motor. The clerk told George that they did not have such a thing in the store but they did have some motors and belts. With George's prodding and help, the ZCMI employees rigged an electrical attachment to eliminate the burden of operating the washing machine mechanism by hand. With her newfangled machine, Lucy became the envy of the neighborhood. Julina Smith, wife of the prophet, came over to witness the marvel and told her husband about the invention. The next time President Joseph F. Smith saw George, he acted miffed and said to him, "Do you know what [you have] cost me? . . . Five electric washing machines."[283]

Though driving a car—which George was more than happy to do soon after the car's introduction[284]—usually cut down the time George spent on the road, he was still away from home much of the time. Even though ever-increasing health issues made traveling difficult for him, George made every effort to be a gracious and humble representative of the Lord. Francis M. Gibbons, who served as a secretary to the First Presidency, explained:

> [George was] fastidious in his grooming and cleanliness, and, because of frail health, he was exceedingly careful about his diet. At home, for instance, he insisted on having separate towels for his face, feet, and body; and a whole wheat concoction was an essential item in his usual breakfast menu. He was also sensitive about odors, and he often carried breath sweeteners to make sure he was not offensive to others. It was difficult to accommodate habits such as these to the realities of frontier living, where running water was considered the ultimate in personal luxury and where bathrooms were a rarity. George Albert's unfailing courtesy and

---

283 Pusey, 241–242.

284 Pusey, 242.

> consideration for the feelings of others prevented him from complaining about the facilities or food provided by his hosts, who always offered the best they had. Nor did he attempt to dictate menus or to insist on special treatment in sleeping or other arrangements. He merely accepted what was offered, expressing genuine thanks for the kindnesses shown to him.[285]

Staying in other people's homes did take a toll on an already-precarious constitution, though. Such stress and strain would soon show its heavy hand, as George found himself unable to fulfill his apostolic duties as he had from 1903 to 1909. Oddly enough, it would seem that just when he was beginning to understand the art of apostleship, he would have to give it up.

285 Gibbons, 54–55.

Chapter 9
SUBMISSION

George Albert Smith seemed to have his share of physical ailments. At six feet tall, he usually weighed a slight 160 pounds. He had dark brown hair, was of light to intermediate complexion, and had blue eyes.[286] His eyes always caused him concern and worry, especially after the sunstroke he'd suffered while working on the railroad.[287] Additionally, in early 1900 George suffered an accident to his left eye that further impaired his eyesight. An operation performed in March 1900 failed to entirely correct his vision.[288] George had written to his boyhood friend Lewis Peck about how scared he was that his eyes might be failing.[289] For the next few years, George constantly complained about his eyes. Just before he was called to be an Apostle, he wrote to Lucy, "My eyes are beginning to bother me again so I will have to hire somebody to do what little eye work I have. . . . I started in to write you a letter every day but will have to give it up for I have rested my eyes several times to write these few lines. The Lord doubtless has a purpose in permitting this affliction and I must be patient."[290] Later that month, he divulged, "If my eyes were as strong as they were four years ago I could do all I have to do and plenty of time left to read, but they are not and I will have to get along as best I can."[291] Because of his eye problems, George left the land office in 1906.[292] Not

---

286 George Albert Smith, unpublished manuscript, George A. Smith Papers, boxes 38, 96.

287 Swinton, 20.

288 Susan Easton Black, "George Albert Smith Led by Love," *LDS Church News*, Aug. 28, 1993.

289 Lewis Peck (Baker City, OR) to George Albert Smith, 11 April 1900, box 20, fld 16.

290 George Albert Smith to Lucy Woodruff Smith, 4 April 1902, George A. Smith Papers, box 136, fld 2, 5.

291 George Albert Smith to Lucy Woodruff Smith, 28 April 1902, George A. Smith Papers, box 136, fld 4.

292 Thomas Kearns (US Senate, Washington DC) to George Albert Smith, 28 Feb. 1903, George A.

one to complain aloud, he documented his concerns in his journal over the next few years as his eye problems continued to plague him:

> January 28, 1904. "Absented myself from a cottage meeting in the 13th ward on account of my eyes."
>
> October 18, 1904. "Eyes are very weak this morning. Not painful unless I use them."
>
> December 14, 1904. "I never saw such smokers as there were present. The menu was excellent, the toasts very good but the smoke was vile. I left before the adjournment on account of my eyes."
>
> October 24, 1905. "Lucy read part of my manual lesson. This she does frequently as I am unable to get it without somebody reading to me."[293]

Part of the problem with George's eyes was that his left eye tended to drift outward. In 1907, George underwent another surgery to correct this problem. The surgery was considered successful, but it produced an altered focus that required a long adjustment period.[294] As recorded in his journal, his eye problems continued:

> Dec. 4, 1907, El Paso, TX. "Eyes very weak."
>
> Dec. 7, 1907, Colonia Juarez, Mexico. "Awoke feeling very well but my right eye is somewhat disabled. It pained me all day."
>
> Dec. 8, 1907, Colonia Juarez, Mexico. "Awoke feeling splendid except for my eyes."
>
> Dec. 12, 1907, Colonia Juarez, Mexico. "Awoke feeling well, my eyes still affected. . . . Wrote a letter to Lucy until my eyes were tired."
>
> Dec. 23, 1907. "Awoke feeling well but my eyes were tired."
>
> Dec. 24, 1907. "My eyes are quite weak. I helped the folks decorate the house for Christmas."

Smith Papers, box 24, fld 6.

293 George Albert Smith, Journal, 28 Jan. 1904 to 24 Oct. 1905, George A. Smith Papers, box 67, book 1.

294 Gibbons, 56.

> March 6, 1908. SLC. "My eyes are tired."
> March 10, 1908, SLC. "My eyes quite weak."
> June 22, 1908, SLC. "Awoke with tired eyes."
> Sept. 24, 1908, Whitesock Springs. "My eyes were very tired."[295]

Eye problems were not the only physical limitation George suffered during the early years of his Apostleship. In fall 1904, George was treated for uric acid trouble. The general fatigue of Apostleship, constant travel, and pressure of duty aggravated George's tenuous health. Staying in members' homes and sleeping in different beds was hard on George. And it seemed that the hostesses would prepare their best recipes for their esteemed guests, but these dishes were often so rich that they were not compatible with George's delicate digestive system. George tried not to offend by rejecting the food he was served, but his digestive problems were a constant struggle as he visited the stakes of Zion. Often, he would just eat the grain concoction he carried with him.[296]

Lucy, having lived with George for ten years prior to his becoming an Apostle, was constantly worried about his frail constitution and warned him not to overwork. She felt, though, that most of the time her warnings went unheeded by her husband.[297]

As the months passed while he served as an Apostle, George struggled more and more with physical weakness and nervousness. By August 1906, while visiting a stake in Canada, he was so sick that he had not eaten a square meal for two days. He also suffered from a nosebleed and recorded that he was full of pain.[298] Despite these limitations, George still went to a conference in Raymond, Alberta, and delivered three addresses. The next weekend he was at a conference in Cardston, Alberta, and then caught a train for Great Falls, Montana, where the train was so crowded that he had to ride on the roof of a boxcar. By 1908, George was traveling more than thirty thousand miles a year.[299]

---

295 George Albert Smith, Journal, 4 Dec. 1907 to 24 Sept. 1908, George A. Smith Papers, box 67, book 2.

296 Gibbons, 235.

297 Lucy Woodruff Smith (Ocean Park, CA) to George Albert Smith, 13 April 1902, George A. Smith Papers, box 22, fld 13.

298 George Albert Smith, Journal, 16 Aug. 1906, George A. Smith Papers, box 67, book 2.

299 Richard Neitzel Holzapfel and William W. Slaughter, *Prophets of the Latter Days* (Salt Lake City, UT:

The inconvenience of transportation in the first decade of the 1900s took its toll on George's weak body. George and his companion experienced unfortunate circumstances in September 1908 that were typical of the day. George and Elder Anthon W. Ivins were visiting Whiterock Spring, Nevada, and spent a night in a wagon. Rain poured the entire night, and George later recorded in his journal that the wagon "cover leaked and we got our clothing wet; it was so wet when we got up that we didn't try to build a fire." Instead, they went without breakfast and hitched up the wagon to continue on their journey on bad roads and with cold wind. Such a traumatic climate would have an adverse effect on anyone, but George especially suffered. After speaking at two meetings, he developed dysentery.[300]

By mid-November, George never felt well and got relief only by vomiting and purging his body. While visiting Charleston, South Carolina, in December, he experienced severe pain in his bowels. By the end of 1908, George's problems with his eyes, cold sores, lame back, dry throat, and painful rheumatism left him physically weak, yet he felt like he was spiritually strong and often worked beyond what was wise.[301]

His extensive travel continued to take a toll on his already-precarious state of health. In January 1909, when a streetcar neglected to stop for him, he ran to the train depot and caught the train but feared he had overdone it in trying to do so. George felt his heart was weak, and he visited the doctor's office when he got home. The diagnosis was that George's heart was not bad, but he needed to rest. Ignoring the doctor's advice, George continued at a feverish pace. During the next few weeks, he drove through several "raging blizzards" to stake conferences, and by February his throat was causing him a great deal of trouble. One awful night, George woke with terrible pain throughout his body. A Dr. Gamble diagnosed him with la grippe, a type of influenza.[302] George recorded, "This was the fifth time I have

---

Deseret Book, 2003), 108–109.

300 George Albert Smith, Journal, 24 Sept. to 27 Sept. 1908, George A. Smith Papers, book 5, journal 4.

301 George Albert Smith, Journal, Nov. to Dec. 1908, George A. Smith Papers, book 5, journal 4, and book 6, journal 5.

302 Stubbs, 101.

had lagrippe, and I believe it has been the hardest siege of all."[303] By March 4, he was well enough to sit up and dictate his first letter since that awful night. Though la grippe was an awful virus, it was not the cause of George's health problems. His greatest ailment was thought to have been nervous tension. What made matters worse was that when George took time to rest and improve his health, he worried he was shirking his duty, and the anxiety he suffered weakened him physically and made him more vulnerable to his other illnesses.[304]

After a period of bed rest, George received osteopathic treatment every day for two weeks. For the remainder of the month, he was depressed and discouraged that he wasn't getting much better and could do no work.[305] Fellow Apostles administered to him, Lucy hovered over him, and group prayers were offered in his behalf, but he continued to be in a state of nervous exhaustion.[306]

George's condition was not a shock to those who knew him. Letters from worried friends reveal that those close to George knew his health was unstable. Samuel O. Bennion, President of the Central States Mission, wrote on March 9:

> I was very sorry to hear of your having been ill and trust that you will have recovered fully by this time. I was not much surprised however, because I think that you are overtaxing your strength. Some say it is better to wear out than to rust out. I believe it is but if you would lay quiet until you began to rust the[n] go to work, I think your physical anatomy would be much better.[307]

By April, George's health was not improving. George attended the first session of general conference but missed the rest of the sessions because he felt unwell. At that point George and Lucy realized that

---

303 George Albert Smith to George B. Lowrie, 4 March 1909, George A. Smith Papers, *Letterpress Book #2*.

304 Gibbons, 178–179.

305 George Albert Smith, Journal, 9 March, 18 March, and 23 March 1909, George A. Smith Papers, book 6, journal 5.

306 Gibbons, 61.

307 Samuel O. Bennion to George Albert Smith, 9 March 1909, George A. Smith Papers, box 32, fld 7.

as a member of the Twelve living near Church headquarters, he could not get the rest he needed. They decided it would be best if George went to Ocean Park, California, to recuperate. The day before George left for California, his uncle Heber J. Sears, who was a doctor, warned George to take it easy. In the following letter, he admonished that things could get much worse if George did not slow down:

> My Dear Nephew,
>
> A letter from your mother brings the sad intelligence that you are down with nervous frustration. I take no satisfaction in saying "I told you so," but I do wish I could say something that could bring you to the realization of the danger you are in. For years I have seen the necessity of a period of complete relaxation and have endeavored to warn you of the consequences that are sure to follow such a period of prolonged tension. Nature is now giving you a warning which you will do well to take. When the nervous system is once broken down that patient is too often a wreck for life. No class of diseases resist so stubbornly the effects of the physician as nervous diseases. In fact there is but little hope after they reach a certain stage. Their manifestations cover a wide range—from slight nervous instability to insanity. I need but call your attention to the number of good people who have gone insane in your own locality and in the same field of usefulness that your own efforts are directed in. Insanity is largely on the increase as statistics will show and let me whisper a very significant fact in your ear: it is only a step from nervous frustration to insanity. For Heaven's sake George—"Side step or step backward" not forward—Cheat the asylum of a victim. Dump your responsibility for a while before the hearse dumps your bones. Once more I will make the plea. If you are doing all this for humanity stay with humanity as long as you can and administer the fancied in broken doses. If the Church requires your life give it to the

> Church in a thinner layer spread over 30 or 40 more years instead of 3 to 5. Could you not do more good in this way? There are more ways of keeping the wor[d] of wisdom than by abstaining from tea, coffee, beer. You are an apostle. While I have only one [foot] in the church yet, in my opinion I keep the Word of Wisdom better than you do. Should there be any dispute on this point I would offer in evidence a body 48 years young in a splendid state of preservation—free from disease and capable of great endurance.
>
> Now George! Wake up—We can't afford to lose you. Give the "other fellows" an inning while you drink lemonade in the shade. Call "Casey to the bat" and you watch the game while the others run the bases for a while if you'll be hauled off in the ambulance before the game is half over.
>
> Give our best love to your family and accept the same for yourself. With a strong hope that you will be good to yourself, I remain, Your affectionate Uncle.[308]

The day after George received this stern warning, he left for California with Lucy's uncle John and aunt Lucy Acomb to seek recuperation at the seashore. The trio arrived in Ocean Park, near Santa Monica, on April 13, 1909. They rented a little house by the beach for twenty-five dollars a month. Living conditions were dramatically different for George in Ocean Park. There were no meetings, no visitors, and no speeches. Instead, George spent time sleeping and walking on the beach. While in California, George saw a doctor in Los Angeles who tried to find the source of George's nervousness and fatigue. The only thing the doctor could diagnose was that his twelfth rib was out of place under the eleventh rib.[309] In addition to George's rest and relaxation, the doctor ordered him to receive treatments once a week.[310] This prescription added to George's

308 Heber J. Sears (Chicago, IL) to George Albert Smith, 12 April 1909, George A. Smith Papers, box 32, fld 11.

309 Pusey, 249.

310 George Albert Smith to Lucy Woodruff Smith, 18 May to 22 May 1909, George A. Smith Papers, box 136, fld 11.

state of depression, leaving him feeling inadequate and thinking he was disappointing everyone around him. George did not know where else to turn except to the Lord. That spring, his life was filled with fervent prayers and priesthood blessings.[311] But he did not get better.

Lucy had returned to Salt Lake and became more and more worried as their separation went on, especially when she felt that George was keeping things from her. In a letter written on April 18, she tried to get George to be more open about his situation: "I just hope you can rest and rest and rest. You've never told me yet one word about the pain in your side. I always feel better when you tell me all about yourself and I never feel worse when you tell me all [not] when you write and say I feel fine. I don't believe it and I just feel hungry to know how you are. Everyone asks after you and wants to know how you get-along."[312]

As the weakness worsened, it seemed that everyone George and Lucy knew was including supplications for his health in their prayers. On May 11, 1909, Lucy's aunt reassured her: "I don't believe for one minute our Heavenly Father will lean a deaf ear to all the petitions that are sent to him for George's benefit."[313]

Florence S. Sears, a cousin of George's, wrote, "We pray for you all every night and I feel and know that the Lord will bless and [restore] his health. I am so glad you have such long hours of absolute rest for that will do so much to help."[314] Clarissa S. Williams penned, "We pray for him always and know that the Lord with surely answer the prayers which are constantly being said for the dear boy."[315] Joseph McRae wrote, "May the Lord bless you dear brother in all your labors and make you strong and well is the prayer of, Your brother."[316] On April 11, George received this message from Lafayette Holbrook in Provo:

---

311 George Albert Smith to Lucy Woodruff Smith (Salt Lake City, UT), 13 April 1909, George A. Smith Papers, box 27, fld 11; and Gibbons, 62–63.

312 Lucy Woodruff Smith (Salt Lake City, UT) to George Albert Smith, 18 April 1909, George A. Smith Papers, box 32, fld 12.

313 Aunt S (San Diego, CA) to Lucy Woodruff Smith, 11 May 1909, George A. Smith Papers, box 32, fld 11.

314 Florence S. Sears to Lucy Woodruff Smith, 19 July 1909, George A. Smith Papers, box 32, fld 11.

315 Clarissa S. Williams to Lucy Woodruff Smith, 29 July 1909, George A. Smith Papers, box 32, fld 11.

316 Joseph A. McRae (Amarillo, TX) to George Albert Smith, 12 April 1909, George A. Smith Papers, box 32, fld 11.

> I am certainly sorry to learn of your poor health, did not realize it was so bad until [Bro. Taylor] informed me. I certainly hope and pray that the trip to the coast will completely restore you to perfect health and vigor, and I believe it will especially if you will throw off all cares, be free and easy, living a sort of a come day go day kind of life while you are there; it is rest and low altitude that you require.[317]

Ellie Woodruff wrote to Lucy on April 18, 1909: "I didn't realize George was so sick. I knew he was all worn out but didn't dream he was so bad. I will give him my faith and prayers and I believe he will soon gain his strength again if we all remember him because it is as you say, there is so much for him to do and the Lord will spare him to do it. A rest is the thing he has needed so long."[318] And President Joseph F. Smith expressed his concerns for George in a letter written on May 8, 1909:

> We were all glad to hear from you but sorry you did not seem to be making better progress in regaining your health. We sincerely hope and pray that you may soon start out for rapid recuperation and recovery of your perfect health and vigor. We remember you earnestly in our prayers from week to week and daily our petitions ascend to the great giver of all good for His blessing to [descend] upon you. We miss you in our Councils and in the efficient service o[f] your ministry and long to see you again as good as new.[319]

In addition to the expressions of faith from President Smith, Lucy also shared that she'd received some spiritual assurance. Writing George about what had transpired, she said, "Last night . . . I had such a comforting influence come to me which told me that you

---

317 Lafayette Holbrook (Provo, UT) to George Albert Smith, 11 April 1909, George A. Smith Papers, box 32, fld 11.

318 Ellie Woodruff (Independence, MO) to Lucy Woodruff Smith, 18 April 1909, George A. Smith Papers, box 32, fld 12.

319 Joseph F. Smith (Salt Lake City, UT, Office of First Presidency) to George Albert Smith, 8 May 1909, George A. Smith Papers, box 32, fld 14.

would be well again if you were to use wisdom in the care of yourself and I know you will. What a comfort the gospel is. You know the Lord makes us come to him and rely on him for which I am grateful."[320]

By the time of his seventeenth wedding anniversary, though George wrote to Lucy, "Seventeen years of wedded bliss—each happier than the last and love and blessing for you,"[321] other ailments were surfacing. He wasn't sleeping well, his nerves were restless, his skin was blistered, he felt very weak, and he was having more trouble with his stomach. The one ray of sunshine was that Lucy and the children joined him in California on June 12, 1909.[322] The arrival of his family seemed a tonic for him as he joined them at play—swimming in the ocean, flying kites, and going to see the races in Santa Monica.[323]

In July, Dr. Samuel Allen of Salt Lake City visited and determined that George's "vital organs were in good condition," and that he "was getting along fine and must continue to rest."[324] By August there was enough improvement that he took his family "to a fast day service in Los Angeles, where he spoke briefly, but he returned exhausted. His old stomach ailment became active again."[325] Even going to one meeting seemed to be too much for George, and a week later he wrote that he did not see that he was improving at all.[326]

Probably seeking some relief from the monotony of bed rest, George decided to take a swim on August 24. As he ventured out into the ocean, all went well with his swim until he started back to shore and was about halfway there when a double-header wave struck him, burying him under the water. George swam to the top only to be hit by another wave that sucked him into the undertow. When he surfaced he was too weak to swim and struggled to the piling of

320 Lucy Woodruff Smith to George Albert Smith, 28 April 1909, George A. Smith Papers, box 27, fld 11.

321 George Albert Smith, Journal, 27 Nov. 1908 to 18 May 1914, George A. Smith Papers, book 6, journal 5.

322 Ibid.

323 George Albert Smith, Journal, June 1909, George A. Smith Papers, book 6, journal 5.

324 George Albert Smith, Journal, 15 July, 16 July, and 17 July 1909, George A. Smith Papers, book 6, journal 5.

325 Pusey, 249.

326 George Albert Smith, Journal, 1 Aug. to 8 Aug. 1909, George A. Smith Papers, book 6, journal 5.

a pier, where he clung while resting and catching his breath. Trying to swim from pile to pile, George found his strength completely gone. Fortunately, he saw a man on the beach who was able to wade out toward him. With the help of this man and the tide, George was able to reach a spot where he could touch the bottom and wade the rest of the way in. After this traumatic dip in the ocean, George caught a nervous chill and had to go directly to bed. "It was as near to drowning as I ever want to be," he stated, and the thought of his narrow escape haunted him for days.[327]

A few days later, Lucy "sent for the doctor and the elders, who stayed with him all night." Suddenly averse to the ocean, George decided he wanted to go home. So the Smiths headed for Utah on August 28, 1909. George nearly collapsed three times before managing to get on a streetcar bound for Los Angeles, where he then boarded a train for Salt Lake City.[328]

Lucy and the children went home, but the doctor insisted that George needed to be away from the noisy children and to stay in a quiet place where he could sleep outside. George went to stay with a nearby family, the Acombs, who borrowed a tent for George to use. Thus "the patient began a long experiment with the 'fresh air' cure" that was popular at the time.[329]

In September George dictated his first letter in more than four months. He also dictated his journal to Lucy, who visited often, rather than trying to write in it himself.[330] Still, his condition had certainly not improved enough for him to fulfill his duties as an Apostle. President Joseph F. Smith, seeing the distress of the junior Quorum member, tried to comfort George in a letter written on September 7, 1909: "I do not want you to worry about anything. . . . Please remember what the Lord said to his apostles: 'Take no thought of what ye shall eat, etc.' I say this to you. The Lord will provide for you, therefore don't worry."[331] But it was George's nature to worry

327 George Albert Smith, Journal, 20 Aug. to 24 Aug. 1909, George A. Smith Papers, book 6, journal 5.

328 Pusey, 249–250.

329 Kirk Gilmore (Salt Lake City, UT), Interview by Mary Jane Woodger, 10 Oct. 2006, transcription in possession of Mary Jane Woodger; and Pusey, 250.

330 Stubbs, 104.

331 President Joseph F. Smith to George Albert Smith, 7 Sept. 1909, George A. Smith Papers, box 27, fld 14.

and to let his nerves get the best of him, despite the reassurances of others.

Loved ones tried to help. John Henry and others gave George numerous priesthood blessings. After one blessing, he seemed a little better, but then he had a nightmare, fell out of bed, and was right back where he started. On September 13, Dr. Allen concluded that George had a strained heart muscle and prescribed a full year of rest.[332] Such a prescription was too much for George to abide by. The next day he ignored Dr. Allen's instructions and attended a meeting of the Quorum of the Twelve, staying "until he was 'tired out.'" Later in the week, George witnessed a procession in honor of US President William Howard Taft and went to the Tabernacle to shake the President's hand. Despite his defiance of the doctor's orders, George felt better and managed to attend part of two sessions of the October 1909 general conference. He even bore his testimony for a few minutes, but when he sat down he was perspiring heavily and his whole body began to tremble. George went home with a nervous chill and then returned to the Acombs' for a month of rest in his tent.[333] George's father and President A. H. Lund gave him another priesthood blessing, but within four days he was in extreme pain from his heart and had a nervous chill.[334] Though he had been obeying the doctor's orders about sleeping outdoors, Dr. Allen suggested that George go to a lower altitude again after only being home for about two months.[335]

Facing a year of bed rest, George read the well-intentioned letter Apostle Heber J. Grant had sent him: "Always praying the Lord to bless you and assuring you that I have faith for your recovery, as I have more than once been healed when in a bad and even a worse condition of health than yours."[336] Elder Grant may have underestimated George's health problems. George's incident at general conference seemed to convince George to follow the doctor's

332 George Albert Smith, Journal, 13 Sept. and 14 Sept. 1909, George A. Smith Papers, box 32, fld 11.

333 Pusey, 249–250.

334 George Albert Smith, Journal, 3 Oct., 6 Oct., and 7 Oct. 1909, George A. Smith Papers, box 32, fld 11.

335 George Albert Smith to R. S. Campbell, 27 Sept. 1909, George A. Smith Papers, *Letterpress Book #2.*

336 Heber J. Grant to George Albert Smith, 23 Oct. 1909, George A. Smith Papers, box 36, fld 22.

advice, but his near drowning and the long distance from home deterred him from another stay at Ocean Park. Instead, George decided to go to the city named after his grandfather—St. George. The Smiths took the train to Modena and then packed a wagon with a bed in the back for George, arriving on November 6, accompanied by George's twenty-six-year-old brother, Nathaniel. Lucy and the children occupied the Rose Jarvis cottage,[337] and Nathaniel set up a tent with a wooden floor for George. The sides of the tent were near the kitchen door of the house, and the small abode also contained a stove for warmth. Nathaniel massaged his brother every night to help alleviate his pain.

Five months later, George found himself in a pitiful condition. For five months, he had not left his bed. For five months, he'd never changed out of his bed clothes. For five months, even arranging his bedclothes caused him to have a nervous chill or to faint and lose consciousness for a second. As George experienced constant weakness, he fell deeper and deeper into depression and began to compare himself to Job. George did admit, however, that Job had been harassed by those who should have been his friends, yet "in my weakness I had friends all around." And it was a balm to George's soul to know that while he was helpless, he was not "compelled to suffer for the necessities of life." But he wondered what purpose there was in his long, drawn-out illness.[338] Still, George and those around him tried to exercise faith in his recovery, and temple workers came twice a week to give him priesthood blessings.[339]

Depression, discouragement, and boredom were taking their toll on George. His impaired eyesight made it impossible for him to read for any length of time, even if the light in the tent had been adequate. Unlike his stay at Ocean Park, where he often disobeyed the advice of his doctors, George now followed his doctors' orders exactly, but he did not feel better. He felt just as weak, just as nervous, and just as useless in his calling.[340]

---

337 "Your Good Name," *The Improvement Era*, March 1947, 139; and George Albert Smith Journal, 10 Nov., 1909, George A. Smith Papers, box 32, fld. 32.

338 George Albert Smith to C. L. French, 26 April 1926, George A. Smith Papers, box 52, fld 17.

339 George Albert Smith, Journal, 3 May 1910, George A. Smith Papers, box 26, journal 5.

340 George Albert Smith, "Your Good Name," *Improvement Era*, L, March 1947, 139.

In December, during a spell of weakness and exhaustion, George had a dream that proved life changing. He later recalled:

> I lost consciousness of my surroundings and thought I had passed to the Other Side. I found myself standing with my back to a large and beautiful lake, facing a great forest of trees. There was no one in sight, and there was no boat upon the lake or any other visible means to indicate how I might have arrived there. I realized, or seemed to realize, that I had finished my work in mortality and had gone home. I began to look around, to see if I could not find someone. There was no evidence of anyone's living there, just those great, beautiful trees in front of me and the wonderful lake behind me.
>
> I began to explore, and soon I found a trail through the woods which seemed to have been used very little, and which was almost obscured by grass. I followed this trail, and after I had walked for some time and had traveled a considerable distance through the forest, I saw a man coming towards me. I became aware that he was a very large man, and I hurried my steps to reach him, because I recognized him as my grandfather. . . . I remember how happy I was to see him coming. I had been given his name and had always been proud of it.
>
> When Grandfather came within a few feet of me, he stopped. His stopping was an invitation for me to stop. Then . . . he looked at me very earnestly and said:
>
> "I would like to know what you have done with my name."
>
> Everything I had ever done passed before me as though it were a flying picture on a screen—everything I had done. Quickly this vivid retrospect came down to the very time I was standing there. My whole life had passed before me. I smiled and looked at my grandfather and said:
>
> "I have never done anything with your name of which you need be ashamed."

> He stepped forward and took me in his arms, and as he did so, I became conscious again of my earthly surroundings. My pillow was as wet as though water had been poured on it—wet with tears of gratitude that I could answer unashamed.[341]

The dream made a deep impression on George, and he wondered if he was meant to continue on the other side of the veil. In a letter he confessed, "I did not know whether my work was completed or not, but I told the Lord that if it was complete and He was preparing to call me home, that I would be ready to go."[342] George surely felt that if he went to his Father in Heaven, he would find peace.[343]

So George made a decision. He began to pray that if he was not to recover, that he be released from his weak body. One night George confided his thoughts to Lucy, asking that she join him in his petition. At first she was adamantly against it, but after relentless pleading on George's part, she gave in. A friend later related that "no one would know what a strain it was on [Lucy's] feelings and [on her] great love for [her] husband and children to accept such a resignation." So George and Lucy prayed together for his release or his recovery. When Lucy joined George in prayer, something remarkable happened. To their astonishment, their prayers marked "the turning point of his betterment in health." Peace came, and George recuperated from his long illness and received "a testimony that he was to live as he was one of the chosen to lead his people sometime in the future."[344] It seemed the Lord had more for George to do in mortality, and though there would be more months of illness and his recovery would be slow, his hopelessness and depression were gone. His submission to the Lord's will seemed to have turned the tide.

A second witness that his mission on earth was not yet finished came to George from his father just a few weeks later. On April 9,

341 George Albert Smith, "Your Good Name," *Improvement Era*, March 1947, 139.

342 George Albert Smith to C. L. French, 26 April 1926, George A. Smith Papers, box 52, fld 17.

343 Shauna Lucy Stewart Larsen (Orem, UT), Interview by Mary Jane Woodger, 23 Aug. 2007, transcription in possession of Mary Jane Woodger.

344 Lucy Woodruff Smith, as related to Bishop K. J. Fetzer and contained in a letter from Bishop Fetzer to the Smith children, 7 Aug. 1953, George A. Smith Papers, box 151, fld 3.

1910, after John Henry had been sustained as Second Counselor in the First Presidency, he testified that George had more to do in mortality: "Keep up good fortitude and good faith; don't waver in your determination to live. . . . Your brethren love you and I am sanguine the Lord loves you and the bitter experience through which you are going is but designed for your purification and uplifting and qualification for an extended life work."[345]

Following his experiences, George returned to testify, "I have been in the valley of the shadow of death in recent years, so near the other side that I am sure that for the special blessing of our Heavenly Father I could not have remained here. . . . The nearer I went to the other side, the greater was my assurance that the gospel is true. Now that my life has been spared I rejoice to testify that I know the gospel is true, and with all my soul I thank my Heavenly Father that he has revealed it to me."[346]

345 John Henry Smith to George Albert Smith, 9 April 1910, George A. Smith Papers, box 29, fld 6

346 George Albert Smith, CR, Oct. 1921, 42.

Chapter 10
RETURNING FROM THE SHADOW OF DEATH

When George returned home, he found a bed made for him out of doors on which he slept well when the dogs and cats would let him. The doctor suggested George wash out his stomach every other day with salt water, which eventually relieved some of his problems. By June 14, George felt well enough to take a trip to the Great Salt Lake. When he reported that the salt water seemed to have a good effect on him, both internally and externally, the doctor advised him to stay on the lake for a few more days. George moved into a large room on Saltair's north pier, and his children took turns staying with him at night. George took two or three dips in the lake each day,[347] and by the end of the summer, the swimming and the air seemed to have done some good and George's health was improving. However, the process was slow. There were still times when his nerves got the best of him, but he always felt that he would be better the next day.[348]

George knew he needed to "use judgment [to] not get any more setbacks," but one day he decided he was well enough to go out on the lake in a boat. A squall developed and the boat drifted in spite of the sailors' efforts to keep the boat on course. Eventually, George donned a waterproof coat and took the wheel. He was sure all the excitement would take a toll on his health, but when he returned to his room, surprisingly, he had no chills and was able to go right to sleep.[349]

George still had some stomach and nerve problems, but as he prayed, he knew the Lord was delivering him from his afflictions and

---

347 George Albert Smith, Journal, 3 May 1910, George A. Smith Papers, box 27, fld 21.

348 George Albert Smith, Journal (Saltair Beach), 25 June 1910, George A. Smith Papers, box 27, fld 21.

349 George Albert Smith, Journal, 1 July to 28 Aug. 1910, George A. Smith Papers, box 73, fld 6.

that his requests for recovery would be granted. By August 28, 1910, George could walk two miles a day, even though it took him longer than it had before his illness.[350]

During the next few weeks, George spent time at Gray's Sanatorium taking a course for his nerves that included "daily hand and electric massage treatments to alleviate the nervousness and the intermittent dizzy spells he suffered." Over the course of a five-week stay at Gray's, George gained fifteen pounds, bringing his weight to almost ideal for his height—160 pounds.[351] By December 19, he was walking as many as six miles a day, but his nerves were still unsteady, and he found he still could not "talk or visit without discomfort."[352]

But little by little, his health was improving. After the new year began, George was attending the Quorum of the Twelve meetings, and on March 4, 1911, he came home from Saltair. At home, however, he was bombarded by new worries. Just two weeks after he returned home, Lucy came down with la grippe and developed complications that necessitated surgery and four long weeks in the hospital. In addition, at April general conference John Henry suffered a serious hemorrhage of the lung from which he would never recover.[353]

Despite his miraculous progress, George was still unable to speak much, and he could not speak at all in public. However, his ability to speak gradually improved, and on September 17, 1911, he attended two meetings and was able to speak for ten minutes. He was even able to take his children Edith and Albert to the circus but could not do much else. George wished that he could do the work he used to do.[354] At the October general conference, he attended all of the daytime meetings but then suffered from a cold for a week. While he was in bed nursing his cold, his brother Winslow came to the house and delivered the news that their father had died. George's response after the shock was, "Well I better get out of this bed and look after the family."[355]

350 George Albert Smith, Journal, 1 July to 28 Aug. 1910, George A. Smith Papers, box 73, fld 6.

351 Gibbons, 72.

352 George Albert Smith, Journal, 28 Nov. 1910 to 22 Jan. 1911, George A. Smith Papers, box 73, fld 6.

353 Pusey, 252.

354 George Albert Smith, Journal, 17 Sept. 1911, George A. Smith Papers, box 73, fld 6.

355 George Albert Smith, Journal, 13 Oct. 1911, George A. Smith Papers, box 73, fld 6.

John Henry Smith died at the age of sixty-three, leaving two wives and fifteen children, four of whom were minors. George was pleased with the reaction of his mother and Aunt Josephine (his father's plural wife) at the death of their husband: "Contrary to the understanding of the world, his two wives are very dear to each other, and in this time of bereavement they comfort and console each other as sisters should."[356] Losing his father and not having his health completely restored, George knew it would be "easy to make a martyr of one's self and so hard to overcome sorrow and distress," but he resisted that temptation as much as possible.[357]

Some comfort came to him on the night of December 2, 1911, when he had a vivid dream involving his father. In the dream he saw himself, his father, and President Joseph F. Smith together. As George approached the two men, President Smith held out a "good sized package" that apparently contained something George wanted. During this exchange, John Henry "sat smiling" and "seemed much interested in what was transpiring" but did not speak. Perhaps the package was a foreshadowing of George's greater responsibility now that John Henry was gone. George also dreamed that he saw his maternal grandfather, Lorin Farr, dressed in a gray salt-and-pepper business suit with a soft hat. His grandfather looked and acted twenty years younger than he had when he'd died. In the dream, as George and his grandfather met, Lorin shook George's hand and talked to him about the family. Afterward George was amazed that he "could feel the warmth of his grandfather's hand and detected that he had a body of flesh and bones." The dream was a great comfort to George and probably helped relieve the grief he was feeling.[358]

But even with such assurances, the stress of his father's death took a toll on George, and by January 5, 1912, he was "out of commission."[359] Knowing he could not push his limits, in February he headed for Ocean Park again, where he slept and rested but refrained from swimming. In April, he traveled to Tucson, Arizona, where he spent several

356 George Albert Smith to Mr. and Mrs. George S. Nye, 16 Nov. 1911, George A. Smith Papers, box 30, fld 17.

357 George Albert Smith (Salt Lake City, UT) to Wayne Decker (New York, NY), 28 Nov. 1911, George A. Smith Papers, box 30, fld 17.

358 George Albert Smith, Journal, 5 Jan. 1912, George A. Smith Papers, box 73, fld 6.

359 George Albert Smith, Journal, 5 Jan. 1912, George A. Smith Papers, box 73, fld 6.

weeks at the Pueblo Club. George enjoyed the dry desert air, and the ample meals served at the club enabled him to build his weight back to 158 pounds.[360] Having taken the necessary downtime, George was able to speak for five minutes at the next October general conference. It was the first time he had addressed a conference crowd in three years, and a year later at the following October conference, he was able to speak for ten minutes "without ill effect."[361] George still had feelings of inadequacy about the small load he was carrying in the Twelve, but as his health slowly improved, he began to again shoulder some of his former responsibilities.[362]

In 1913, George's health continued to improve, and Lucy was as well as she had ever been.[363] In his biography of George Albert Smith, Francis M. Gibbons explains, "To say that George's health had been restored would be an unwarranted exaggeration. During the remainder of his life, he was frail and subject to occasional sieges of illness," but in 1913, there was "definite improvement in his condition and a return to relative normalcy."[364] With his continuing struggles with fatigue, weakness, influenza, neuritis, and other ills, George always worried that his health might degenerate and that the frustrating years of unproductivity would be repeated. In his journal he confided:

> I do know that I cannot continue to work as long hours as I am now and I am trying to find some way to ease up so that my health will not break. My brethren are considerate of me but the fact is that there is so much more work than we can do properly that all are working beyond their strength and I would not like to be the one to fail when the others are busy. I am grateful for all my blessings and will be pleased to work as long as the Lord gives me strength.[365]

---

360 Gibbons, 75–76.

361 Pusey, 257.

362 Robert T. Hill (Los Angeles, CA) to George Albert Smith, 30 Aug. 1913, George A. Smith Papers, box 39, fld 2.

363 George Albert Smith to Mr. Dale L. Pitt (Flat River, MO), 16 Dec. 1913, George A. Smith Papers, box 39, fld 11.

364 Gibbons, 78.

365 Pusey, 305.

Throughout 1914, George was well enough to be fully active in the Quorum. But the year also brought great concern for George and everyone else as the seeds of war began to take hold. After World War I began in 1914, George thought many times that if the Europeans had accepted the gospel and had not rejected the elders of the Church, then they would not be in their present difficulties and many lives would have been saved.[366] When Japan declared war on China in August 1914, as terrible as the war was, George was convinced that "no doubt good will come out of it because it will break down some of the barriers that were raised by the aristocracy to prevent the teaching of the truth." George acknowledged the hand of the Lord and knew that He would eventually open the way for missionaries to teach the truth.[367]

As talk of war swirled around everyone, George continued to increase his labors, and by February 1915, George wrote, "I am taking my place with [the] brethren and doing equally as much work as I used to do but am doing it in a more moderate way."[368]

The next few years passed pleasantly for the Smiths as George busily fulfilled his responsibilities as an Apostle. As the Latter-day Saints served their country during the war, George became a voice of comfort and solace. He advised young men serving in the military to make up their minds to be good soldiers and to bring credit to Utah and the Church. He advised one soldier to "read the scriptures and store your mind with the truths the Lord has revealed to the children of men[; to] attend to your prayers regularly, and by example let everybody know that you [believe] in the divine mission of Jesus Christ and of Joseph Smith."[369] He often advised Latter-day Saint servicemen to read Alma, beginning in chapter 56, and to learn from the experiences of the two thousand sons of Helaman.[370]

366 George Albert Smith to Mr. Fera Decker (Provo, UT), 18 Aug. 1914, George A. Smith Papers, box 41, fld 14.

367 George Albert Smith to Hon. Pliny T. Sexton (Palmyra, NY), 13 Aug. 1914, George A. Smith Papers, box 41, fld 14.

368 George Albert Smith to Reed Smoot (Washington, DC), 19 Feb. 1915, George Albert Smith Papers, box 43, fld. 6.

369 George Albert Smith to Eugene Gay (Camp Kearney, CA), 26 Feb. 1918, George A. Smith Papers, box 42, fld 25.

370 George Albert Smith to Mr. Paul Bean, 17th Calvary (Douglas, AZ), 9 May 1918, George A. Smith

By September 1918, the Church had more than twelve thousand men serving in the United States military, and George wrote in a letter that as far as he was aware, there was not one LDS soldier who complained or did anything "to obstruct the operation of the Draft."[371]

Amid the turmoil of World War I, the Smiths experienced a joyful interlude when their daughter Emily, who had become a registered nurse at LDS Hospital, was sealed to Robert Murray Stewart—a returned missionary and law student—in the Salt Lake Temple on February 1, 1918. George officiated at the ceremony. A reception was then held at the Smith home for about two hundred guests. George felt his "good girl" would become a "splendid wife."[372] George and Lucy's second daughter, Edith, was nearly grown too, and reminded George of himself. He would say to her, "You know, Sweetheart, I just can't figure out how anyone could be as good looking as you are and still look like me."[373]

Another joyous experience occurred when the Smiths sold their West Temple property and bought a spacious brick bungalow at 1302 Yale Avenue, next to an adjoining property Lucy had purchased earlier and that George soon dedicated.[374]

As the Smiths settled into their new home, the war hit closer to the hearts of the Smith family when Emily's groom was drafted. The worldwide flu pandemic of 1918 also reached the Smith home, and by August, George, Lucy, Edith, and Albert were all miserable with the flu.[375] Albert also suffered an attack of inflammatory rheumatism, which affected his heart.[376] He was taken to the hospital to have his

---

Papers, box 45, fld 14.

371 George Albert Smith to William S. Kline (Albany, NY), 17 Sept. 1918, George A. Smith Papers, box 44, fld 10.

372 George Albert Smith, Journal, 1 Feb. 1918, George A. Smith Papers, box 67, fld 8.

373 Pusey, 259.

374 George Albert Smith to Nicholas G. Smith (Cape Colony, South Africa), 31 May 1919, George A. Smith Papers, box 46, fld 10.

375 George Albert Smith to Herbert B. Naw, Lieutenant Chaplain (342nd Field Artillery American Expeditionary Force, France), 12 Nov. 1918, George A. Smith Papers, box 44, fld 16.

376 George Albert Smith to Lewis Peck (Cove, OR), 24 Sept. 1918, George A. Smith Papers, box 44, fld 21; and George Albert Smith, Journal, June to July 1918, George A. Smith Papers, box 67, fld 8.

tonsils removed in an attempt to help him recover more quickly.[377] When George and Lucy, who were not well themselves, arrived at the hospital to visit Albert, he was asleep but covered with blood as the result of a hemorrhage. George was very concerned that Lucy's overworking and her worry over their boy would endanger her health.[378] That month, George explained his concerns to a friend: "There has not been a day for ten years that somebody has not been ailing in my home."[379]

In Washington, DC, Emily used her nursing skills to bless young men who had been injured and to help with the Stewart household income. George was pleased that his daughter was using her training and experience to help those in distress and that she could aid her husband financially as well. He advised his daughter, "I do not want Murray to feel that it is not proper for you to help, financially, if the opportunity offers. That is a mistaken idea that some people have; and the result is that a man has 'his nose on the grindstone' all his life, when with the additional help his wife could give, they would both be comfortable in middle life."[380]

Because of the flu epidemic, all stake conferences and other public gatherings were cancelled, and George conducted Sunday services in his own household over the next few weeks.[381] In September, Lucy called George's attention to the fact that he had "not been very cheerful for some time." George tried to hide his feelings but recorded in a letter that "deep down in my soul there is an anxiety and yearning that I cannot express. If only I had the physical strength to be a part of the great war machine, it would relieve in part the feelings that I now possess."[382] Although George's physical condition

---

377 George Albert Smith to Charles A. Callis (Chattanooga, TN), 2 Aug. 1918, George A. Smith Papers, box 43, fld 22.

378 Stubbs, 324; and George Albert Smith, Journal, June to July 1918, George A. Smith Papers, box 67, fld 8.

379 George Albert Smith (Salt Lake City, UT) to Zelpha W. Burt (Delta, UT), 29 Aug. 1918, George A. Smith Papers, box 39, fld 6.

380 George Albert Smith to Emily Smith Stewart (Dupont, WA), 30 Oct. 1918, George A. Smith Papers, box 45, fld 2.

381 Pusey, 263.

382 George Albert Smith to Brigadier General Richard W. Young (Paris, France), George A. Smith Papers, box 45, fld 11.

prevented him from actively participating at the front, at home he was a part of the Executive Committee of Utah, charged with raising money for the war fund.[383] He felt that America was "fighting for the liberty of mankind," and as a Church member, he was "more deeply interested in the outcome" of the war than others.[384]

At the October 1918 general conference, George became so ill with pneumonia that he had to leave the meeting and was taken to the hospital. He had learned from the past that he shouldn't push his limits and knew he would have to rest or he would lose his life.[385]

How delighted George must have been when the Armistice was signed on November 11, 1918. However, his joy was tempered when President Joseph F. Smith died on November 19, 1918. Though George was sure that "everything [would] go on about as usual," he wrote in a letter that President Smith had been "most tender and affectionate" toward George, especially since the passing of his own father, and with the prophet's death, George wrote that a "peculiar feeling came over me and a vacancy that nothing can fill."[386]

By December, conditions in the George Albert Smith home were improving, and George wrote to the new prophet, President Heber J. Grant, that he would, with proper care, be able to perform any duties the prophet assigned him. George pledged his support to President Grant by saying that he would do anything he desired of him to further the work of the Lord.[387] As 1918, World War I, and the flu epidemic came to an end, George settled into his new home feeling better than he had in a long time, "in health and spirits." Looking back over the war years in Utah, George felt the state had been blessed in many ways. He wrote, "Crops have been unusually heavy and the prices have been high enough to keep the farmers good natured."[388] As 1919 dawned, George's life was one of "contentment

383 George Albert Smith to Joseph Rivett and family, 14 Dec. 1918, George A. Smith Papers, box 44, fld 24.

384 George Albert Smith to Lewis Peck (Cove, OR), 24 Sept. 1918, George A. Smith Papers, box 44, fld 20.

385 George Albert Smith, Journal, 4 Oct. 1918, George A. Smith Papers, box 67, fld 8.

386 George Albert Smith to Chaplain Calvin S. Smith (Headquarters 362nd Infantry American Expeditionary Force), 17 Dec. 1918, George A. Smith Papers, box 45, fld 4.

387 George Albert Smith to Heber J. Grant, 11 Dec. 1918, George A. Smith Papers, box 44, fld 4.

388 George Albert Smith to Joseph Rivett and family, 14 Dec. 1918, George A. Smith Papers, box 44, fld 24.

and happiness, with good food and comforts." At the same time, he realized there were thousands dying of starvation and little children "crying for want of a crust of bread."[389] Little did George realize that very soon, he would witness firsthand what war could do to humanity.

389 George Albert Smith, Chairman for the Utah Committee for Armenian and Syrian Relief, to Presidents, Counselors, and Bishops of Alpine, Nebo and Utah Stakes, 7 Jan. 1918, George A. Smith Papers, box 45, fld 12.

A very young George Albert Smith, shown here at about four years of age.

Class members with which George Albert Smith attended school in Salt Lake City; he is standing alone at the extreme right, holding his hat.

George Albert Smith (right), age 16, with his friend John Howard.

Early portrait of a young George Albert Smith.

Lucy Emily Woodruff in her wedding gown. George Albert Smith and Lucy were married May 25, 1892, in the Manti Temple.

A portrait of George Albert Smith taken in 1892—the same year he was married—just before he left to serve in the Southern States Mission. He and Lucy served together in the mission from 1892 to 1894. Here he is wearing a seal-skin hat and a buffalo-skin coat that had beaver-skin patches on the elbows; he wore both the hat and coat for many years.

George Albert Smith atop the Salt Lake Temple at its dedication in 1893. He is third from the right on the back row; Lucy is next to him, wearing a feather hat.

President George Albert Smith and Lucy Woodruff Smith at Niagara Falls on their much-postponed honeymoon in November 1894.

George Albert Smith.

Missionaries George Albert Smith (seated) and Henry Foster.

George Albert Smith, circa 1912–1914.

George Albert Smith, who was sustained an Apostle on October 6, 1903.

Lucy Woodruff Smith with daughters Edith, left, and Emily.

George Albert Smith with his son, George Albert Smith Jr.

Elder George Albert Smith at the unveiling of a marker honoring Father Escalante and his party in Provo, Utah, September 25, 1931.

Elder George Albert Smith and his daughter, Emily Smith Stewart (left), in the garden of Ralf E. Woolley in Honolulu, Hawaii, on November 11, 1936.

Devoted to the Scouting program, President George Albert Smith received the Silver Beaver award in 1932 and the Silver Buffalo award in 1934 from the Boy Scouts of America.

Elder George Albert Smith with Helen Keller in 1941, whom he escorted in his role as president of the Society for the Sightless. Miss Keller spoke to an audience of six thousand in the Tabernacle.

The Quorum of the Twelve, 1943. Front row, l. to r., Pres. G. A. Smith, G. F. Richards, J. F. Smith, S. L Richards, J. A. Widtsoe, J. F. Merrill; back row, l. to r., C. Callis, A. E. Bowen, H. B. Lee, S. W. Kimball, E. T. Benson, M. E. Petersen.

The First Presidency, 1945: J. Reuben Clark, George Albert Smith, David O. McKay.

President George Albert Smith at his desk in the Church Administration Building.

President George Albert Smith, center, with United States President Harry S. Truman, 1945.

President George Albert Smith visiting Church members in Mexico in May 1946; twelve hundred returned to Church activity as a result of his visit.

Hundreds of Church members covered President George Albert Smith with floral leis as he disembarked from his ship in Honolulu in 1950 to commemorate the centennial of the gospel's arrival in Hawaii and establishment of the Hawaiian mission.

President Smith visits with four-year-old Virginia Stockdale.

President Smith dedicating the This Is the Place Monument, July 24, 1947.

President Smith visiting with representatives of the Navajo Indian tribe, October 23, 1948, near the time he set up the Church Indian Committee.

Mourners line up outside the Church Administration Building to view the body of President George Albert Smith at his viewing on April 5 and 6, 1951.

Chapter 11

A MISSION ABROAD WILL PROLONG YOUR LIFE

During a fast and testimony meeting on March 21, 1919, President Heber J. Grant announced that George Albert Smith would preside over the European Mission.[390] Three months earlier, in January, President Grant had privately informed George about the call. George was excited about the prospect of serving in Europe, but Lucy and other members of the family were apprehensive, wondering if George's health would worsen with the dampness of England and the rigors of being a mission president. There was also concern for Edith, who had not completely recovered from the flu, and Lucy's health was also tenuous. Despite these reservations, George was determined to fulfill the assignment. George's resolve surely became all the more firm when President Grant prophesied that "a mission abroad will prolong your life."[391]

Travel was difficult right after World War I, so the journey to Europe was postponed until late spring, and there was some concern that Lucy and the children would not be able to join George on his assignment. George had a hard time securing passports, and, as late as April 28, the British government was still not willing to let all of the Smiths come.[392] Finally, the passports and visas were secured, but Lucy still felt unsure about their future in Europe. In planning the trip, she said to George, "Let's see if we can make it to Omaha. If we get that far, we can try for New York, and if we get to New York perhaps we can make it to England."[393]

---

390 Stubbs, 137.

391 Gibbons, 90; and Heber J. Grant to George Albert Smith, 27 Jan. 1919, George A. Smith Papers, box 41, fld 12.

392 George Albert Smith to Nicholas G. Smith (South Africa), 28 April 1919, George A. Smith Papers, box 46, fld 10.

393 Pusey, 266.

On May 29, George was set apart as the President of the European Mission. President Grant voiced the blessing, and in it he counseled George that as he went to Liverpool, he was to "seek earnestly and diligently for the guidance of His Holy Spirit." George was assured that he had been "called on this mission by the inspiration of the Lord" and would "return in safety." The prophet blessed George "with increased capacity in making friends for the Church, and in touching the hearts of those with whom [he came] in contact." And to top it off, George was promised that he would "have increased vigor of body" and "increased health." He was also told that the Lord had preserved his life, that "he [had] healed [him] and made [him] sufficiently well that [he was] able to go on this mission."[394]

Such promises gave George confidence as he left Utah on June 4, 1919, accompanied by Edith, Albert, and three elders; Emily and her husband, Robert Murray Stewart, moved into the Smiths' Yale Avenue home. The journey across the ocean was as pleasant as could be hoped for, and George even thought, "If we had owned the ship we couldn't have been treated any better."[395] The Smiths arrived in Liverpool, England, on June 25, 1919, greeted by Elder George F. Richards, whom George would replace as the European Mission President.[396] The Smiths then headed for the mission home, Durham House, at 295 Edge Lane:

> Durham House, which had a private section for the mission president and his family, also served as the quarters for some of the elders working in the mission office, as a way station for various missionaries and other members passing through Liverpool, and as a place of worship for some of the local Saints. The age of the mansion, the heavy use it had received, and the scarcity of materials and furnishings created by the war had given the once-proud building a dowdy, used-up appearance.[397]

---

394 Setting apart blessing of George Albert Smith as President of the European Mission, Heber J. Grant as voice, George A. Smith Papers, box 100.

395 George Albert Smith to Ralph J. Pugh (London, England), 26 Aug. 1921, George A. Smith Papers, box 47, fld 6.

396 Gibbons, 91.

397 Gibbons, 91.

Upon looking over his new home, George wrote, "It isn't like home, but we hope to get used to it."[398]

George's responsibilities as the European Mission President included serving as the editor-in-chief of the *Millennial Star,* which by 1919 had been in print for nearly eighty years. He was also in charge of all Church affairs in Great Britain and western Europe. George arrived in Liverpool in less than robust health, and his weak condition during his first year in England cast doubt on the accuracy of President Grant's prediction. George was practically an invalid and had to be "carried to and from means of transportation." When one of the missionaries went home and reported to Church members of George's precarious health, people began to speculate that he would have to return to Utah. After hearing of the concern the returned missionary's report had caused, George responded, "[He] has seen me break down two or three times and I think it gave him a scare, but the fact is, I am just about as well as I was when I left home."[399]

Despite George's limitations, he met with many of the high officials of the British government, and "through his gift of making friends, walked into their hearts" as he tried to solve the problems facing the European Mission and the mission home.[400] Three problems now stared George in the face. The first was the scarcity of supplies due to the war and the difficulty of obtaining any supplies due to hindrances from the local government: "The Smiths were made just as uncomfortable as possible, due to the fact that everyone felt that foreigners had no business in England at a time when there was shortage of everything needed to make one comfortable."[401]

The second problem was the virulent anti-Mormon feeling prevalent in the area. When the Smiths arrived, they encountered intense hostility. Before leaving the States, George had contacted many prominent friends, asking them for letters of introduction to their acquaintances in England. In this way, he perhaps hoped to counteract the prejudice right from the start.[402]

398 George Albert Smith, Journal, 24 June 1919, George A. Smith Papers, box 67, book 8, cited in Gibbons, 266.

399 George Albert Smith to Robert Murray Stewart, 28 Feb. 1920, George A. Smith Papers, box 173, fld 9.

400 James Gunn McKay, "A Tribute to George Albert Smith," 1932, George A. Smith Papers, box 100, fld 8.

401 George Albert Smith to John A. Widtsoe, 24 Feb. 1928, George A. Smith Papers, box 55, fld. 23.

402 George Albert Smith Correspondence, 1919, George A. Smith Papers, box 41, fld 9.

Much of the prejudice stemmed from British newspapers that were attacking the Church. Their brand of yellow journalism produced stories of missionaries enticing girls to go to Utah "to be enslaved as polygamous wives." Although George appealed to the newspapers, asking them to refute the slander, in most cases they refused. George did succeed, however, in convincing some of the editors "that they had been imposed upon," and a few newspapers ceased publishing anti-Mormon slander.[403] Though George had been prepared for what he might face, anti-Mormonism was a shock to his family, especially to fourteen-year-old Albert, who attended a lecture where they called President Joseph F. Smith "Dirty Joe"; said that the Mormon plan of salvation was synonymous with "throat cutting"; and claimed that "when the girls are taken to Utah by the elders, they are given to the authorities who use them for a vile purpose and then they cut their throats to save their souls."[404]

The entire time George was in England, he fought the perception of Mormon elders as lustful polygamists who enticed young women to join them in an immoral lifestyle. The surge of anti-Mormon propaganda intensified when the sensational films *Trapped by the Mormons* and *Married to a Mormon* were released, and anti-Mormon street meetings were held only a block from the mission home. Pusey records, "Some ministers contributed to the hostile environment with fanciful tales of tragedies supposed to have befallen Mormon converts. Against this tide of adverse publicity, the emaciated Apostle set out to win the hearts of the British people with love and understanding."[405] George's reaction to intensifying persecution was to try to calmly reason with those who were misinformed, particularly business and government leaders with whom he met to foster goodwill toward the Church. As previously mentioned, George especially tried to create positive relations with newspaper editors and journalists. On October 26, 1919, he thanked editor W. D. Black for an article favorable to the Church that had appeared in his paper.[406]

403 George Albert Smith, Mission Report, 4 June 1919, George A. Smith Papers, box 46, fld 25.

404 George Albert Smith Jr. to Emily Smith Stewart, 14 July 1919, George A. Smith Papers, box 173, fld 5.

405 Pusey, 266–274.

406 Gibbons, 96.

The third problem facing George was a shortage of missionaries. When World War I began, there had been between seven hundred and eight hundred missionaries in the European Mission, with three hundred to four hundred of them serving in England. When George arrived in 1919, there were only twelve missionaries in England.[407] The shortage of missionaries was directly related to the shortage of food in England. Because food was scarce, government officials did not want to worry about feeding foreigners, and it was, therefore, difficult for American elders to obtain permission to enter the country.[408]

While working on visa problems and trying to obtain approval to bring more Americans into the country, George also kept busy acquainting himself with the members and missionaries in Great Britain. Within six weeks, beginning on August 19, 1919, he traveled to Nottingham, Sheffield, Birmingham, and Hull, England; Cardiff and Bristol, Wales; Dublin, Ireland; and Glasgow, Scotland. On his excursions, George was accompanied by members of his family or by his assistant, Elder Junius F. Wells. During this time, Elder Wells was of great service to George. "When George Albert Smith would be talking, Junius F. Wells would sit behind him and when he wanted a certain date or experience, whatever he was talking about, he would turn around and say: 'Now Brother Wells what about that?' George . . . would say . . . Brother Wells is like [a] card index [system] . . . You pull out a card and its there."[409]

Lucy and the children accompanied George to Dublin in late September, and they experienced a "stormy passage" while crossing the Irish Sea. Two weeks later, traveling to Glasgow, the Apostle experienced an "attack of nervousness and extreme weakness." He held his scheduled meetings despite his illness, but after his return home, he was confined to bed for two days and missed a conference in Liverpool. After his recovery, he held meetings in Manchester, West Hartford, and Newcastle.[410]

---

407 George Albert Smith to Heber J. Grant (Santa Monica, CA), 10 Feb. 1919, George A. Smith Papers, box 45, fld 23.

408 George Albert Smith to John A. Widtsoe, 30 Oct. 1928, George A. Smith Papers, box 55, fld 16, cited in Stubbs, 141.

409 Cecil John Henry Tyrell, Interview, 21 July 1987, LDS Archives (Salt Lake City, UT), OH912.

410 Gibbons, 96.

As he had while traveling in the southern United States, George would often engage fellow train travelers in conversations that turned to the topic of the gospel. One memorable conversation took place when George shared a compartment with a Presbyterian minister. During the interchange, George told the minister he was a member of the Church. "Aren't you ashamed," the astonished minister asked, "to belong to such a group?"

"My brother," George Albert replied, "I would be ashamed of myself not to belong to that group, knowing what I know." He then launched into an explanation of Latter-day Saint beliefs.

"Why do you come over here and invite our people to leave this wonderful land and go to America?" the minister challenged. "Do you come over here to divide our families? Why don't you leave us alone, and why don't you go and preach the gospel to the heathens like we do?"

"We do," came the reply.

"Where do you go?"

"England."

The minister was annoyed, and George Albert hastened to say that he had intended no offense. Then it was his turn to press the questions:

"What is a heathen?"

"A man who does not believe in the God of Abraham, Isaac, and Jacob."

"Haven't you any such people as that here in England?"

"Plenty of them."

"Surely you are not going to complain at me and my associates, if you have not converted them, if we come over here to help you?"

"Well, I guess that is right."

George Albert then pressed his advantage. "You have a misconception of the purpose of The Church of Jesus Christ of Latter-day Saints in this land," he said. George continued:

> We are asking all you fine people over here to keep all the glorious truths that you have acquired in your churches . . . from your scriptures, [and from] your educational institutions. . . . Keep also the fine characters you have developed and the love and beauty that are in your

> hearts from having lived in this wonderful land. Keep all this. It is a part of the gospel of Jesus Christ. Then let us sit down and share with you some of the things that have not yet come into your lives that have enriched our lives and made us happy. We offer you these things without money and without price. All we ask you to do is hear what we have to say, and if it appeals to you, accept it freely. If it does not, then we will go our way to somebody else that we hope will be more fortunate.[411]

In October, George and Elder Wells went to London to work on the visa problem. George fervently prayed that their trip would be a success. The American ambassador had secured an interview for George with Sir Robert Horne, the minister of labor in Great Britain, but when George got to Horne's office, he was told that the minister would be leaving that day for Scotland and would be gone for three weeks. George pled for just five minutes of the minister's time. Sir Robert agreed to postpone his trip and to meet with George later that afternoon. During the meeting, Sir Robert assured George that he would issue instructions to his department to allow 250 missionaries to arrive as fast as they could get there.[412]

Obtaining passports and visas was also a problem for missionaries outside of England. In November, Elder Wells and Albert accompanied George as he traveled to Switzerland. In Switzerland, George visited the Swiss minister of foreign affairs, Dr. Charles R. Paravicini, who was so impressed with George's diplomacy that he requested the "Swiss Cantons to open their doors to the Mormon missionaries."[413] Meeting people in such high stations as that of Dr. Paravicini did not intimidate George:

> Feeling entirely at home with persons of high or lowly rank, he rejected the idea of class distinctions. When his friends urged him to meet someone because he was "a very important person," George had a standard reply. "Of course, he is," he would say. "Everyone is

411 *Sharing the Gospel,* 199–200.

412 Pusey, 268.

413 Gibbons, 97.

> important. I don't think you can classify human beings on the basis of their importance. Some people may be more influential than others; some may be more capable, some more prominent, and some may have greater responsibilities than others, but no one is more important than anyone else."[414]

Despite his comfort with such "important" people, after such big trips George would sometimes be weak and would have to rest for a time. When George went to bed to conserve his energy, he often took his work with him and asked missionaries to take dictation at his bedside. George's burdens began to weigh heavily on him, and by New Year's Day 1920, he suffered a "breakdown" and was unable to work for nearly three weeks.[415] During this time, Lucy's health was also weak, and as the "mistress of Durham house," Lucy's physical strength was not always "equal to the task" of her heavy responsibilities.[416] While in England, she served as the President of the Relief Society in the European Mission and also attended meetings of the International Council of Women.[417]

By April 1920, despite Sir Robert's promises, there were still only twelve missionaries in Great Britain. George wrote, "Evidently the government of Great Britain is trying to keep our Elders from entering any of her territory, but the Lord is our strength and his servants are in his hands."[418] After going to London several times to see government officials, George finally received word on June 1 that the missionaries would be allowed to come.[419]

That summer, George spent five weeks visiting the branches of the Church in Norway, Sweden, Denmark, Holland, and Belgium. One experience that would have an effect on George for the rest of his life took place, fittingly, on July 24, Pioneer Day. In 1920, most travel from England to the European continent was done by boat or

---

414 Memorandum by George Albert Smith Jr. to Merlo Pusey, 23 Feb. 1960, cited in Pusey, 269.

415 George Albert Smith, Journal, Jan. 1920, George A. Smith Papers, box 67, book 8.

416 Elias to Lucy Woodruff Smith, 1 Jan. 1920, George A. Smith Papers, box 133, fld 27.

417 Lucy Woodruff Smith to the officers of the Relief Society of the European Mission, 20 Jan. 1921, George A. Smith Papers, box 133, fld 29.

418 George Albert Smith, Journal, 4 April 1920, George A. Smith Papers, box 67, book 8.

419 George Albert Smith, Journal, 1 June 1920, George A. Smith Papers, box 67, book 8.

train, but airline passenger service had recently begun, even though at the time people considered it risky. At the suggestion of Elder Wells, George took his first flight.[420]

Taking young Albert and Elder Wells with him, George boarded a single-engine Air Force cast-off plane with two open cockpits piloted by a Royal Air Force World War I veteran. Before leaving the ground, George turned to his young son and promised, "If we ever get out of this thing alive, I'll never get into another one." At first "the machine jumped around a good deal," and George felt insecure without anything to hang on to, but for about two-thirds of the flight the ride was smooth and quite pleasant. After landing, while walking across the field, George said to Albert, "The next time I do a trick like that I'm going to keep one foot on the ground all the way."[421] Despite that response, his first flight seemed to have impressed George, and after it was over he had to admit that "flying [was] a very pleasant and interesting experience."[422]

Working with individual elders in the mission seemed to be one of George's favorite responsibilities, and his teachings and faith surely had a great effect on these young men's lives. For instance, he once told an elder who had been assigned to a town where the missionaries had been repeatedly denied permission to hold street meetings, "Now remember, give the Lord a chance. You are going to ask a favor. Give the Lord a chance. Ask him to open the way." The elder went to the chief constable's office to ask permission to hold street meetings in the town. "Well, what street corner would you like?" asked the constable. The elder responded, "I don't know this city as well as you do. I would not ask for a corner that would be undesirable, or where we would block the traffic. Would you mind going with me to select a corner?" The constable agreed to accompany him. It took just fifteen minutes and the missionary had "one of the best corners in town" and "permission to preach the gospel of Jesus Christ where it had not been preached on the streets since before the war." When the young

---

420 George Albert Smith Jr., "President Smith's First Airplane Ride," George A. Smith Papers, box 124, clipped magazine article pasted in scrapbook 1, 228–229; George A. Smith to Robert Murray Stewart, 2 Aug. 1920, George A. Smith Papers fld 10; and George A. Smith to Clarence Howard, 8 Aug. 1926, George A. Smith Papers, box 52, fld 23.

421 Ibid.

422 George Albert Smith to Robert Murray Stewart, 2 Aug. 1920, box 52, fld 10.

elder later told President Smith about the incident, President Smith said, "Just think of a missionary asking the chief constable to pick a corner on which to preach the gospel!" The missionary had proven, as President George Albert Smith said, that "the Lord has a way of accomplishing things that we are unable to do, and never asks us to do anything [without making] the way possible."[423]

Another missionary on which George had a great impact was Elder Elbert Curtis. Elder Curtis took dictation from George, and the first time he did so, it was late in the day. After taking the President's dictation, Elder Curtis ate supper and then joined a group visiting in the mission home living room. As George noticed his young charge, he asked him, "Did you finish typing those letters, Brother Curtis?"

"No, sir," Elbert replied, "I left some of them to finish in the morning."

"Brother Curtis, when we are doing the Lord's work we continue until it is finished," George gently corrected.[424]

Later, Elbert Curtis would say, "I personally sat at his table and slept under his roof for many months as his secretary in Liverpool, England. I loved him like my own father and cannot measure his influence in my life."[425]

Another missionary learned a lesson from George while praying:

> [President Smith] asked a new missionary just off the boat to pray as the mission-home group kneeled down together before going to bed. The red-faced young man was unable to utter a word. With patience adroitly mixed with determination, George Albert coached him through a prayer. Every missionary came to realize that behind his good humor was an unshakable determination to make their work succeed.[426]

Such was the influence that George had on the missionaries who were fortunate enough to serve under his tutelage. While George

423 Gibbons, 213–214.

424 Pusey, 267.

425 "Thousands Mourn Leader's Death; Church, Civic, Business Leaders Pay High Tribute," *Deseret News*, 5 April 1951, LDS Archives (Salt Lake City, UT), ms 00289.

426 Pusey, 267.

encouraged the missionaries to do their best, he was also careful not to put too much pressure on them. Often he instructed, "we crowd people into the water for their own hurt if we are not careful, especially if they happen to be emotional. It is always safer and better to be sure they are convinced beyond question of the truth of the work."[427]

By fall 1920, George felt the conditions of the Church in Europe were much better than when he had arrived: new missionaries were arriving regularly, Church membership was growing, and prejudice was diminishing. Therefore, George must have been quite surprised when a letter came from President Heber J. Grant in November expressing concern for George's health and suggesting he return to Utah for the winter.[428] George respectfully replied, "The work here [is] just getting on its feet and I think a few months longer will not hurt me and I prefer to remain until things here are in better condition." As the months rolled along, George hoped his decision to stay was wise.[429] He was nursing a cold when he received a cable informing him that his mother had passed away on February 4. Just three months later, word came that Lucy's father had died. It must have haunted George's thoughts that if he had gone home for the winter, he would have been able to see his mother once more before she died, and Lucy would have been able to see her father. Then, during the spring of 1921, Lucy contracted asthma and began to suffer from coughing spells.[430] Despite their ill health and grief over the passing of loved ones, the work continued, and George realized that there was one other duty he needed to perform before his mission closed.

Before leaving Utah, George had been asked to represent ZCMI in touring England and Scotland with a delegation from the American Goods Association as guests of the British Chamber of Trade. For more than a month, George and sixty-five other American merchants were entertained in most of the larger cities of England and Scotland. While

427 George Albert Smith to German E. Ellsworth (Chicago, IL), 15 Dec. 1913, George A. Smith Papers, box 35, fld 4.

428 Pusey, 270.

429 George Albert Smith to Heber J. Grant, Nov. 1920, George A. Smith Papers, box 67, book 8.

430 George Albert Smith to Reed Smoot (Washington, DC), 19 Aug. 1921, George A. Smith Papers, box 47 fld 10.

on the tour, George saw many of Great Britain's tourist attractions and met many influential people. He made quick friends with most of the other merchants, but there was one "pompous Englishman who made belittling remarks about the Mormons in the party [which] caused some of the other delegates to remain aloof from the Smiths. George reported the discourtesy to the chairman and offered to leave if his presence were causing any embarrassment. The chairman begged him not to do so and said he would try to bring about a change." However, the rude comments continued and came to a head one day when the man turned to George and asked, "I say, Mr. Smith, just what does that funny little button you always wear represent?" As he asked the question, the man flipped over George's lapel on which he wore the emblem of the Sons of the American Revolution. George responded, "I'll tell you, my friend, that represents the time that my great-grandfather licked your great-grandfather." All of those listening broke into laughter and applause. After that incident, the man was put in his place, and he no longer bothered George with belittling comments.[431]

In June, President Grant wrote another letter mentioning his concern that remaining in England's damp climate might be detrimental to Lucy's health; however, he ensured George that he could stay as long as he felt it necessary for the good of the work.[432] This time, since the concern was for Lucy and not for him, George decided they would leave England. Orson F. Whitney was assigned to be the new mission president, and he arrived with his wife and a party of elders on June 12. George spent a month orienting Elder Whitney to the European Mission and saying good-bye to the Church members there.[433] In his last message to the Saints of Europe, he admonished them to be faithful. Printed in the *Millennial Star,* it read:

> We must not forget, Latter-day Saints, that we have been made partakers of the Gospel of Jesus Christ and the responsibility is on us to share our blessings

431 Emily Smith Stewart to T. Earl Pardoe, 12 May 1948, George A. Smith Papers, box 96, fld 1.

432 Heber J. Grant to George Albert Smith, 29 June 1921, George A. Smith Papers, box 42, fld 9.

433 Gibbons, 103.

> with our fellow creatures. We have been warned and should continue to warn our neighbors. The Lord has spoken in our day and organized his Church. He has conferred divine authority on men and his all-powerful arm is making bare to prepare the way for his Second Coming.[434]

On July 10, 1921, a party was thrown in honor of the Smiths, and five days later they left Liverpool on the *Melita.* Arriving in Montreal, the Smiths then traveled to the Joseph Smith farm in Vermont to join President Grant and a large group of Church members gathered to celebrate Pioneer Day on July 24.[435] The Smiths then visited the Joseph Smith Sr. farm and the Hill Cumorah in Palmyra, New York. Leaving Palmyra, the Smiths traveled by train to Chicago and then on to Salt Lake City, arriving on August 3, 1921. They had been gone for twenty-six months.[436]

As George looked back over his tenure as President of the European Mission, he stated that never before had two years passed so rapidly.[437] It almost seemed like a dream as he thought over his experiences in Europe.[438] George had been able to subdue some of the prejudice against the Church, and his ability to make friends had been a great asset to his Heavenly Father as he had found a way for North American missionaries to once again serve in the European Mission. The Lord had also kept His promises in fulfilling President Grant's blessing. What were the odds of George serving under such constant stress and pressure but coming home feeling better than when he had left? After his experience as a mission president, George agreed with what President Heber J. Grant had predicted; he wrote: "If I had not gone to Europe for three years [I doubt] if I would be alive today. My mission there made a new man of me physically."[439]

---

434 "Long Missionary Service One of Great Contributions during Career of Leader," *Deseret News*, 5 April 1951, LDS Archives (Salt Lake City, UT), ms 00310.

435 Pusey, 274.

436 Pusey, 106.

437 *Sharing the Gospel,* 11.

438 George Albert Smith to Wilford Owens Woodruff (Liverpool, England), 27 Aug. 1921, George A. Smith Papers, box 47, fld 16.

439 George Albert Smith to Heber J. Grant, 6 March 1919, George A. Smith Papers, box 45, fld 23.

Chapter 12
A NEW MAN

Refreshed after his service in the mission field, George returned with Lucy to their home on Yale Avenue, to the haven they had created before their mission to Europe. Inside the home George and Lucy displayed objects of art and culture; above all the most treasured items in their house were the more than two thousand books in their library.[440] Behind the house, on their third acre of land, George grew an abundance of vegetables and fruits, including plums, peaches, gooseberries, currants, cherries, apples, and grapes. Additionally, he dedicated another third of the property to flowers,[441] with sometimes as many as three thousand tulips in bloom.[442]

As the 1920s progressed, George and Lucy settled into family life. And their family was quickly growing. One of their greatest joys came on May 25, 1929, when their second daughter, Edith, married George Oscar Elliott in the Salt Lake Temple. George recounted how pleased he was that Edith had chosen a wedding dress that was both modest and beautiful.[443]

On special occasions, like his own birthday, George would gather the family together around his blue rocker. These family meetings would often stretch on for hours; while the adults discussed "adult affairs," the children were allowed "to slip away to the sand pile or the story book."[444]

---

440 George Albert Smith Correspondence, 3 May 1923, George A. Smith Papers, box 46, fld 7; and Stubbs, 194.

441 Stubbs, 195.

442 George Albert Smith to George Hancock, 19 May 1925, George A. Smith Papers, box 54, fld 20.

443 George Albert Smith Correspondence, 3 May 1923, George A. Smith Papers, box 46, fld 7; and Stubbs, 194.

444 Martha Stewart, "My Grandfather's Influence in My Life," unpublished manuscript, George A.

Christmas was one of George's favorite holidays and was laden with family traditions. On Christmas Eve, near midnight, the doors to the dining room would open to reveal Lucy in front of a table with a beautiful cloth, a wonderful Christmas arrangement, and an abundance of food. Before enjoying the feast, the family would kneel to express gratitude and ask for forgiveness.[445] George would hang a huge stocking, assuring the children that "Santa would never be able to get all the things he wanted in a regular-sized stocking."[446]

George's time with family was divided once again, however, with his obligations to the Church. President Rudger J. Clawson of the Quorum of the Twelve gave George numerous stake conference assignments during the remainder of 1921 that frequently took George away from home. George traveled all over the Intermountain West to places such as Panguitch, Kanab, and Logan, Utah; Snowflake, Arizona; and Juarez, Mexico.[447]

Besides attending frequent conferences, George was also an active member of the community. He became the chairman of the executive committee of the *Deseret News*, a member of the General Board of Religion Classes, a member of the Salt Lake City Chamber of Commerce, and chairman for the Centennial Committee for the Church. George also served as a member of various temporary committees, such as the reception committee for the visit of US President Warren G. Harding in 1923; the executive committee for the July 24 celebration; the state committee responsible for conducting the Defense Test in Utah; and the committee to relieve unemployment in Salt Lake City.[448]

In 1922 George also participated in the first radio broadcast to originate from Salt Lake City.[449] George often exclaimed, "I am as busy as a cranberry merchant at Thanksgiving, with more to do than I can possibly attend to!"[450]

Smith Papers, box 172, fld 36.

445 Evelyn B. Woodruff, Interview by Ronald Walker for the James Moyle Oral History Program, 23, 1 Sept. 1981, Salt Lake City, Utah, LDS Archives (Salt Lake City, UT), ms D200, fld 612.

446 Stubbs, 208.

447 Gibbons, 108.

448 George Albert Smith Correspondence, 1921–1930, cited in Stubbs, 186; and Emerson R. West, *Profiles of the Presidents,* 3rd ed. rev. (Salt Lake City, UT: Deseret Book, 1974), 247.

449 Gibbons, 280.

450 Stubbs, 191.

On September 21, 1922, George was called as the general superintendent of the YMMIA, the calling he had previously held on a stake level. The Lord knew of George's knack for building young people. George would serve in this position for the next thirteen years. Along with his counselors, Richard R. Lyman and Melvin J. Ballard, and many other high-profile leaders in the community, George built a strong leadership support system. Never one to hold long meetings, George streamlined board meetings and gave more autonomy to board members. He tried to have a "leadership of love" that "tied [the presidency] to board members in unity and tightness."[451]

The YMMIA board worked tirelessly to emphasize character-building activities that would boost young men's testimonies. The M-Men basketball program was organized in stake and regional competitions, culminating in an all-Church tournament. The association also sponsored music and dance festivals held at Saltair and at the University of Utah stadium. The YMMIA also worked to increase coordination between themselves and their female counterparts, the YWMIA. Accordingly, the *Young Women's Journal* was combined with the *Improvement Era* in 1929.[452]

In accordance with his concern for the young men of the Church, George took a keen interest in the Scouting program. In 1912, as an advisor to the YMMIA, George was one of a group that recommended the Church apply for a national charter to establish a Church Scouting program under the umbrella of the Boy Scouts of America. The aims of Scouting—"to foster loyalty to God and country and to develop physical, mental, and moral strength"—were in line with the goals of the YMMIA. And the Boy Scout goal of doing one good deed each day particularly encouraged Christlike living. Along with other Church leaders, however, George felt the Church's Scouting officials should "be appointed by priesthood authority" and that the Church should be allowed to "change the policies of the national organization to harmonize with Mormon doctrine and goals."[453]

In George's opinion, no other program in the world could develop the character of boys like Scouting. George believed that "only in

---

451 Richard R. Lyman to George Albert Smith, 2 March 1937, box 67, fld 1; and Gibbons, 110.

452 Gibbons, 110–111.

453 Gibbons, 112–113.

cases where the bishops did not understand the Boy Scout program or were lukewarm in their support of this movement, did it fail to help young boys. He urged the bishops to choose the right type of man to be the scoutmaster and to give him real support, both of his own and especially that of a strong troop committee, composed of men with some years of experience."[454]

George gave more than lip service to Scouting—he also gave "foot service." Walking the streets of Salt Lake City, George personally called on businessmen to collect funds for the Scouts. Though the majority of the boys in the program were Latter-day Saints, he found that those not of the LDS faith were just as generous to the program as were Latter-day Saints.[455]

George also worked hand in hand with the Scouts themselves. In addition to his executive responsibilities, George often camped with Scouting groups. On one Independence Day he accompanied the Scouts—including twenty-two boys from his home ward's Troop 41—on a caravan trek to Wyoming. George sang campfire songs, told pioneer stories, and dedicated Independence Rock "in memory of rugged ancestors who had passed that way almost a century before."[456] Even though he went on the camping trips as a leader, he never missed an opportunity to serve: "If someone wanted a drink of water, if there was wood to be gathered, if there was food to be cooked, he was the first to respond. The horses were always tended before he thought of himself. If someone needed help, he was always there."[457]

George's successful efforts on behalf of the Scouting program did not go unnoticed. In the 1920s he was elected to the BSA Regional Executive Committee for the Twelfth Region, comprising California, Nevada, Arizona, and Utah. In a letter, George wrote, "By 1926, this region was leading all others in the United States in the excellence of its scouting program, and in the number of scouts enrolled in troops,

---

454 George Albert Smith to W. W. Henderson, 14 Dec. 1926, George A. Smith Papers, box 52, fld 24; and Stubbs, 226.

455 George Albert Smith to Joseph E. Cardon, 27 Dec. 1926, George A. Smith Papers, box 52, fld 14.

456 Gibbons, 114.

457 Stubbs, 233.

and Utah led the region."[458] In 1932, George became the first Utahn to be elected to the National Council of the Boy Scouts of America. That year he was presented with the Silver Beaver Award, the highest award bestowed by a local council. Two years later, the National Council awarded George the Silver Buffalo Award, the highest honor obtainable in Scouting.[459] As a nationally prominent Scouting leader, George gave himself and the Church much positive exposure.

George's involvement with the Sons of the American Revolution (SAR) also provided positive national exposure. He headed the Utah delegation to the May 1922 national SAR convention held in Springfield, Massachusetts, and was soon after elected as a vice-president general in the organization.[460] Soon, George's eloquence as a speaker was appreciated by chapters throughout the country:

> Audiences enjoyed his enthusiastic delivery, his apt use of anecdotes, his friendly personality, and his skillful treatment of historic and patriotic theme. And his earnestness and frankness carried conviction to his listeners. At a banquet in Oregon, he gently chided the local chapter for its failure to pray at its meetings. It pleased him that afterward several expressed approval of these remarks though they were considered to be quite unorthodox for an SAR gathering.[461]

Whenever he spoke, George was always introduced by the president general as a Mormon and as "Vice-President General George Albert Smith, the man we all love."[462] George was actively involved in the SAR for many years and developed many friendships that "were a source of much satisfaction."[463]

Another organization George lent his energies to was the Society for the Sightless. George became its president in 1933 and served in

---

458 George Albert Smith to Charles C. Moore, 16 April 1929, box 88, fld 4.

459 Stubbs, 231–232.

460 Gibbons, 121.

461 Gibbons, 122.

462 George Albert Smith, Journal, Oct. 1925, George A. Smith Papers, box 67, book 10.

463 Pusey, 276.

that office for the next sixteen years.[464] Part of his efforts with the society included the building and dedication of a new home for the blind in Salt Lake City and the printing of the first Braille edition of the Book of Mormon. In 1941, the society was honored with a visit from Helen Keller, who spoke to an audience of six thousand in the Tabernacle. As president of the society, George had the opportunity of escorting Miss Keller. He recorded that the audience was entranced as she delivered her speech.[465]

As evidenced throughout his life, George highly valued people and had a special gift for making friends. Whether a relative or a stranger, Mormon or atheist, those who met George were immediately endeared to him. One doctor George met while on a trip to Hawaii remarked, "If there were more people so unselfishly interested in the welfare of their fellowmen as I found you to be there would be no excuse for changing this existence in the hope of finding a better one."[466]

One such example of George's talent for friendship took place after he attended the Century of Progress Exposition in Chicago, which was held from 1933 to 1934. George was impressed with the exhibit and wished to personally thank the director. Inquiring, he was told that the director of the exposition was a man by the name of Dawes. George assumed that the director was Henry Dawes, the brother of Charles G. Dawes, a former vice-president of the United States and ambassador to Great Britain—a man George knew well. Having some free time, George called Mr. Dawes's secretary to request an appointment. However, Mr. Dawes's secretary informed George that there were already a hundred people waiting to see her boss about getting jobs. George responded, "Well that may be true, but I am probably the one man he would like to see, because I have a job."[467] With that, the secretary gave George an appointment and helped him bypass the crowd of anxious job applicants.

When the door opened to the director's office, George was introduced to Mr. Dawes—a Mr. Dawes completely unfamiliar to George, who

464 Gibbons, 203–204.

465 Pusey, 298–299.

466 J. E. Strode to George Albert Smith, 4 Jan. 1937, George A. Smith Papers, box 62, fld 1.

467 George Albert Smith, "Editor's Page: Searching for Family Records," *Improvement Era*, XLIX, Aug. 1946, 491.

quickly learned that Ambassador Dawes had more than one brother. Though Rufus Dawes was very pleasant, George was embarrassed at his mistake and tried to get out of the situation as quickly as possible. Even after George congratulated Dawes on the successful fair and reminded him of the crowd waiting for his attention, Dawes insisted George stay. So George sat down and began to converse with Mr. Dawes. He asked, "Mr. Dawes, where do your people come from?"[468] George then talked about the Church's interest in family history and the genealogical library in Salt Lake City. In the midst of this conversation, Dawes excused himself to another room and came back with a small box. He then opened the box and took out a package wrapped in white tissue paper. Inside the box was one of the most spectacularly bound books George had ever seen: "It was well printed and profusely illustrated, and the cover was elegantly embossed with gold." The book contained the family history of Dawes's mother's line, the Gates, and had cost Dawes $25,000. When Dawes asked if it would be of any worth to George, he replied that yes, it would be of great worth. Without further commentary, Dawes gave the book to George.[469]

George was in a state of disbelief at what had happened. He later wrote, "Twenty-five thousand dollars worth of genealogy placed in my hand by a man whom I had met only five minutes before! . . . I was amazed. Our visit continued but a short while longer. I told him how delighted I was to have it and that I would place it in the genealogical library in Salt Lake City." Later George received a copy of a similar record of Dawes's father's line from Charles G. Dawes. The Church had received $50,000 worth of genealogy just because George had been polite to someone. However, George knew it was more than that—he felt the acquisition had been a result of inspiration.[470] True to form, George's gift for friendship had brought great blessings.

At another time, George conversed with a prominent Catholic bishop. During the conversation, the bishop asked George why Latter-day Saints had such a high standard of morality. The following was George's response:

---

468 Ibid.

469 Ibid.

470 George Albert Smith, *Improvement Era*, XLIX, Aug. 1946, 491.

> From my mother's knee I have been taught that this body of mine should be kept sacred, as the tabernacle of an immortal spirit. I was taught when I was a child that to be clean in my living was most important. In fact, . . . upon one occasion my father called me to him when I was just a young man, and he said, "My son, I have something I want to say to you." . . . I loved my father; I almost worshiped him, and anything that he said to me sank deep into my soul. He said, "My son, there are reports of evil in the community; bad men and bad women are coming in from different parts of the country, one or two at a time. I hope that you will avoid them, but if by any chance any wicked man were to enter into our home and attempt to take the virtue of your mother or your sister I want you to know from your father that I would expect you to defend that virtue with your life. Then," he said, "that is not all. I lay the same obligation upon you with reference to every other man's wife and daughter."
>
> That sank into my soul, and has been as armor to me as I have traveled through the world, and it has been a joy to me to hold up to our Father's other children that standard of virtue: not only shall we not have our own despoiled, but we should see to it that no other man's family should be despoiled.[471]

The bishop looked at George and said, "I thank you for that suggestion. I have never heard anything just like that. I hope you will have no objection if I repeat it as I go among my people."[472]

George always kept in touch with the people he met in his travels. Writing letters provided a way to express thanks, make friends, and plant seeds of the gospel. Over the years, he wrote thousands of pages of correspondence to the well-known and the unknown. Stubbs records that "many felt he wrote the nicest letters they had ever received, and indeed he had that knack."[473] George believed that

471 George Albert Smith, CR, Oct. 1944, 96–97.

472 Robert and Susan McIntosh, eds., *The Teachings of George Albert Smith: Eighth President of the Church of Jesus Christ of Latter-day Saints* (Salt Lake City: Bookcraft, 1996), 122–123 (hereafter cited as McIntosh).

473 Stubbs, 288.

telling people how he felt was like "presenting flowers to people while they were still alive instead of at their funerals."[474]

Much good came from George's letter writing as he created friends for the Church. For instance, George corresponded with George Hancock, a noted teacher in England, for years. In a letter dated December 19, 1925, Mr. Hancock told George of a confrontation he'd had with an English cleric:

> I had had at one lecture a chat with one of the leaders of the Church of England about Salt Lake City. He was bitter against you good people and so I had a good grueling with him, at the finish I found out that he had got his knowledge from some ignoramus editor of a newspaper who scarcely knew where Salt Lake was. . . . You can depend upon me always supporting your church, state and people. I told one big audience, if our English folk were half as energetic, kind and good as the Utah people things would be different here.[475]

Ever the missionary, George clearly had more in mind for Mr. Hancock, as shown in a letter written to him on May 11, 1926:

> I am also satisfied that if you were to understand the Gospel as it is taught by the Latter-day Saints you would find in it all the beautiful things that you have learned in any other Church organization, and in addition many other wonderful teachings that would enrich your life, and it would offer to you the opportunity some day to hold the Priesthood.[476]

Though Mr. Hancock never joined the Church, George remained a faithful correspondent and friend.[477]

As previously stated, George extended his generosity not only to close friends and relatives but to anyone who happened to cross his path. When traveling, if "a pullman porter was especially thoughtful

474 George Albert Smith to J. E. Gorman, George A. Smith Papers, box 52, fld 18.

475 George Hancock to George Albert Smith, 19 Dec. 1925, George A. Smith Papers, box 50, fld 21.

476 George Albert Smith to George Hancock, 11 May 1926, George A. Smith Papers, box 50, fld 21.

477 Gibbons, 219.

or courteous, George Albert would take time out of his busy schedule to write him a letter of commendation."[478] He wrote to thank, to make friends, and to bring people to the gospel—and his efforts were undaunted: "His correspondence was voluminous, and never a one-shot affair. He would write again to those who did not respond to his letters. George kept up a correspondence with one man in England for more than fifteen years."[479]

Along with the letters, George would send Church magazines, copies of the Book of Mormon, and other books. He frequently gave to his friends copies of the standard works of the Church; *The Vitality of Mormonism,* by James E. Talmage; *Mr. Durrant of Salt Lake City,* by Ben E. Rich; *Essentials in Church History,* by Joseph Fielding Smith; books on Zion and Bryce Canyon National Parks; radio talks by Church leaders; and various missionary pamphlets and booklets.[480] In one ten-year period, George sent twelve hundred books and pamphlets to those he had met on his travels.[481] Especially during Christmas, George would share his testimony with friends of other faiths, including "prominent people whom he did not know personally."[482] As one Salt Lake businessman commented, George was the best public relations man in the West.[483]

In his travels, George used various modes of transportation. In 1923, George and Lucy joined a party of 163 people traveling by train to Canada to attend the Cardston Alberta Temple dedication.[484] When Western Airlines inaugurated its passenger flights out of Salt Lake City to the West Coast in August 1927, George used the airline for the first time to fulfill an assignment.[485] After his first flight in 1920, George flew whenever he could as air travel became more

---

478 Pusey, 301.

479 Francis M. Gibbons, *Dynamic Disciples—Prophets of God* (Salt Lake City, UT: Deseret Book, 1996), 188.

480 George Albert Smith, list of books sent to his friends, 1935–1945, unpublished manuscript, George A. Smith Papers, box 103, fld 1.

481 Truman G. Madsen, *The Presidents of the Church* (Salt Lake City, UT: Deseret Book, 2004), 134 (hereafter cited as Madsen).

482 Gibbons, 209.

483 "Passing of a Saint," *Time*, 16 April 1951, 65.

484 Pusey, 278.

485 Gibbons, 199.

available. He was not joined by everyone in thinking that flying was the new way to travel, though. Moreover, some of the Brethren, especially J. Reuben Clark, were very opposed to flying, and Elder Clark used all his influence to keep George and other members of the Twelve out of the air because he felt it was too dangerous.[486] When people would remind George of the many people who were killed on flights, he would answer, "There are more people die in bed than any place else. Can't I go to bed either?"[487] During the 1920s and 30s a rash of plane crashes supported the criticism of airline transportation. But George continued to defend the industry. Using his talent with the written word, his written correspondence countered the negative press and applauded the advantages of air travel while downplaying the dangers.[488]

George used his gift for friendship, his knack for writing, and his enthusiasm for flying to bless the Church's historical efforts. George first visited the Hill Cumorah in 1901. At that time, the historical site was owned by George Sampson, "a sulky fellow who had no use for Mormons." George Sampson was not interested in selling the property and would not even let George climb to the top of the hill.[489] In 1907 George was in Palmyra again to look into purchasing the Joseph Smith farm. After talking with the owner of the farm, M. Avery Chapman, George bought the property for $20,000.[490]

George heard that Pliny T. Sexton had purchased the Hill Cumorah property since George had been there last. Hearing of the sale of the Joseph Smith farm, Mr. Sexton called on George. From then on, George carefully sustained a friendship with Sexton. From the beginning, George let Sexton know that he wanted to buy the Hill Cumorah for the Church.[491] During the time of their correspondence, a Latter-day Saint couple, Mr. and Mrs. Willard Bean, were asked to live at the Joseph Smith farm. George often asked Bean to keep an eye on the Hill Cumorah and to let him know if

486 Gibbons, 200.

487 Emily Smith Stewart to T. Earl Pardoe, 12 May 1948, George A. Smith Papers, box 96, fld 1.

488 George Albert Smith to Glen Perrins, 6 Jan. 1930, George A. Smith Papers, box 58, fld 1.

489 George Albert Smith to Lucy Woodruff Smith, 8 Sept. 1901, George A. Smith Papers, box 135, fld 25.

490 George Albert Smith, Journal, 10 June 1907, George A. Smith Papers, box 67, book 4.

491 George Albert Smith to Pliny T. Sexton, 8 March 1909, George A. Smith Papers, *Letterpress Book #2*, box 28.

there was ever an opportunity to buy the sacred property.[492] George also encouraged Bean to maintain a friendship with Sexton.[493] With George's constant communication, Sexton began to feel that the Church, with George as its representative, would be willing to pay an overpriced amount to get the hill in its possession. George said, "Mr. Sexton seems to think that we will pay a great big price for it."[494]

George felt Sexton's price would eventually come down, and he was willing to travel to New York to purchase the Hill Cumorah when the time was right.[495] Little did George know when he began this quest that it would take twenty-seven years to fulfill. Not until February 1928, when Pliny Sexton had passed away and the Hill Cumorah became part of Sexton's estate, was George able to purchase it for the Church.[496] This significant purchase gave the Church a total of 283 acres in the area and included the whole of the Hill Cumorah.[497] George's drive to help gain these properties for the Church stemmed from the fact that "he believed if you do not memorialize—if you don't put up monuments and mark significant places in your history—you will forget and neglect them."[498]

In his efforts to help preserve the past, George linked himself with other like-minded individuals. He called a group of friends who shared his historical interests to meet in his home in August 1930.[499] Out of this meeting came the organization of the Utah Pioneer Trails and Landmarks Association, with George as its first president. To raise funding, the organization held "plains dinners" in almost every stake in the Church. Through the MIA and George's efforts with the association, many historical markers and monuments were placed across the Intermountain West.[500]

Aside from traveling to obtain and memorialize Church history sites, George also traveled extensively to visit Latter-day Saints in

492 George Albert Smith to Willard Bean, 23 Jan. 1922, George A. Smith Papers, box 43, fld 5.

493 Gibbons, 137–138.

494 Gibbons, 138.

495 George Albert Smith to Willard Bean, Jan. 23, 1922, George A. Smith Papers, box 43, fld. 5.

496 Stubbs, 250–254.

497 Russell R. Rich, *Ensign to the Nations* (Provo, UT: BYU Publications, 1972), 499.

498 Madsen, 225–226.

499 Stubbs, 255.

500 John D. Giles, "The MIA Preserves History," *Improvement Era*, XXXVIII, Feb. 1935, 83.

far-flung stakes. In 1925 alone he traveled approximately 37,000 miles.[501] But even with such extensive travel, there were still apostolic duties at home. One such duty was to chair the committee preparing the observance of the Church's centennial on April 6, 1930. Organized with just six members one hundred years earlier, the Church now had more than 700,000 members in 104 stakes and 29 missions in many nations. The celebration commenced at the April conference, which lasted four days. In the evenings during the conference—and for a month after—a colorful pageant, "Message of the Ages," was presented to capacity audiences. George felt the performance of this pageant exceeded the committee's expectations, and he was pleased with the results of his careful planning.[502]

Though the work in the Church was blossoming, troubles lay ahead for the country. With the collapse of farm prices, increase of unemployment, and stagnation of industry, the 1930s brought distress for the entire country. Reports of Latter-day Saints who were struggling flowed in to Church headquarters from nearly every community. At the close of 1931, George reflected that it had been "a year of anxiety for the world." Unemployment was everywhere, and George saw "no prospect of a change" unless people became humble and righteous. If they would make that change, George was "sure the Lord would bring peace again." As George saw the suffering of those around him, he was grateful for his many blessings—grateful for his family's relative prosperity, and grateful for his and his family's much-improved health.[503]

501 George Albert Smith Correspondence, 1925, George A. Smith Papers, box 50, fld 13.

502 Pusey, 281–282.

503 George Albert Smith, Journal, 31 Dec. 1931, George A. Smith Papers, box 67, book 10.

Chapter 18
CONFLICTS

The Great Depression affected nearly everyone, including George and the Church. George found that as his income began to shrink, paying his bills was not easy.[504] As a board member of many corporations, he struggled with the pressure to trim others' salaries and dividends since he knew of the distress it would cause employees. The strain George felt created some tension between him and President Heber J. Grant, who also served on the ZCMI board. After a board meeting in July 1932, George found himself disagreeing with the actions of the board to cut retired employee pensions.[505]

> President Grant insisted that no legal commitments had been made and that the company could not afford to continue, in the depths of the depression, the policy it had adopted when times were good. George Albert replied that the company was bound by the requirements of good faith to honor its pledges, regardless of how its business was faring.[506]

A few months following this incident, George resigned from the board. This was just the first of "many distressing circumstances" that kept George's "nerves tingling."[507]

504 Pusey, 284.

505 George Albert Smith, Journal, 17 July 1932, George A. Smith Papers, box 73.

506 Pusey, 284–285.

507 George Albert Smith, Journal, 22 Nov. 1934, George A. Smith Papers, box 73; and Martha Ray June Stewart Hatch (Socorro, NM), Phone Interview by Mary Jane Woodger, 16 Aug. 2007, transcription in possession of Mary Jane Woodger.

Another stress that started in 1920 upset George's nerves for several years. It began when George and Lucy's daughter Emily Stewart, who was serving on the Primary General Board, was called by Primary General Superintendent Louise B. Felt to take a hospital training course in Denver to supplement her training as a registered nurse. Emily could then supervise the Primary Convalescent Hospital for Crippled Children.[508] After completing the training course, she implemented many of the ideas she had learned in Denver, some of which were contrary to those held by May Anderson, the secretary of the Primary, who had also studied convalescent hospitals.[509] In 1925, May Anderson became Felt's successor, and a severe conflict began to develop between Emily and May.

By 1931, Emily was so concerned with the policies governing Primary Children's Hospital that she went to Presiding Bishop Sylvester Q. Cannon, who served as an advisor to the Primary organization with Elder David O. McKay.[510] Bishop Cannon advised Emily to bring up her concerns at the next board meeting. When she brought up her concerns on December 9, 1931, everyone sided with President May Anderson's views except for Emily and one other board member.[511] The meeting was emotionally charged, and some board members wept and even got on their knees, asking for President Anderson's forgiveness for opposing her views. Anderson then accused Emily of saying things that were not true. Emily became so emotional "she declared she had been 'crucified in the midst of her youth.' The Primary could not go on, she added, until the decks were cleared."[512]

Not able to compromise, the two quarreling sisters met with Elder McKay and Bishop Cannon on January 11, 1932. The meeting resulted in a decision to release Emily from her calling since the two women could not work together in a peaceful manner. After the hearing, Emily went to her father's office and told him the whole story. That night George didn't sleep at all, his nerves went to pieces, and the next day things did not get any better. George wrote in his journal that he was "sorely grieved at the injustice to [his] daughter."[513]

508 Pusey, 285.

509 Gibbons, 152.

510 Ibid.

511 Gibbons, 152–154.

512 Pusey, 285–286.

513 George Albert Smith, Journal, 12 Jan. 1932, George A. Smith Papers, box 73.

George could not feel any peace about what had happened as he attended a stake conference in Idaho that weekend. The nervous exhaustion of the whole situation forced him to stay in bed for a day when he returned. George then decided to defend his daughter and attended a meeting with Elder McKay, Bishop Cannon, and Elder Melvin J. Ballard. George hoped some good would come from the meeting, but the very next day he found that May Anderson had asked the rest of the board members to support her in releasing Emily. All but two board members agreed.[514]

Several conversations took place between George and Elder McKay over the course of almost a year. The next February, George brought up his daughter's case at a meeting of the First Presidency and the Twelve, arguing that a mistake had been made and that it "should be corrected and [Emily] vindicated." The meeting's conclusion was that Emily should bring her husband and meet with Elder McKay, Bishop Cannon, and the Primary superintendency.[515]

At that meeting, Emily and her husband asked that she be reinstated to the board.

Bishop Cannon concluded that, under the circumstances, reinstatement would be a "farce," and Elder McKay concurred. The two General Authorities did ask President Anderson to retract statements accusing Emily of lying in front of the board. Elder McKay also suggested that Emily might be happier in another assignment. True to his word, he later called Emily to the General Board of the Sunday School, but she declined. The offense continued to fester, and at one point, "two neutral members of the Twelve were asked to look into the dispute and seek a solution, but nothing came of it. The conflict went again before the First Presidency, which decided that its termination was imperative." In all of this, George continued to champion his daughter's cause. Finally, President Grant "admonished George Albert that he should accept the decisions of his brethren without further protest." To George's credit, he followed his leader's instructions without animosity or wavering loyalty. But the ordeal took a toll on his weak condition, probably even more so when Emily's church attendance drastically declined thereafter.[516]

---

514 Pusey, 286.

515 Pusey, 287–288.

516 Shauna Lucy Stewart Larsen (Orem, UT), Interview by Mary Jane Woodger, 23 Aug. 2007,

Despite George's initial defense of his daughter, none of the other Brethren seemed to hold any animosity toward George. As hard as the ordeal over Emily was, George's obedience to and love for the Lord's prophet carried him through the nerve-wracking situation.[517]

Unfortunately, there were other nerve-wracking situations in the works. In 1935, while George was in Chicago, he received word that his brother Winslow Farr Smith and his son-in-law George O. Elliott had been indicted in Montana along with three others "for using the mails with intent to defraud" in relation to their positions with a mortuary company. George was sure they were entirely innocent, and wrote that it was "a wicked act to jeopardize them as [had] been done."[518] George believed that

> the problem had begun when the Deseret Mortuary Company of Salt Lake City started to reduce the price of funerals and other mortuary services until finally they had engendered the bitterness of all the other morticians in the country. They had been doing this for several years prior to the indictment and various undertakers had tried in every possible way to make trouble for them and finally they had succeeded in inducing the District Attorney in Montana to bring a case against them.[519]

Winslow Smith was a director of the company, but he never received a salary for acting as such. He had never sold any stock, nor received any commissions, and he never wrote a letter concerning the company. George O. Elliott received a very modest salary for being the company bookkeeper and secretary, but as such he had "never mailed a stock certificate. He owned no stock. If these two were in any way involved it was because of some technical thing that had been done by the corporation."[520] Evidently, the owners of the mortuary had sold

---

transcription in possession of Mary Jane Woodger.

517 Gibbons, 154.

518 George Albert Smith to Gus Backman, April 1935, George A. Smith Papers, box 53, fld 32.

519 Stubbs, 320.

520 Stubbs, 321.

some stock through the mail to some people in Montana,[521] but as far as George knew, his brother and son-in-law were innocent, as he explained in a letter to Senator William H. King:

> [They] were not connected with the sale of the stock and had nothing whatever to do with the representations which were made by those who sold the stock in Montana . . . they had made no representations of any character to induce persons in Montana to acquire stock . . . their connection with the company was nominal and not active, and was not of such a character as to identify them with any acts or omissions which would come within the so-called mail-fraud status.[522]

The case was particularly difficult for George, because he shouldered the majority of the financial costs. In the midst of the Great Depression, he spent nearly $6,000 to keep his relatives out of jail.[523] It also cost George tremendous physical energy, and he often stayed home to rest his nerves during the tedious proceedings.[524] During the trial, he suffered from lumbago, or acute lower back pain, and Lucy was bedfast.

Many came to George's aid during this tense situation. During the two years that the case dragged on, George's personal friends volunteered to help George and his family by traveling to Montana to serve as character witnesses. However, to George's dismay, Winslow and George Elliott were both found guilty in 1937, but they were fined and had their jail sentences suspended—much lighter punishment than any of the others convicted in the case. When George heard the decision, he and his daughter Edith (George Elliott's wife) knelt down to thank the Lord for their deliverance. George was relieved that neither his brother nor son-in-law would have to spend time incarcerated.[525]

Though the conflicts of the 1930s had been difficult for George to bear, surely none would prove more difficult than what he would face

---

521 Ibid.

522 William H. King to George Albert Smith, 16 May 1935, George A. Smith Papers, box 106, fld 34.

523 George Albert Smith to George Albert Smith, Jr., 21 Jan. 1937, George A. Smith Papers, box 62, fld 2.

524 George Albert Smith to Nicholas G. Smith, 10 Feb. 1937, George A. Smith Papers, box 62, fld 3.

525 George Albert Smith to George Albert Smith Jr., 2 Feb. 1937, George A. Smith Papers, box 62, fld 3.

in 1937, when what had been his greatest joy would turn into a long good-bye.

Chapter 14
THE LONG GOOD-BYE

Lucy's six-year battle with neuralgia and arthritis began in 1932. After watching her suffer all day long on New Year's Day and hoping she would get better, George took her to the hospital the next night at seven. The distress of Lucy's illness was even harder on George than his own ailments had been for him. By January 22, Lucy was no better, and George was much worse, having experienced a nervous setback. For the next five months Lucy was very ill at home. A year later, in January 1933, George took Lucy to the hospital again.[526]

George and Lucy were both sick until that April, when George's health seemed to improve but Lucy continued to suffer. By May, Lucy was distressed, and George was at a loss about what to do. They had the advice and care of three physicians, and a trained nurse was hired to stay with Lucy day and night for four months, but Lucy did not get better. The only thing that seemed to bring Lucy temporary relief was a priesthood blessing George gave her. George hoped the Lord would heal Lucy soon, but by October of that year she was still weak and suffering from considerable pain, and by Christmas 1933, Lucy was still ill.[527]

Even in the midst of their suffering, however, George and Lucy experienced moments of joy. In July 1935, all the adult members of George's family, including Lucy, were present at the sealing of Albert Smith and Ruth Nowell. Lucy had to be carried up the steps of the temple in a chair, but she seemed to handle the ordeal

526 Gibbons, 155; and Stubbs, 324.

527 George Albert Smith, Journal, 1932–1933, George A. Smith Papers, box 68, books 1 & 2.

well.[528] George officiated at the marriage and was delighted with the accomplishments of his last child. Prior to his marriage, Albert had served a mission in Germany and Switzerland, had been the student body president of the Harvard Business School Association from 1933 to 1934, and had been appointed to the editorial board of the *Harvard Business Review*—which, according to George, was "the highest distinction that Harvard confer[red] upon its pupils."[529]

George was pleased with his son's character as well as his achievements. Writing to Albert, he commended him, saying:

> It is very pleasing to us to find that you make friends by being manly and dependable. That is the finest foundation a young man can lay for future life. . . . As I sit in the office and see the pictures that are on my desk and on the wall, and realize that my grandfathers and my father bequeathed to me great possibilities, and that in my children there may live these possibilities, I am profoundly grateful.[530]

Eventually, Albert graduated from Harvard Business School, as would Albert's three sons after him.[531] Each of George and Lucy's children achieved various academic accomplishments: Emily graduated as a nurse, Edith received her master's degree in history from the University of Utah, and Albert graduated from the same university with a bachelor's degree and later received his doctorate degree in business administration from Harvard University.[532] And by the time Albert was married, all of George and Lucy's children had been sealed in the temple to their spouses, another source of great joy to George amid his tense concern for Lucy's situation.

By the end of 1936, Lucy was still not very strong, and George's daughter Emily was also suffering from a serious illness but was

528 Gibbons, 160.

529 George Albert Smith Correspondence, Jan. 1934, George A. Smith Papers, box 58, fld 17; and Stubbs, 204.

530 George Albert Smith to George Albert Smith Jr., 28 Aug. 1925, George A. Smith Papers, box 93, fld 7.

531 George Albert Smith V (Morris Plains, NJ), Phone Interview by Mary Jane Woodger, 16 Aug. 2007, transcription in possession of Mary Jane Woodger.

532 Stubbs, 204.

improving.[533] Another New Year's Day came, and George found the Smith family in a precarious situation:

> Lucy was unable to be up at all; a nurse tending her had fallen and hurt herself; Emily had been ill for a couple of months, Edith was expecting her second child at any time . . . ; Emily and Murray's son, Robert, Jr., was ill with a glandular infection; the mortuary case involving his brother, Winslow, and son-in-law, George Elliott, was pending; and George Albert himself was not feeling the best physically.[534]

George did very little traveling during 1937; seeing the difficulties he faced, the Brethren relieved him of the responsibility of attending stake conferences. George also wanted to stay as close to home as possible because of Lucy's serious illness. He avoided any overnight assignments and tried to be close to a telephone at all times.[535]

Whenever George was away, both he and Lucy experienced great anxiety. In addition to Lucy's illness, George also became sick, contracting a strand of flu that sapped all of his strength. George was forced to spend a considerable amount of time at home for nearly two months.[536] The family prayed fervently for Lucy's restoration, and George knew the Lord could heal his wife if it was His will.[537]

By the end of March, after nearly five and a half years of illness, the doctors gave George little encouragement that Lucy would live much longer. The doctors felt she would only continue to grow weaker. It became a question of *when* she would pass away, not *if* she would. Lucy now required around-the-clock care.[538]

On April 4, George's birthday, the family gathered at the Smith home for the blessing of Edith and George Elliott's second child, a girl to be named Nancy Lucy. Lucy was strong enough to be out of bed and seated in a chair, but that evening she had a heart attack and

533 George Albert Smith, Journal, 31 Dec. 1936, George A. Smith Papers, box 68, books 1 & 2.

534 Stubbs, 325.

535 Stubbs, 326.

536 Ibid.

537 Stubbs, 326–327.

538 Gibbons, 159.

the family feared they would lose her.[539] For the next ten days, Lucy "had a series of attacks," becoming weaker with each one. Albert came to Utah from Boston because the family did not expect Lucy to live much longer but, much to their surprise, she continued to linger, and at times her health even improved in small ways.[540]

By April 24, Lucy was well enough to go on a ride with George. In a letter, George confessed that he felt "that the Lord can heal and that prayer is efficacious," but on May 25, George and Lucy's forty-fifth wedding anniversary, George may have wondered if it would be their last anniversary.[541] By July 12, George wrote that Lucy "was so weak she could hardly speak loud enough for me to hear." However, at the same time, George was amazed at her "marvelous vitality." He had long felt that Heavenly Father was not going to heal Lucy, and he was praying that she would be relieved from her pains and distresses, though she still clung to life.[542]

George recorded on August 17 that Lucy had slept for most of the last forty-eight hours. The doctor informed George that she could remain that way indefinitely, but amazingly Lucy seemed to improve in September. She was trying to rally, but by October she was weak again, her heart fluttering and throbbing.[543] George noted in his journal that Lucy seemed to long for relief through death.[544]

On October 14, while George was attending a General Authority meeting, word was sent that Lucy had had a sinking spell. George excused himself immediately and went home. Following George's departure, the Brethren gathered and prayed for Lucy, and she subsequently seemed somewhat better.[545] But the small improvement was not permanent.

On November 5, George was speaking at the funeral of a man in his ward, James B. Wallis. As he finished his remarks and sat down,

---

539 Stubbs, 327.

540 Ibid.

541 George Albert Smith to John Delaney (Napa, CA), 17 May 1937; John Delaney Correspondence 1937–1950, LDS Archives (Salt Lake City, UT), ms 2380; and George Albert Smith, Journal, April to July 1937, George A. Smith Papers, box 68, book 2.

542 George Albert Smith to German Ellsworth, 12 July 1937, George A. Smith Papers, box 60, fld 19.

543 George Albert Smith, Journal, 17 Aug. to 8 Oct. 1937, George A. Smith Papers, box 68, book 2.

544 Gibbons, 167.

545 George Albert Smith, Journal, 14 Oct. 1937, George A. Smith Papers, box 68, book 2.

a slip of paper was handed to him; he was immediately needed at home. George left the chapel at once, but Lucy had breathed her last breath before he arrived. George went to her room and kissed her and then offered a prayer of gratitude for the life of his wife.[546] He then notified Albert to return home at once for the funeral. Though George and his family felt sad, there was a comfort in the assurance of a future reunion with Lucy. She had suffered for more than six years, and George believed she was with dear ones beyond the veil—especially her mother, for whom she had longed so much as a child.[547]

At her funeral, "the Yale Ward chapel overflowed with relatives and friends who assembled to honor Lucy Woodruff Smith and her family."[548] President Heber J. Grant attended the funeral, as did all the other General Authorities. George selected Melvin J. Ballard and J. Golden Kimball to speak, as they were especially dear to the Smiths. Lucy had served on the general board of the YWMIA for twenty-nine years while Elder Ballard had served as a counselor to George in the YMMIA superintendency. These two boards had worked so closely together that "Lucy had looked on Elder Ballard as one of her file leaders and as a special friend because of the relationship between him and her husband. And ever since the days early in her marriage when she had worked in the mission field under his leadership, she had looked on J. Golden Kimball as a surrogate father."[549] Words spoken at the funeral told of Lucy's talents and of the gifts she had shared with those around her. A friend had once said to her, "You need only to open your mouth and the words seem to flow without effort."[550] Long-time associate of the YWMIA, Clarissa Beasley, said, "She was our friend, our loyal understanding friend. Simple and modest in dress and in conduct, one felt instinctively that any form of sham or insincerity was out of place in her presence. She was thoroughly genuine."[551] Soon after Lucy's death, Richard R. Lyman wrote to George:

546 Pusey, 93.

547 George Albert Smith, Journal, 3 Nov. to 5 Nov. 1937, George A. Smith Papers, box 68, book 2.

548 Gibbons, 164.

549 Ibid.

550 Gibbons, 165.

551 Ibid.

> The extremely sad but long expected news has just reached us with the lovely picture of our lovely Lucy on the front page where it deserves so much to be. Few women have had such an honor and very few have deserved it. . . . I don't know that there ever was a more perfectly mated couple than Lucy and yourself. . . . Lucy was a wise and able and ambitious girl. She did the work of a man as map-maker and office woman when in her youth. She had a clear mathematical mind. . . . She came into your life and home to be your fond and devoted wife.[552]

After the funeral, George wrote that he felt "no presence of death in [his] home." He wrote that it was "almost as if I could walk into Lucy's bedroom any time and find her there." It was soon decided that Emily and her family would move in with George. Edith lived right next door, and the constant presence of grandchildren was a great comfort to their grandfather.[553] A few years after Lucy's death, George wrote to another man who had lost his wife and expressed his feelings:

> I know that the gospel must give you great satisfaction and the assurance of eternal life enables you to push on and make the most of mortal life. I am glad to know your wife is at rest, particularly in view of the fact that there was not much prospect of her enjoying health again. Now she will be waiting for you and your children, and it will be up to you to keep in touch with your family and encourage them to so live that they will be with you both again when this earth becomes the Celestial Kingdom. . . . I know something about the feelings of separation, but the Lord has been very good to me, and I've been kept so busy that I haven't had any time to worry. I was glad when Lucy passed on, because she had been ill for so long.[554]

552 Richard R. Lyman to George Albert Smith, 17 Nov. 1937, George A. Smith Papers, box 67, fld 27.

553 George Albert Smith to Richard R. Lyman (London, England), 10 Dec. 1937, George A. Smith Papers, box 67, fld 27.

554 George Albert Smith to Lewis Peck (Cove, OR), 20 Nov. 1942, LDS Archives (Salt Lake City, UT),

Soon after the funeral, George traveled to the East coast to hold a stake conference and to attend a meeting of the National Executive Board of the Boy Scouts of America in New York. On that trip, George visited LDS boxer Jack Dempsey, who at one time had been the heavyweight champion of the world. Because Dempsey had been born in the small Mormon town of Manassa, Colorado, he was known as the "Manassa Mauler." George was interested in the fighter because of his Mormon roots, and he and his brothers "periodically contacted him to express their friendship and support."[555] On the trip, George wrote that his "nerves almost gave out after the long strain" of Lucy's illness and death, but he hoped that he would regain his strength.[556]

By December 20, George realized the toll Lucy's death was taking on him. He became aware that he had worn out his nerves; his strength was greatly diminished, so he took time to recuperate.[557]

Christmas Day 1937 was difficult without Lucy, although George still felt her influence in their home.[558] Right after the holidays, President Grant gave George an assignment to tour the missions of the South Pacific, possibly with the thought that it might help ease George's transition to life without Lucy. George accepted this duty and received a blessing in January from the prophet that gave George great solace before he left.[559]

In the blessing, President Grant assured George that "God will be your constant guide and companion." President Grant also expressed gratitude that George's life had "been preserved, notwithstanding . . . that for many years you have been in such a precarious condition that few of your friends felt you could live." He warned George "to guard your strength, to study to preserve your health, and endeavor not to overdo." George was also told to rely on his companion for the trip, Rufus K. Hardy, "as far as possible" and "to turn over work to him."

---

ms 15591.

555 Gibbons, 169.

556 George Albert Smith to Wilfred Corr (Pasadena, CA), 20 Dec. 1937, George A. Smith Papers, box 66, fld 35.

557 George Albert Smith to Don McCombs (Steilacoom, WA), 20 Dec. and 16 June 1937, George A. Smith Papers, box 67, fld 29.

558 George Albert Smith to Alice E. Davidson (Salt Lake City, UT), 29 Dec. 1937, George A. Smith Papers, box 67, fld 4.

559 Gibbons, 170.

He was blessed that he would "go in peace and return in safety"; that he would "have great joy in [his] labors among that people"; that he would "be inspired . . . to teach them the Gospel of Jesus Christ"; and that he would have a "wonderful spirit and blessing in gaining the love and confidence of those people" they were to visit. He was also promised that "through your faith and faithfulness every desire of your heart in righteousness" would be given him, and that he would have "the ability necessary to fulfill this important mission."[560]

George left Utah on January 17, 1938, and on the following day he sailed from San Francisco on the ship *Lurline.* Arriving in Honolulu on January 28, he went right to work, holding meetings with Church members and missionaries. Rufus K. Hardy and Matthew Cowley joined him on February 7.[561]

After their stay in Hawaii, George and his companion sailed to Pago Pago, Samoa. Their boat was met by a seventy-foot-long war canoe. When George landed at the dock, he was greeted by two thousand Saints and four brass bands. Two hundred Relief Society sisters dressed in white led a parade to the mission home. Over the course of the next few days, George attended the Forty-Ninth Annual Samoan Conference, or *huitau.*[562] This *huitau* commemorated the arrival of the gospel in Samoa. At this meeting George was delighted with the seventy converts who were baptized after the morning session. For the afternoon session of the conference, the island's entire police force was called in to handle the crowd of Saints, estimated at four thousand.[563] Unfortunately, "the good health that George had built up [in the first part of the tour] seemed to wane in Samoa. His heart was skipping beats, and he again felt worn out. Despite this he continued his rounds of conferences, meetings, inspections, and sightseeing and gave blessings to 148 persons."[564]

Next, George toured the New Zealand Mission with Matthew Cowley, who was arriving to take his place as president of the mission, and he met with nearly all of New Zealand's nine thousand Saints. The New Zealand

560 Setting-apart blessing of George Albert Smith to visit the missions in the Pacific Islands, Heber J. Grant as voice (Salt Lake City, UT), 13 Jan. 1938, George A. Smith Papers, box 96, fld 16.

561 Preston Nibley, *Presidents of the Church,* 13th ed. rev. (Salt Lake City, UT: Deseret Book, 1974), 293.

562 "Tour of Pacific Isles Highlight of Career," *Deseret News,* 5 April 1951, LDS Archives (Salt Lake City, UT), ms 00313.

563 Ibid.

564 Pusey, 298.

huitau lasted for four days. George spoke at all the sessions and met with missionaries in a carved house for eleven hours. At the end of the *huitau,* Princess Te Puea, a respected Maori leader and benefactor, requested that George visit her and give her a blessing. After his visit, Princess Te Puea presented George with a *kakahu tarriko,* a native Maori robe, as a gift of gratitude. [565]

From New Zealand, George and President Hardy went to Australia, where they traveled more than ten thousand miles to conduct a conference in every branch on the continent.[566] Presidents Smith and Hardy were the first General Authorities to visit some of these places in Australia, and so for most of the Australian Saints, the visits were a memorable occasion.[567] While in Brisbane, George took the opportunity to visit with Ina Inez Smith Wright, a daughter of Alexander Smith, son of the Prophet Joseph Smith. George also addressed the Boy Scout executives and leaders of Australia in several meetings and addressed the Australian people over the radio.[568]

While traveling from Australia to Tonga, George and his companions experienced rough seas almost as soon as their vessel left the mainland. George apparently was so worn out from his touring that he slept through the whole ordeal. When someone asked him the next morning how he'd handled the storm, he asked what storm they were talking about. In Tonga, George participated in a sunrise baptismal service and then surprised the natives when he rode a bicycle two miles back to the mission headquarters.[569]

Following his successful tour of the Pacific, George's ship docked in Los Angeles on July 11, 1938. Waiting for him on the pier were Emily and Edith and their children, who had traveled from Salt Lake City to greet him.[570] Having kept his mind and heart busy with the labors of the gospel in lands far away, George now resumed his activities at home as an Apostle of the Lord Jesus Christ.

---

565 Stubbs, 340–341.

566 "Tour of Pacific Isles Highlight of Career," *Deseret News*, 5 April 1951, LDS Archives (Salt Lake City, UT), ms 00313.

567 Gibbons, 177–178.

568 "Tour of Pacific Isles Highlight of Career," *Deseret News*, 5 April 1951, LDS Archives (Salt Lake City, UT), ms 00313.

569 Ibid.

570 Gibbons, 188.

Chapter 15

HIS CREED AND TEACHINGS

When George was called as an Apostle, he wrote down some goals for his life. The following came to be known as his creed:

> I would be a friend to the friendless and find joy in ministering to the needs of the poor. I would visit the sick and afflicted and inspire in them a desire for faith to be healed. I would teach the truth to the understanding and blessing of all mankind. I would seek out the erring one and try to win him back to a righteous and a happy life. I would not seek to force people to live up to my ideals but rather love them into doing the thing that is right. I would live with the masses and help to solve their problems that their earth life may be happy. I would avoid the publicity of high positions and discourage the flattery of thoughtless friends. I would not knowingly wound the feeling of any, not even one who may have wronged me, but would seek to do him good and make him my friend. I would overcome the tendency to selfishness and jealousy and rejoice in the successes of all the children of my Heavenly Father. I would not be an enemy to any living soul. Knowing that the Redeemer of mankind has offered to the world the only plan that will fully develop us and make us really happy here and hereafter I feel it not only a duty but also a blessed privilege to disseminate the truth.[571]

571 Bryant S. Hinckley, "Greatness in Men," *Improvement Era*, XXXV, March 1932, 295.

What were the odds that the little rascal who had teased young Lucy and terrorized the neighbors would write such a creed? George had been transformed over the years, and he went on to teach others what he had learned.

His teachings as an Apostle always centered on loving people. George once said to a friend "that he [George] lacked the prowess to be an athlete, that he was too homely to win popular favor, and that his weak eyes prevented him from becoming a scholar, but he could excel in human kindness. So, he made kindness his specialty."[572] Throughout the Church, tales of his kindness began to circulate as he exemplified the creed he had written.

With his kindness, George helped others overcome prejudices against the Latter-day Saints. He was determined "to break down the animosity that exists . . . even in the minds of good men and good women, and teach them the gospel," and he believed that the gospel "is the power of God unto salvation unto all those who believe and obey it."[573] One thing he repeatedly taught was that all people are God's children, and no matter in what circumstances human beings find themselves, Latter-day Saints should be willing to give help and aid when possible. George made this teaching his own personal quest.

For instance, J. Winter Smith reported that one time George helped him get a job and gave him advice about another job he was considering. George recommended several things to the young man and gave him encouragement. He was not only kind to J. Winter, but he was also kind to everyone in J. Winter's family. Although J. Winter was not always in Utah and "didn't have much personal contact with" George, George wrote him encouraging letters. Once, when J. Winter "was in charge of a big project in California, [George came to California and J. Winter] had the pleasure of having him as a guest in [his] home." J. Winter remarked that those around George could feel what J. Winter called "the radiation of his spirituality." Before George left California, J. Winter's wife was ill, so George volunteered to give her a blessing.[574] Based on the kindness George had shown him, J.

572 Owen Reichman, Interview by Merlo Pusey, 27 May 1959, cited in Pusey, 301.

573 *Sharing the Gospel,* 10.

574 J. Winter Smith, Interview by Maureen Ursenbach for the James Moyle Oral History Program, 12 Oct. 1972, Salt Lake City, UT, LDS Archives (Salt Lake City, UT), OH 48.

Winter greatly admired George and considered him to be one of his very close friends.

Fellow Apostle Joseph Anderson said George tried very sincerely to love everybody. Throughout George's life, the more a person had gone astray, the more George seemed to sympathize with that person because of his or her greater need for love.[575]

George's care for others often took precedence over any care he had for himself. For example, on one occasion when he was ill, George went to the depot to say farewell to a cousin who was returning to his tour of duty in World War I. The small act of kindness left quite an impression on the soldier returning to war-torn Europe. Upon his arrival in Europe, the soldier wrote to George, "Dear cousin, there are too many of us and too few like you."[576]

But George "did not confine himself to helping only those whom he considered 'worthy.'" He also made a practice of aiding those who had made serious mistakes, even those who had committed crimes. Through letters and personal visits, George would attempt to seek out the erring ones and win them back to a righteous life, as is illustrated by the kindness he showed to one particular gentleman he met while traveling in Atlanta, Georgia. The man approached George and told him of his brother, who was being held in the Utah State Prison for killing a man. The man pleaded with George, "My brother was always a good boy, and I do not believe that he should remain in that penitentiary. If you will help him to get out and send him home I will see to it that he is properly received and given another chance." Apparently, the young man in prison had shot another person in self-defense. George promised to help in whatever way he could and visited the young man in prison upon his return home. After visiting with the man, George felt he would be better off at home with his family, as "he did not seem to be a bad sort of person." With George's help and influence, the young man was eventually released with a pardon and shipped home to be with his family.[577]

Even when a person had wronged George, George had a desire to love and forgive. One legendary example took place when the buggy

575 Joseph Anderson, Interview by Shari Anderson Lindsay for the James B. Moyle Oral History Project, 28 Nov. 1975, Salt Lake City, UT, LDS Archives (Salt Lake City, UT), ms 343.

576 Charles Merrill to George Albert Smith, 21 Nov. 1918, George A. Smith Papers, box 40, fld 4.

577 George Albert Smith to Charles A. Callis, 16 Dec. 1925, George A. Smith Papers, box 50, fld 3.

rope was stolen from George's buggy. When George heard about the theft, he was not angry but said, "I wish we knew who it was, so that we could give him the blanket also, for he must have been cold; and some food also, for he must have been hungry."[578]

In his dissertation on George Albert's life, Francis M. Gibbons records, "A 'good deed a day' was more than a platitude to George Albert Smith. It was a compelling idea that motivated him to regularly and aggressively look for opportunities to serve and lift others. And through consistent application, the idea ultimately became a fixed habit." No matter where he was or what he was doing, George seemed to always find an opportunity to help someone along the way.[579]

George's children were often witnesses to his acts of kindness. One day his daughter Edith came to his office, and as they were leaving, Edith reminded her father to put on his coat because it was very cold outside. George replied that he did not have a coat. Edith remembered that he had worn a coat to work in the morning. When she pressed the issue, her father admitted that he had given his coat to someone he felt needed it more than he did.[580]

George's kindness was just as well known to the General Authorities. G. Homer Durham of the Seventy once wrote of George that "his kindly deeds will become legendary and grow with the years. Many were poignant. More than a few have tremendous dramatic force. A few may have been pedestrian, but even if so, the kindly, soul-warming force behind each will live and grow."[581]

One such experience that lived and grew with time was the story of the fourteen-year-old girl who claimed she was hitchhiking from Los Angeles to Iowa. George picked her up on a Utah highway. After hearing her story, he delivered the young hitchhiker to the home of his sister, who was a social worker in the Travelers Aid Society. His sister called the girl's parents, and the girl was returned safely home.[582]

George also helped many with their financial concerns and, in doing so, was generous with not only his means but also his patience

578 Charles Merrill to George Albert Smith, 21 Nov. 1918, George A. Smith Papers, box 40, fld 4.

579 Gibbons, 135.

580 Pusey, 302.

581 G. Homer Durham, "A Daily Good Turn," *Improvement Era,* LIV, June 1951, 479.

582 Pusey, 302.

and forgiveness. He always tried to give others the benefit of the doubt. One day a tall, fine-looking young man who said he was the son of a stake president came into George's office and said he'd had all of his belongings stolen and was now devoid of any respectable clothing. He asked George for a loan of $7.50. George gave the young man the money, and the young man gave him a personal check in return. When the check was returned by the bank marked "No account," George sent a letter to the stake president whom the boy said was his father, saying, "If he is not your son of course I will not expect to see him any more, but if he is, some day I am sure he will pay the bill."[583]

Another such case occurred one day when George received a call from a mother who told him that her son was in need of financial help if he were to finish his university training. George was in a difficult financial situation himself at the time but felt that the boy was deserving of help, so he took out a loan of $250, which he in turn loaned the boy for his education.[584]

George felt great empathy for the poor and for those "who had felt the bondage of debt and hard times," possibly because of the financial rough times he himself had experienced during the Depression. And so George was willing to come to the assistance of those who were suffering financially. He often allowed others to postpone repaying him until they were able to do so. He would tell them "not to worry about repaying the loan until they found it convenient, for he would get by." For one man who was struggling to pay back his loan, George wrote, "I knew that you would pay it as soon as you could, and when I let you have it I had an idea that the time would be longer than you anticipated, so don't worry."[585]

Another example of George's generosity occurred when he sent $400 to a member of the Church in Arizona who had fallen into debt and lost his home. The money was enough to pay off the debt, and George also volunteered to raise more money to help the man build a new home. He only requested that his name remain anonymous.[586]

583 Stubbs, 273–274.

584 Stubbs, 271.

585 Stubbs, 272.

586 Pusey, 240.

George was not only generous with money, but he also shared his food with people nearly every day in his home on Yale Avenue. During the Depression, most of the men who ate at the Smiths' table "insisted that they were working men who could not find anything to do and must have something to eat or starve."[587] George made a rule to never to turn anybody away, even if they smelled strongly of liquor or tobacco; even if the scent were strong enough to knock him down, George invited them in if they said they were hungry.[588]

In addition, George often gave priesthood blessings to the sick and made visits to encourage, uplift, and counsel those who were struggling. On these visits, he brought flowers from his own garden to brighten and uplift his friends.[589]

In his many travels, George often stayed at members' homes, and after each stay, George was emphatic that he write a thank-you note. He was always appreciative of kindnesses shown to him and genuinely desired to express his gratitude. Often he sent along with the note a photograph he had taken while visiting.[590]

George also had a gift for bringing peace to troubled hearts. On one occasion when George traveled to Las Vegas, Nevada, to hold a stake conference, "trouble was brewing" as George discovered that the Church members in the area were often arguing with one another. As he met with the stake presidency and high council, George was determined to find the cause of the bickering and bad feelings that plagued them. At the conclusion of the conference, all were in tears and unified as they put their arms around one another.[591]

Years later, at George's funeral, J. Reuben Clark Jr. remarked that George "was one of those few people of whom you can say that he lived as he taught."[592] And just as George dedicated his life to kindness, love, and charity, he taught members of the Church how to develop the right attitudes and perspectives to help them live

---

587 Stubbs, 274.

588 George Albert Smith to James Duckworth, 14 Sept. 1936, box 59, fld 20; and George Albert Smith to Jessie S. LeSieur (Los Angeles, CA), 23 Dec. 1914, George A. Smith Papers, box 41, fld 24.

589 George Albert Smith to J. E. Cannon, n.d., George A. Smith Papers, book 52, fld 18.

590 Stubbs, 285.

591 Pusey, 281.

592 J. Reuben Clark Jr., "Address Delivered at Funeral of George Albert Smith," 7 April 1951, *Church News, Deseret News* (Salt Lake City, UT), 11 April 1951; and George Albert Smith, CR, April 1944, 31.

righteously and charitably. Reminiscent of the lesson he learned from his father, George explained to Latter-day Saints:

> When I have been tempted sometimes to do a certain thing, I have asked myself, "Which side of the line am I on?" If I determined to be on the safe side, the Lord's side, I would do the right thing every time. So when temptation comes think prayerfully about your problem and the influence of the Lord will aid you to decide wisely. There is safety for us only on the Lord's side of the line.[593]

George taught that we are placed on earth to overcome temptations. As we learn to be charitable to one another, he averred, those passions are overcome.[594] And if a person fails to overcome those passions and allows temptation to become sin, George was clear about with whom the responsibility falls:

> We choose where we will be. God has given us our agency. He will not take it from us, and if I do that which is wrong and get into the devil's territory, I do it because I have the will and power to do it. I cannot blame anybody else, and if I determine to keep the commandments of God and live as I ought to live and stay on the Lord's side of the line I do it because I ought to do it, and I will receive my blessing for it. It will not be the result of what somebody else may do.[595]

In addition to the importance of agency and staying on the Lord's side of the line, George emphasized the importance of keeping a proper perspective. One story he shared was about two individuals with very opposite behaviors who would grow up to be quite famous:

> The boys both went to school, but the first boy did not take much interest in school. He learned to steal. He learned to be so skillful that finally he associated with

593 George Albert Smith, "A Faith Founded Upon Truth," *Church News*, 17 June 1944, 9.

594 George Albert Smith, CR, April 1905, 61.

595 George Albert Smith, CR, Oct. 1932, 27.

> two or three men in robbing a bank. Later they held up a mail stage and one of the men on the stage was killed. Later they held up a train. . . .
>
> The other boy went to school and got an education. He became an associate of fine people and he grew up with a reputation in the community. He was one of the finest men they had.
>
> One day the papers came out with the statement that "Public Enemy No. 1 was shot to death in the city of Chicago." Public Enemy No. 1 in the United States was John Dillinger—the first boy I talked about. He went from one bad thing to another until finally he was shot to death.
>
> The other boy was Paul McNutt, governor and chief executive of the state of Indiana, who has held responsible government positions, one of them being Governor-general of the Philippine Islands.
>
> What was the difference between those two boys? They were about the same age. It was the viewpoint they had of life. The one boy was being taken down hill all the time. The other boy was always going upwards.[596]

During the years of the Great Depression, George helped Latter-day Saints have a good attitude about their circumstances. He warned:

> I hope we are not going to become bitter because some men and women are well-to-do. If we are well-to-do, I hope we are not going to be self-centered and unconscious of the needs of our Father's other children. If we are better off than they are, we ought to be real brothers and sisters, not make-believe. . . . We must not fall into the bad habits of other people. We must not get into the frame of mind that we will take what the other man has. Refer back to the Ten Commandments, and you will find one short paragraph, "Thou shalt not covet." That is what is the matter with a good many

596 Sharing the Gospel, 149–151.

> people today. They are coveting what somebody else has, when as a matter of fact, many of them have been cared for and provided with means to live by those very ones from whom they would take away property.[597]

George also taught Latter-day Saints to be concerned with making happy homes rather than with making large fortunes.[598] He believed that making a happy home began with focusing on marriage. He warned men that if they neglected to marry and raise children, exaltation would be much less likely. Family life was one of the duties of mortality, he said, and he did not believe it likely that bachelors would be in heaven.[599] He encouraged parents to be patient and loving to children because "they will eternally abide with us on the other side, if we and they are faithful."[600]

Earthly families, George taught, were the beginning of eternal relationships. Especially after losing Lucy, George took the opportunity to talk about the blessing of a good woman in the life of a priesthood bearer. He encouraged men to put their arms around their wives, show them appreciation, and treasure motherhood.[601] Likewise, he taught that children were a great blessing.[602] After observing that some Latter-day Saints seemed to care more about their pets than about having children, he warned:

> No Latter-day Saint woman, understanding or comprehending the gospel of Jesus Christ, will refuse the legitimate opportunity to bear sons and daughters in the image of God. No man properly realizing his privileges and opportunities would do anything to prevent himself from being a father in Israel, and having the privilege of rearing and educating children created in the likeness of our Father whom we worship. But

---

597 George Albert Smith, CR, Oct. 1949, 172.

598 "Mormon Elder Visits Helena," *Montana Daily Record,* 1 Oct. 1914.

599 Gordon Noel Hurtel, "Not As High Rank in Heaven For Bachelors As Benedicts, Says Mormon Apostle Smith," *The Constitution,* 14 July 1907.

600 George Albert Smith, CR, Oct. 1905, 29.

601 George Albert Smith, CR, April 1943, 90–91.

602 George Albert Smith, CR, Oct. 1907, 36–37.

> our brethren and sisters in some parts of the world fail to understand that, and, in the place of sweet, innocent children, and the prattle and joyous laughter of those of whom our Father has said, "Their angels are ever present with me" (see Matthew 18:10), we find dogs, birds and cats receiving the affection and taking the place of those jewels that the Lord intended should embellish the crown of every good man and woman in the world, who are capable of being fathers and mothers.[603]

As the Church moved through the Great Depression, George taught that the gospel of Jesus Christ could solve every problem afflicting mankind.[604] Referring to the Lord's commandments as "the rent we pay for the blessings of life," he was diligent in helping Latter-day Saints understand that keeping the commandments brings joy and happiness.[605] In October 1935, at one of the worst periods of the Depression, he disclosed in general conference:

> You will pardon me if I have talked with intense earnestness. It is not because I am angry—I am hurt; my feelings are wounded at the indifference, the carelessness, yea blindness, of many who belong to this great Church, because I know what the result will be. The Lord himself has spoken. Now let us go to our homes and wherein they are not in order, let us set them in order, get the Spirit of the Lord and keep it, observe the commandments of God that we may obtain his blessings, and let us demonstrate day by day by loving kindness and charity, and consideration to one another in these trying times, that we do know that God lives.[606]

The gospel was simple for George. If you kept the commandments, God would watch over, protect, and bless you. If you were righteous,

---

603 *Teachings,* 118–119.

604 George Albert Smith, CR, April 1925, 68–69.

605 George Albert Smith, "Origin of Man and Prophecy Fulfilled," *Liahona,* Jan. 1980.

606 George Albert Smith, CR, Oct. 1935, 122.

you would experience real happiness.[607] He also spoke of the consequences that would come to the unrepentant. In April 1937, as Hitler began to amass his troops and look past his borders for domination, George warned: "The world will soon be devastated with war and carnage, with plague and all the distresses that the Lord has promised unless they repent; but he has indicated that they will not repent, and distress must come."[608] George's voice became a source of instruction as he insisted that "all wars that have ever occurred have happened because of unrighteousness."[609]

As America gathered its strength for retaliation against Japan after the attack on Pearl Harbor on December 7, 1941, George lent his support as a member of the War Fund Committee and in other ways. Although he felt that the world was in a "deplorable condition" and had great sympathy for the young men who would soon "face the horrors of war," he saw no excuse to hate the Japanese, Germans, or any other people. In a general conference a few years after the war, George declared, "I do not have an enemy, that is, there is no one in the world that I have any enmity towards. All men and all women are my Father's children, and I have sought during my life to observe the wise direction of the Redeemer of mankind, to love my neighbor as myself."[610]

George also recognized the opportunities for missionary work that the war brought to Salt Lake City as many moved there to take war-related jobs: "We go all over the world," he said, "to find a few people who will listen to the gospel while right at our doors are thousands of newcomers who need friendship."[611]

Though stake conferences were suspended for six weeks during the summer of 1942—along with the discontinuance of institutes, conventions, and auxiliary stake meetings—George and other General Authorities were not off duty. Throughout World War II, the Brethren counseled Church members to plant gardens, bottle fruit

607 Gibbons, 355.

608 George Albert Smith, CR, April 1937, 36.

609 George Albert Smith, "Some Thoughts on War, and Sorrow, and Peace," *Improvement Era,* XLVIII, Sept. 1945, 501.

610 George Albert Smith, CR, April 1949, 87.

611 Pusey, 308.

and vegetables, and store coal.[612] During these troubling times, George also reminded Latter-day Saints that it was a blessing to have prophets to guide and direct them. In 1943, he observed that there were "thousands of people who would walk any distance . . . that they might see the face and touch the hand of the Prophet of the Lord, and yet there are many [Saints] who disregard his counsel." George reminded them how the Saints had once ignored the prophet when he had asked them to vote against repealing the Eighteenth Amendment, which established the prohibition of alcohol, and he now pleaded with congregations during this critical time to listen to the prophet.[613]

Throughout the war and in the years after the war, George became a great steadying voice. Pusey writes, "He did not close his eyes to evil or difficulty, rather he maintained a deep-seated conviction that the right would triumph. He insisted on communicating very directly with his audiences, leaving no opportunity for back-benchers to snooze or gather wool. His rather high-pitched voice was strong and vibrant with emotion and conviction."[614]

George constantly bore his testimony during the war years, declaring that "God lives . . . Jesus is the Christ . . . Joseph Smith was the medium in this latter day of restoring the gospel of our Lord and organizing the Church that bears the name of the Redeemer of mankind."[615] And we can safely assume that his testimony would be the power that would sustain him in the great responsibilities he would have placed upon his shoulders in the coming months.

612 Gibbons, 238.

613 George Albert Smith, CR, Oct. 1949, 47.

614 Pusey, 228–229.

615 Gibbons, 329.

Chapter 16

HE DID INTEND FOR ME TO BE HERE

Though many observed George's cheerful demeanor, he was still experiencing problems with his health. George had bad dreams that interrupted his sleep, his heart seemed jumpy during the night, and going into his eighth decade, he found that he moved much more slowly than he once had.[616] His brethren in the Quorum were considerate of him, but he knew that they were also working beyond their strength, and he did not want to be "the one to fail when the others [were so] busy."[617]

However, in June 1943, an event took place that would further tax George's energy. President Rudger J. Clawson of the Quorum of the Twelve passed away, and as George helped plan Elder Clawson's funeral, one of the Brethren suggested that George be sustained as the new President of the Quorum of the Twelve. George told his colleague that it was too early to think of sustaining him. He was glad, however, to serve the Lord in any capacity. As George anticipated this new calling, many prayers were uttered on his behalf, petitioning God that he might "retain his faculties and his physical strength to carry on in his leadership."[618]

On July 8, President Heber J. Grant set George apart as President of the Quorum of Twelve Apostles. In the blessing, George was paid a great compliment: "No more devoted and splendid worker has ever been among the leaders of the Church than yourself, excepting, of course, the Prophet Joseph Smith."[619]

616 Gibbons, 305.

617 Pusey, 305.

618 Pusey, 307.

619 Ibid.

The following Sunday, George, as the new President of the Quorum, called his family together and asked for their support in his new calling. Emily and Murray, Edith and George, and the grandchildren all gathered, but Albert and his family did not travel from their home in Boston. George asked his family members if they would do their "utmost to keep peace and harmony within his own home and to live in accord with the commandments of the Lord." He told his children and grandchildren that if they "lived as true Latter-day Saints," he would be honored and respected in his new calling.[620]

George moved to a larger office in the southeast corner of the Church Office Building. Later that summer, Spencer W. Kimball and Ezra Taft Benson were called to fill the two vacancies in the Quorum. In September, George's good friend and fellow Apostle, Richard R. Lyman, said, "Under the direction of George Albert Smith the members of the Council of the Twelve are sure to be tied together by bonds of genuine affection, and unitedly and individually every member will have the freest possible opportunity, encouragement, and inspiration to do his best."[621]

Richard R. Lyman and George Albert Smith had known each other since they were boys, and Richard had served as George's assistant in the YMMIA.[622] Since their childhood, they had played and worked side by side. For more than a quarter of a century, they had served in the Quorum of the Twelve together. Therefore, George was shocked when he heard of Richard R. Lyman's misconduct—Richard was unlawfully cohabiting with a woman other than his wife in a relationship that was a violation of the law of chastity. George hoped that this shocking news was heresy and that the charges were unfounded. But if they did prove to be true, George's duty as President of the Twelve was to protect the integrity and spiritual standing of the Quorum. No one, not even a close friend, "could trifle with the sacred obligations" held by Apostles of the Lord. George ordered a full investigation of the charges. He was so shaken by these events that on November 11, when Joseph Fielding Smith and Harold B. Lee came to his home to report on the investigation,

620 Pusey, 308.

621 Gibbons, 256.

622 Gibbons, 109.

George had to stay in bed and listen to the report there. Their findings established Richard R. Lyman's guilt, leaving George in a horrible state of grief. He just could not understand how "such a fine, helpful associate all these years" could have fallen.[623]

Then, on November 12, George had a dream that he was with Richard in his car in a very unsettled and disagreeable part of the country. It was late at night and they had no lights. When George woke up he was much disturbed and remained in bed until late. That day, at a meeting of the Quorum of the Twelve, Richard R. Lyman admitted that the charges against him were true. He had been immoral. The Brethren were in tears, but George recorded in his journal that Elder Lyman did not seem "to realize his wrong." The Quorum voted unanimously to excommunicate him from the Church and then agreed that a notice should be published without delay. George felt the devil had surely done his worst.[624]

Arriving home after the meeting, George was exhausted. Leaning on a piece of furniture, he summoned Emily and Edith and sent them to the Lyman home to comfort Sister Lyman. That night George had a "miserable nightmare." Waking with a start, "he seized the hickory cane that Col. Thomas L. Kane had given to his grandfather. Thus armed, he searched the house for intruders, but all was quiet."[625]

As hard as it had been, George had done his duty. The next day he stopped by the Lyman home before going to the office. There he found Amy Brown Lyman, general Relief Society president of the Church, prostrate with grief. Richard was there, but he seemed as though he were "in a dream." Richard had been so kind and helpful to George whenever George had been in distress, but George didn't know how to comfort Richard in return. Richard's condition was unaccountable to him.[626] The ordeal so exhausted George that he had to stay in bed for quite some time afterward.[627]

---

623 Pusey, 309.

624 George Albert Smith, Journal, 5 Nov. to 12 Nov. 1943, George A. Smith Papers, box 68, book 7.

625 Pusey, 312.

626 Pusey, 309–310.

627 Shauna Lucy Stewart Larsen (Orem, UT), Interview by Mary Jane Woodger, 23 Aug. 2007, transcription in possession of Mary Jane Woodger.

During this trying time the Lord was preparing Richard's replacement. Before the announcement of Elder Lyman's excommunication, Mark E. Petersen, who was working as the general manager of the *Deseret News,* had a dream in which he saw the newspaper headline, "Lyman R. Richard Dies." In the dream Petersen was called to the Twelve to fill Lyman's vacancy. The day after Petersen had this dream, he sent a reporter to the Church Administration Building to inquire about the health of the Brethren, especially that of Elder Lyman. Advised that everyone appeared to be well, Elder Petersen still maintained the feeling that some unforeseen incident would remove Elder Lyman from the Twelve and that he would be called to replace him. When the announcement of Elder Lyman's excommunication was put in his hand for publication, that feeling was strongly confirmed and remained with him during the months before his call to the Quorum of the Twelve Apostles in April 1944. When President Heber J. Grant extended the call to him, Elder Petersen related the dream and his spiritual promptings to the prophet, who confirmed that the Lord had used this means to reveal the call to Elder Petersen in advance.[628]

In December 1943, after George had seen to some business in New York City, he traveled to Boston to spend eight days with Albert and his family for the Christmas holiday. George not only saw Albert as his son, but also as a "counselor and confidant." During the more stressful times in his life, such as the excommunication of Richard R. Lyman, George often "expressed the wish that Albert were near to help and counsel him."[629] George must have been pleased the following summer when Albert called him and announced that he had become a full professor in Harvard's graduate school of business administration. In September, Albert purchased a new home, and George must have had mixed feelings about the news—proud that his son had achieved so much but sad that his son would never live on the lot near his home that had been reserved for him on Yale Avenue.[630]

During 1944, as the entire country was consumed by the events of World War II, George said in a conference address that the

628 Peggy Petersen Barton, *Mark E. Petersen* (Salt Lake City, UT: Deseret Book, 1985), 85–86.

629 Gibbons, 258.

630 Gibbons, 285.

present times were worse than the times of the Flood, of Sodom and Gomorrah, of Nineveh, and of "the destruction in this country at the time of the crucifixion of the Savior." George lamented that there were too many people who did not believe in God or in the divine mission of Jesus Christ. He said it seemed there were millions of nonbelievers.[631] But after the Allied troops' 1944 invasion of France and the Yalta Conference in February 1945, it looked like the war might be coming to a close. And though things looked better from a global perspective, George found there were still concerns close to home.

Five years earlier, while at a conference in Los Angeles in 1940, President Grant suffered a stroke. President Grant continued to serve in his calling but at a much reduced pace. By April 1945, he'd become more feeble. On April 30, 1945, George was asked to give President Grant, who was lying in bed, a blessing. He did not seem to be in pain, but "was lethargic and restless" as George pronounced upon him "a blessing of comfort, peace, and freedom from pain."[632]

On May 7, Germany surrendered to Allied forces. Two days later, George left for Chicago to reorganize a stake. On May 14, with his work in Chicago completed, George boarded a train for New York to attend to some business. At four AM, George was awakened by a railroad official who informed him of the death of President Grant. George quickly dressed, left George Q. Morris to take care of the business in New York, and boarded another train headed for Utah. On the way home, George slept for twelve hours and ate a light breakfast at noon. He was met at the depot in Utah by his family, George F. Richards, and Joseph Fielding Smith. The first place George went after arriving in Utah was to the former prophet's home to see President Grant's widow, Augusta.[633]

George conducted President Grant's funeral service and was the keynote speaker.[634] Three days after the funeral, George arose at seven AM and, fasting, went to the temple. There he was sustained as President of The Church of Jesus Christ of Latter-day Saints—prophet, seer, and

631 George Albert Smith, CR, April 1948, 179, 180.

632 Gibbons, 269.

633 George Albert Smith, Journal, 14 May to 18 May 1945, George A. Smith Papers, box 68 fld 8.

634 Gibbons, 272.

revelator—by unanimous vote. George F. Richards was the voice for his ordination. Tears flowed freely as everyone expressed confidence in their new prophet. After he was set apart, George sat down in one of the three chairs on the far side of the altar. The other two chairs were reserved for George's chosen counselors—J. Reuben Clark and David O. McKay, who had previously served as President Grant's counselors.[635]

Elder Harold B. Lee's reaction was probably typical of those who were at George's sustaining that day. He later said,

> There was something that happened to me in that meeting. I was willing then, as always, to listen to the brethren and to follow them, but as they took their places at the front of our council room, there came into my heart a testimony and an assurance that these were the men who had been chosen by God's appointment, and I knew it because of the revelation of the Spirit to my own soul.[636]

After such an intense day, George went to bed that night feeling weary.[637] Once George had been sustained, ordained, and set apart as the President of the Church, he became acutely aware of his inadequacies:

> When one friend offered him congratulations, George responded, "I am heavy-hearted when I consider my own inadequacy against the capacity and experience of my counselors. I have chosen two counselors who are mental giants. I don't feel that I can match them."
>
> "Well," his friend replied, with a calculated challenge in his voice, "maybe the Lord has made a mistake."
>
> "What is that you're saying?" the incredulous president asked.
>
> His friend repeated the challenge.
>
> "Oh, no," he reflected, speaking more to himself than to his visitor, "the Lord has not made a mistake.

635 Pusey, 314.

636 Harold B. Lee, *Improvement Era*, LIII, 3 Dec. 1950, 1007.

637 George Albert Smith, Journal, 21 May 1945, cited in Stubbs, 356.

> He did intend for me to be here." In a flash he seemed to see that, if his succession to the presidency was God's will, talk of his inadequacy was pointless.
>
> Turning to his visitor with an obvious feeling of relief, he said, "Thank you. Thank you for coming."[638]

And so, as he accepted the responsibility of prophet, seer, and revelator and the leader of The Church of Jesus Christ of Latter-day Saints, George felt assured that the Lord indeed had intended for him to be there.

---

638 Pusey, 314–315.

Chapter 17
BINDING WOUNDS

George did not have time to ruminate about his appointment to the highest office in the Church; he had much to do and learn. The day after his ordination, as he presided at his first meeting of the Church Finance Committee, "his eyes were opened to an aspect of the Church about which he had little knowledge." But his experience in serving on various boards and committees, as well as his humble attitude and willingness to ask questions, enabled him to quickly adjust to his new role.[639]

The inspiration to call two counselors who had previously served in the First Presidency was a blessing. Some were surprised that George had chosen David O. McKay to be one of his counselors, especially because of David's involvement in the General Primary Board controversy with his daughter. However, George's "triumph of love and duty over wounds of the past brought a general release of goodwill and fraternal affection. All the Brethren were aware of the hurdle George Albert had cleared" in choosing David O. McKay as a counselor.[640]

Presidents Clark and McKay knew that President George Albert Smith was not as familiar with First Presidency duties, but they did not worry about his inexperience as he did. His counselors were well aware that George had "great qualities that neither of [them] possessed."[641] However, their knowledge of past policies and practices was invaluable in helping George chart the future of the Church:

---

639 Gibbons, 278.

640 Emerson R. West, *Profiles of the Presidents*, 3rd ed. rev. (Salt Lake City, UT: Deseret Book, 1974), 58.

641 J. Reuben Clark, Interview by Merlo J. Pusey, 17 May 1959, cited in Pusey, 316.

> Whenever he received a letter or discourse of substance, he would say, "I wonder what Reuben thinks of this?" and he'd be up on his feet and heading to President Clark's office. . . . President Clark, hunched over his work, would look up, strike his hand on his desk, and exclaim, "President Smith, you don't come to me, I come to you. You are the president and I am the counselor. When you want me, you call me." The reminder was soon forgotten when President Smith had another question and would say, "I wonder what Reuben thinks of this?"[642]

No one, including his counselors, could doubt that George was the right person for the job. Before being ordained as prophet at age seventy-five, George had been disciplined and practiced in loving others during the forty-two years he served as an Apostle. Known for his love and kindness, George came into the presidency at a time when the nation and the world needed these attributes to help heal the wounds incurred by hard economic times and the events of war.

George set the tone of his administration in a meeting with the Twelve on June 7, 1945, where he "counseled the Brethren to love the people into living righteously." George engendered love and tolerance based on his understanding "that every other person in the world had a viewpoint somewhat different from his own." He therefore "made allowance for such differences. In sizing up other people, he gave each one credit for operating from a viewpoint which, at least for the moment, he believed to be sound." George's living example of this philosophy fostered good morale among Church leadership.[643] He was especially influential among "a powerful group of younger leaders," which included Henry D. Moyle, Harold B. Lee, and Marion G. Romney. He served as a kind of "father figure" and in private often referred to these grown men affectionately as "kids."[644]

Soon after George was called as prophet, the Brethren learned that his method of reaching decisions was a little different from what

642 Swinton, 32.

643 Pusey, 317.

644 Gibbons, 276.

had been practiced before. In the past, "some of his predecessors had been inclined to go before the Quorum with firm decisions and merely ask for support." George's method, however, was to fully discuss the problem and then say, "Brethren, I'd like to have your opinions." For George, "this was not a mere formality but an invitation to candid expressions." If they did not reach a consensus after their discussion, he would ponder the matter further and then bring it up again later.[645]

The summer after George became President, the world experienced great devastation. On July 28, 1945, the United States Senate ratified the United Nations Charter, and then in August, two atomic bombs were dropped on Hiroshima and Nagasaki, Japan. George worried that "with the discovery of the atomic bomb, the power to destroy ha[d] been greatly increased." With "nearly a third of a million people killed by one such bomb," George asked Church members to "consider the destruction that would follow the dropping of bombs upon the great cities of the world." As George scrutinized the politics of the day, he deduced that "there seem[ed] to be no intelligence in man or wisdom among the sons of our Heavenly Father who dwell upon this earth, through which, he has found a way to neutralize the effects of the atomic bomb." With such a development, George was even more determined to teach that "there can be no certain protection to the people of the world in the future except by keeping the commandments of God and the counsel he has given to his children through his servants the prophets."[646]

When Japan surrendered on August 14 and when the treaty ending World War II was signed aboard the battleship *Missouri* on September 2, George was filled with new hope because he knew that "freed from the grinding demands of war, the Church would now be able to move out again aggressively in its worldwide proselyting efforts."[647]

Shortly after Japan's surrender, George spoke at a funeral near Tremonton, Utah, for four brothers in the Borgstrom family who had

---

645 Pusey, 316.

646 George Albert Smith, "Pres. Smith's Leadership Address," *Church News*, *Deseret News*, 16 Feb. 1946, vol. 4, no. 8, 8.

647 Gibbons, 285–286.

been killed within six months of each other while serving in the military. Family members, military brass, government officials, and reporters from the national press attended the funeral. It was later reported that "President Smith gave the most magnificent talk on the Church. He gave the parents comfort, and he had all those hardened army officers in tears."[648]

In the *Improvement Era* in 1945, George reminisced:

> Once again, through the goodness and mercy of our Father in heaven, we have lived to see the end of another war. . . . What a terrible thing this war has been. It seems a pity that intelligent people will continue, from generation to generation, to make war upon one another and destroy one another, just to satisfy the selfishness of a few people who want to dictate terms to the world. . . . What about this war? Why is it? There is only one explanation for the war that is now concluding, and that is that the people of this world refused to honor God and keep his commandments. . . . So we may know that war is the result of unrighteousness, not righteousness. All war that has ever occurred has happened because of unrighteousness.[649]

In response to US President Harry S. Truman's call for a day of prayer, George encouraged members of the Church to set aside a day for "prayer and thanksgiving marking the end of hostilities." He also delivered a sermon at a V. J. (Victory over Japan) service held in the Tabernacle on September 4.[650]

George carried on with his other Church duties, dedicating the Idaho Falls Temple on September 23, 1945, just before October general conference. He officiated at all the dedication sessions.[651] On September 30, George attended a reception to welcome Matthew Cowley home from his seven-year mission to New Zealand. Just five

648 Swinton, 38.

649 George Albert Smith, "Conference Address," *Improvement Era*, XLIX, Nov. 1946, 762–763.

650 Gibbons, 286.

651 Henry A. Smith, "Idaho Temple Dedicated by Pres. Smith," 24 Sept. 1945, *Church News, Deseret News*, LDS Archives (Salt Lake City, UT), ms 00274.

days later, George asked Elder Cowley to accept a call to the Quorum of the Twelve. In Elder Cowley's first address as an Apostle, he spoke of George: "I have had his arms about me in my maturity. I think it was he who set me apart for my first mission. He married me to my good wife. He took me upon my second mission—and now this!"[652]

With the Lord's calling of Elder Cowley, old wounds may have been healed, wounds caused long before when Matthew's father, Matthias Cowley, had been removed from the Quorum of the Twelve—something that happened not long after George had joined the Quorum. After Elder Matthew Cowley had been called as an Apostle, Laura Brossard, Matthew's sister, expressed to George her great pleasure in the selection of her brother. In response, George said, "The mills of the gods grind slowly, but they grind exceeding fine."[653]

That first conference George presided over as prophet, seer, and revelator of the Church would, for the first time, "be a full-fledged conference, without restrictions on attendance, since October, 1941, due to the interruption of World War II."[654] Speaking as the Church's new President, George explained how awkward the transition from Apostle to prophet had been for him: "You voted to sustain the Quorum of the Twelve, the quorum that I belonged to for so many years that I felt like a stranger, almost, when I walked out of it to occupy the position as President of the Church."[655]

As other General Authorities spoke, it became clear that they felt their new prophet was anything but a stranger. Elder Oscar A. Kirkham of the First Council of Seventy said:

> I want to bear testimony to the knowledge that comes with intimate association, of how kindly this man has been in his judgment, the inspiration of his leadership, and his outstanding love of youth. . . . It is not only here in this land that he is loved. Just a few days ago I was in Canada with John Stiles, executive commissioner

---

652 Matthew Cowley, CR, Oct. 1945, 50.

653 Pusey, 319–320.

654 *Salt Lake Tribune*, 6 Oct. 1945.

655 George Albert Smith, CR, Oct. 1945, 22.

> of the [Boy] Scouts of Canada, who expressed to me personally his great delight in the coming of new responsibilities, as he said, "to the man I love, George Albert Smith."[656]

Church Patriarch Joseph F. Smith said in his address,

> It is not for me to say what particular mission President George Albert Smith has ahead of him. This I do know, however, that at this particular time in the world's history, never was the need for love among brethren so desperately needed as it is needed today. Furthermore, I do know this, that there is no man of my acquaintance who loves the human family, collectively and individually, more profoundly than does President George Albert Smith. Those two things coming in conjunction, the need for love, [and] his presidency at this time, have for me at least, peculiar significance.[657]

President George Albert Smith's remarks at the closing session of the conference illustrated the great love he had for people from all walks of life, regardless of their religious preferences:

> Today as I stand here I realize that in this city, in the Catholic Church, the Presbyterian Church, the Methodist, the Baptist, the Episcopalian, and the other churches, I have brothers and sisters that I love. They are all my Father's children. . . .
>
> Let us not complain at our friends and our neighbors, because they do not do what we want them to do. Rather let us love them into doing the things that our Heavenly Father would have them do. We can do that, and we cannot win their confidence or their love in any other way.[658]

656 Oscar A. Kirkham, "Conference Address," *Improvement Era,* XLVIII, Nov. 1945, 677.

657 Joseph F. Smith, CR, Oct. 1945, 31–32.

658 George Albert Smith, CR, Oct. 1945, 173–174.

As foreshadowed in this first general conference, the overarching theme of everything George Albert Smith would say and do in the next six years was loving others.

Even after being sustained as prophet, George was reluctant to receive special treatment. For instance, when it was suggested that the Church buy a new Cadillac for his use, George replied, "I'd rather have a Ford. I wouldn't feel right riding around in a Cadillac." After some persuasion by the Brethren, however, he was convinced that "a larger automobile would be more in keeping with his needs, his comfort, and his position." But even while being driven around in a Cadillac right after conference, George humbly told his family, "I have not wanted this position. I have not felt equal to it. But it has come to me, and I will fill it to the best of my ability. I want you all to know that, whatever you are doing in the church, from ward teaching to presiding over a stake, if you do it to the best of your ability, your position is just as important as mine."[659]

In serving to the best of his abilities, George was particularly concerned about binding the wounds sustained as a result of the war and teaching the people what they needed to do to avoid such destruction again: "We are living in a sick world, in a time when, as we read in the scriptures, the wisdom of the wise shall perish, and the understanding of their prudent men shall be hid." He further instructed, "It will be necessary for people . . . to repent of their sins, correct their lives, and live in such a righteous way that they can enjoy the spirit of our Heavenly Father."[660]

George focused on relieving the hungry Saints in Europe following the collapse of the Nazi regime. On October 18, 1945, the General Authorities under his direction had food and clothing sent immediately to war-torn countries. The most critical need was fuel for cooking and for heating of homes. During the war, American Relief Societies had made and stored quilts. With the end of the war, the quilts were included in parcels that were sent to Saints in war-torn Europe. Aside from quilts, the packages also included needles, thread, darning cottons, dehydrated soups, and other needed items. The Church also began producing much-needed vitamins, and members everywhere

659 Pusey, 315–316.

660 George Albert Smith, CR, Oct. 1947, 6.

conducted clothing drives to help assist Church members devastated by the war.[661]

On a visit to Welfare Square "to inspect the results of these clothing drives," George demonstrated his love for the people and dedication to the project: "As he stood before the open boxes where clothing was being gathered to be shipped to Europe, he removed his coat and laid it on one of the piles. Despite the protests of his associates, he insisted and returned to the Church offices without his coat."[662]

These shipments were but a precursor to an even larger project that would help the Saints in Europe—a project that would involve a meeting between George and the President of the United States, although this would not be the first time that George had visited with a President. In fact, George was personally acquainted with eight US Presidents. He'd met President William McKinley at the Music Hall in Buffalo, New York. George had called on President Warren G. Harding when George had been elected a vice-president general of the SAR. And, as previously mentioned, George was also acquainted with President Theodore Roosevelt, who had once admonished him that he "never want[ed him] to come to Washington while [he was] president of the United States without coming to see [him]."[663]

George also corresponded with Presidents William Howard Taft, Calvin Coolidge, and Herbert Hoover, and after the devastating October stock market crash in 1929, George briefly visited with his distant relative Franklin D. Roosevelt.[664] And so, when George walked into the oval office for an audience with President Harry S. Truman, visiting with the nation's executive power was not something new for him. George later described his visit:

> I said: "I have just come to ascertain from you, Mr. President, what your attitude will be if the Latter-day

---

661 Joseph Anderson, *Prophets I Have Known* (Salt Lake City, UT: Deseret Book, 1973), 102 (hereafter cited as Anderson).

662 Anderson, 103.

663 George A. Smith, Journal, George A. Smith Papers, box 124, fld 10, 11–12.

664 George Albert Smith, "A Few Notes for Preservation," George A. Smith Papers, box 124, scrapbook 1, 11–12; and George Albert Smith to Bolton Smith, 6 June 1929, George A. Smith Papers, box 56, fld 8.

> Saints are prepared to ship food and clothing and bedding to Europe."
>
> He smiled and . . . said, "Well, what do you want to ship it over there for? Their money isn't any good."
>
> I said: "We don't want their money."
>
> He looked at me and asked: "You don't mean you are going to give it to them?"
>
> I said: "Of course, we would give it to them. They are our brothers and sisters and are in distress. God has blessed us with a surplus, and we will be glad to send it if we can have the co-operation of the government."
>
> He said: "You are on the right track," and added, "we will be glad to help you in any way we can.". . .
>
> After we had sat there a moment or two, he said again: "How long will it take you to get this ready?"
>
> I said: "It's all ready."
>
> The government you remember had been destroying food and refusing to plant grain during the war, so I said to him:
>
> "Mr. President, while the administration at Washington were advising the destroying of food, we were building elevators and filling them with grain, and increasing our flocks and our herds, and now what we need is the cars and the ships in order to send considerable food, clothing and bedding to the people of Europe who are in distress. We have an organization in the Church that has over two thousand homemade quilts ready."[665]

President Truman quickly opened the way for Latter-day Saint welfare services to be extended to Europe. George then appointed Elder Ezra Taft Benson as President of the European Mission with a special one-year assignment:

> 1. To attend to the spiritual welfare of the saints in Europe.
> 2. To provide for the physical needs of saints relative to food, clothing, and bedding.

665 George Albert Smith, CR, Oct. 1947, 5–6.

3. To direct the reorganization of the mission.
4. To prepare the way for the return of missionaries to Europe.[666]

In January, Elder Benson flew to London, immediately organizing relief operations where food and warm clothing were distributed. Eventually, the Church would send 127 forty-ton carloads of food, clothing, bedding, and medicine,[667] greatly blessing thousands in Europe who had been living in disarray and hopelessness.

Another issue George faced in 1945 surfaced when George's friend Andre Anastasian came with his wife and daughter for a visit. During the course of their conversation, they "talked about the equality of the negro and [the] association of races," and Anastasian was especially interested in the Church's policy of denying Blacks the priesthood. George knew that "the policy would remain in effect until it was changed by revelation," and on November 22, 1945, he explained to his friend, "'The Lord has the last decision . . . and if we will be fair to all, he will bless us.' Little did he know that this 'last decision' would be made known thirty-three years later to his young associate, Spencer W. Kimball."[668]

Though the revelation to change the policy was not part of George's mission, in May 1946 he was able to dispel some hard feelings caused by prejudice in Mexico. A large number of Church members felt they should have a Hispanic prophet and had broken away from the Church in Mexico, establishing their own church. These Latter-day Saints taught incorrect principles and were causing disharmony and stilted progress in the Church.[669]

George arrived in Mexico City on May 20 to speak at five sessions of a "special conference which was the largest and most significant event held in the Mexican Mission up to that time." George encouraged the people who had broken away from the Church to come back to the fold. As a result of his efforts, some who

666 *Church History as Viewed through the Lives of the Presidents of the Church* (Provo, UT: The Church of Jesus Christ of Latter-day Saints Church Schools, Seminaries and Institutes of Religion, 1966), 82.

667 Gibbons, 303.

668 Gibbons, 301.

669 Joseph Anderson, Interview by Shari Anderson Lindsay for the James Moyle Oral History Program, 28 Nov. 1975, LDS Archives (Salt Lake City, UT), ms D200252, 1.

had distanced themselves from the Church for more than ten years decided to return to Church activity, and there was a great feeling of unity and love during the meetings. As George left the chapel, "the entire assembly rose to their feet," and "as he passed down the aisles many hands were outstretched to touch his as he went by."[670] Twelve hundred members who had left the Church returned as a result of his visit. One of the reconciled leaders bore his testimony of President George Albert Smith's divine commission: "There is only one President of the Church, and that is President George Albert Smith."[671] In addition to his success in bringing so many back into Church activity, George presented a leather-bound copy of the Book of Mormon to Mexico President Avila Camacho. Upon receiving the Book of Mormon, Camacho said, "My curiosity has been aroused considerably over that book; I would like to have one."[672]

Wherever George went, he repeated his long-standing teaching that if people would simply love one another, they would be happy. In 1946, marking one year of service as prophet, seer, and revelator of the Church, George remarked, "What a happy world it would be if men everywhere recognized their fellow men as brothers and sisters, and then followed that up by loving their neighbors as themselves."[673] Truly, George's years as prophet would continue to be some of the happiest the Saints had ever known. For the next five years, as George continued to talk about happiness and about keeping the commandments, Latter-day Saints would experience peace, tranquility, and happiness. What were the odds that George Albert Smith could accomplish such a tremendous task in such a short time? The war had been over for less than a year, but George's great capacity to love and forgive people had overcome the odds.

---

670 "Visit to Mexico Aided Return of 1200 Members into Church," *Deseret News*, 5 April 1951, LDS Archives (Salt Lake City, UT), ms 00306.

671 Joseph Anderson, Interview by Shari Anderson Lindsay for the James Moyle Oral History Program, 28 Nov. 1975, LDS Archives (Salt Lake City, UT), ms D200252, 1.

672 Anderson, 107.

673 George Albert Smith, Conference Address, *Improvement Era*, XLIX, Nov. 1946, 762–763.

Chapter 18
THE PRESIDENCY

Though George entered the First Presidency in his eighth decade, he was insistent that his age not be a handicap. One of his favorite sayings was, "I would rather be 78 years young than 50 years old."[674] In his efforts to maintain a youthful energy while serving as the Church President, George kept a rigid dietary routine. He typically ate a light breakfast, consisting generally of prunes and a dish of steamed wheat with cream. One time when he saw his secretary, Arthur Haycock, eating cold, shredded-wheat cereal, George said, "You might as well cut the end off the broom or gather the shavings off the carpenter's floor as eat that. Why don't you have some of mine?" When his secretary did, he found that "the more he chewed, the bigger the wheat grew until he nearly choked."[675]

George was devoted to his regimen, and everywhere he went he took a jar of wheat; the size of the jar depended on how long he was going to be gone. Sometimes the wheat even spilled over to dinner; at restaurants, Arthur often told the server, "We're having roast beef, and he's having boiled wheat."[676] George's favorite dinner was a piece of bread with molasses and butter. While eating this dinner, George tried to have the three ingredients come out even, and there was always a little celebration when he succeeded. He was never able to eat much at one sitting, and when others teased him about his small meal portions, George teased back, saying, "But I've got to keep my girlish figure!"[677]

---

674 Pusey, 342.

675 Swinton, 32.

676 Swinton, 33.

677 Shauna Lucy Stewart Larsen (Orem, UT), Interview by Mary Jane Woodger, 23 Aug. 2007,

After reading his morning newspaper, George had someone drive him to the office, usually his secretary, D. Arthur Haycock, or his son-in-law Robert Murray Stewart. Along the way, someone else nearly always got an invitation to ride with him, whether it was a student on the way to school, a person going to work, or someone waiting for a bus. George and his driver often had to drive many miles out of their way in order to drop off the extra passengers.[678]

George usually arrived at his office by nine AM. The morning was typically "taken up with visitors, meetings, correspondence, and more visitors. Meetings with the Brethren . . . in the presiding councils of the Church and of the various auxiliary organizations and institutions of the Church consume[d] a great deal of President Smith's time."[679] Whenever possible, George liked to go home for lunch, where he usually ate a soft-boiled egg, milk, homemade bread, and bottled fruit.[680] He would then rest for an hour or two before returning to the office. The commute took so much time that George had "a room made available to him in the Hotel Utah adjacent to the Church Administration Building, so he could slip over there for a little snooze without taking too much time from his crowded schedule."[681]

Many of George's evenings were devoted to meetings, public dinners, and other functions, but he liked nothing better than a quiet evening at home. Although living with grandchildren could be trying at times, the grandchildren were happy to have their grandfather in the household, and his teenage grandchildren often felt he was more prepared to listen to them or let them be a bit more disrespectful than their own parents were.[682] Younger grandchildren enjoyed sitting on George's knee, listening to pioneer stories while stroking his goatee. They also visited their grandfather at his office downtown, where he gave each of them a shiny dime from a drawer he kept full of coins to share with young visitors.[683]

---

transcription in possession of Mary Jane Woodger.

678 Swinton, 30.

679 D. Arthur Haycock, "A Day with the President," *Improvement Era*, LIII, April 1950, 288–289.

680 Swinton, 32.

681 Gibbons, 287.

682 Robert Murray Stewart (Ames, IA), Phone Interview by Mary Jane Woodger, 8 Aug. 2007, transcription in possession of Mary Jane Woodger.

683 George Albert Smith V (Morris Plains, NJ), Phone Interview by Mary Jane Woodger, 16 Aug. 2007,

When George spent time relaxing at his home on Yale Avenue, he liked to recline in a large-base rocking chair Lucy had given him.[684] He often said, "If heaven is anywhere near to being as nice as Yale Avenue I'll be happy there," which shows the great love he had for that home as he began to advance in years.[685]

Though George's daughter Emily managed his household well, "he was aware that Emily was sometimes undiplomatic with visitors and that her attempts to shield him occasionally prevented him from seeing people whom he loved and officials who needed his counsel." Emily herself carried a substantial burden, and in September 1947 she suffered a heart attack, although she recovered soon thereafter.[686]

When possible, George enjoyed being outdoors and seeing the neighborhood. Once in a while he'd walk around his yard with a cane. Greeting his neighbors, he'd show his interest in them by asking, "How are you today? How are things going?"[687] One winter day, George met a neighbor on one of his walks who was out shoveling snow without a coat or gloves; he looked cold. George gave him his overcoat without a second thought.[688]

His ordination as prophet "did not alter the habits of kindness he had practiced all his adult life. He continued to make unsolicited, surprise calls on the sick or despondent, to speak at funerals, and to be an advocate for the underprivileged and the minorities."[689] Even with all his other duties, he dedicated his time to serving others by comforting those in distress, performing temple marriages, and visiting widows, relatives, and friends, including Richard R. Lyman and his aunt Gusta Grant.[690]

Though he was a prophet to thousands, George remained concerned with individual people. One such individual who observed his kindness

---

transcription in possession of Mary Jane Woodger; and Robert Murray Stewart (Ames, IA), Phone Interview by Mary Jane Woodger, 8 Aug. 2007, transcription in possession of Mary Jane Woodger.

684 Robert Murray Stewart, "A Normal Day in the Home of George Albert Smith," *Improvement Era*, LIII, April 1950, 287.

685 Pusey, 331.

686 Pusey, 342.

687 Evelyn B. Woodruff, Interview by Ronald Walker for the James Moyle Oral History Program, 23, 1 Sept. 1981, LDS Archives (Salt Lake City, UT), ms D200, fld 612.

688 Joseph Anderson, Interview by Shari Anderson Lindsay for the James Moyle Oral History Program, 28 Nov. 1975, LDS Archives (Salt Lake City, UT), ms D200252, 1.

689 Gibbons, 306–307.

690 Pusey, 323.

was Evelyn Woodruff, who worked as a receptionist in the Church Administration Building. When she was having marital trouble, he reassured her, "Evelyn, you've done your best. The only mistake you made was that you didn't come to us for help. We could have helped you and maybe saved [your husband]."[691]

Along with Evelyn, others who enjoyed George's kindness were his cousins, who had chosen a different path and were members of the Reorganized Church of Jesus Christ of Latter Day Saints:

> [George] was determined to avoid any conduct that would drive a wedge further between branches of the generic family of Asael Smith, from whom both he and the president of the Reorganized Church had descended. So after Israel Smith succeeded to the presidency of the Reorganized Church, George called on him in Independence, Missouri, whenever he was in that area, to cement good relations. And when Israel Smith was in Salt Lake City, he reciprocated by visiting his cousin George Albert Smith in the Church offices.[692]

George once told Israel Smith, "There is no desire on our part to quarrel. Rather, I want to be able to say to your grandfather, the Prophet Joseph, when I meet him on the other side, that I have been kind and friendly with his posterity and have made every effort to help them to see the light of the gospel."[693]

Another family George was very concerned about was the posterity of Father Lehi. George ensured that his teachings of love for all God's children were put into practice when it came to the Native American population. On September 13, 1946, George met with Spencer W. Kimball and told him, "Now I want you to look after the Indians—they have been neglected. You watch all the Indians. I want you to have charge and look after all the Indians in all the world and this includes those in the Islands also." Elder

691 Evelyn B. Woodruff, Interview by Ronald Walker for the James Moyle Oral History Program, 23, 1 Sept. 1981, LDS Archives (Salt Lake City, UT), ms D200, fld 612.

692 Gibbons, 355.

693 Pusey, 349.

Kimball was delighted as he saw in this assignment a fulfillment of his patriarchal blessing.[694]

With Elder Kimball as chairman, George set up the Church Indian Committee. George's interest in the Lamanites' welfare took him to numerous Native American reservations and villages in Utah, Arizona, New Mexico, Mexico, Hawaii, and Tonga, where he blessed those who were sick, taught the gospel, and sat at celebrations with tribal leaders.[695] George also traveled to Washington, DC, where he called on the commissioner of Indian Affairs, the President of the United States, and other high-ranking officials to seek assistance for the Native Americans. George had "friends in many tribes in various parts of America. Visits to his office by Native Americans from nearby and faraway reservations [were] frequent, and more than once [they had] been guests in his home."[696] One time George sat on a hard bench for forty-eight hours, waiting for a chief to see him. The chief was testing him, but George was willing to face the difficult task so he could meet with the chief.[697] When George was criticized for the amount of time he spent with the Native Americans, he would look the questioner in the eye and declare:

> I am an old man, and in the normal course of events, I will soon be called home, and when I get to the other side of the veil I am going to seek out Father Lehi. When I find him, I will look him straight in the eye and say to him, "Father Lehi, I want you to know that while I was on the earth, I did everything in my power to bring the gospel of Jesus Christ to your posterity;" and I don't want to have to hang my head.[698]

George often held meetings with tribal leaders. At one of these meetings some of the ministers of other denominations who also

---

694 Spencer W. Kimball, "Weep O World, For the Indian," *Improvement Era*, L, May 1947, 291–292; see also Boyd K. Packer, "President Spencer W. Kimball: No Ordinary Man," *Ensign,* March 1974, 12.

695 Swinton, 39.

696 John D. Giles, "George Albert Smith—Friend of the Lamanites," *Improvement Era*, LIII, April 1950, 292.

697 Madsen, 234.

698 D. Arthur Haycock, "A Tribute," *BYU Speeches of the Year*, 9 Sept. 1980, 4.

worked with the tribes complained that Mormon missionaries had visited non-LDS patients in the hospital. George responded, "My friends, I am perplexed and shocked. I thought people went to the hospital to rest and get well. If I were ill, it would please me very much if any good Christian missionary of any denomination would be kind enough to visit me and bind up my wounds and pour on the sacred oil."[699] Such diplomacy opened many doors of opportunity to serve and spread the messages of the gospel.

George's teaching that all people are God's children also permeated the heart of his grandson, George Albert Smith V, and even influenced the person that this grandson eventually married. When he met his future wife, who came from the Ukraine and had a very different background and economic status, his grandfather's teachings helped him to move forward in the relationship.[700]

As the responsibilities of the presidency mounted, George became aware of the need to find a private secretary to keep track of his affairs, as Joseph Anderson, the secretary to the First Presidency, was spread far too thin. Arthur D. Haycock, a staff member of the *Improvement Era,* was "loaned" one day to work with George on a project. While working with President George Albert Smith, "Arthur soon realized he was being 'checked out' for a permanent position. After two weeks, the magazine was notified to get someone else; Arthur had a new job."[701] Arthur did much more than secretarial work; he became George's constant companion, driving him wherever he needed to go. He read George his mail and took dictation for letters. Sometimes Arthur found the correspondence quite interesting, such as one letter that caused him to burst out in laughter. When George asked, "What in the world was in that letter?" Arthur told him, "There's a good soul who wants to know what your feeling is on cocoa and cremation. I can't think of two less related subjects." George quipped, "Write and tell him they're both hot." [702]

Though George rarely became angry, Arthur found that George

---

699 Pusey, 324–325.

700 George Albert Smith V (Morris Plains, NJ), Phone Interview by Mary Jane Woodger, 16 Aug. 2007, transcription in possession of Mary Jane Woodger.

701 Swinton, 16–17.

702 Swinton, 18–20.

"couldn't abide a man whose wife had put him through school only to be replaced by a girl at the office whose hair was always in place."[703] Arthur also witnessed George's fondness for children when he accompanied the President to the one-hundredth anniversary celebration of the Seventeenth Ward, where George had grown up. Just as they were getting ready to leave, a five-year-old girl came up to George and whispered, "President Smith, I love you." George thought that "of all the wonderful things said" to him on that occasion, "that was the sweetest thing that happened."[704]

George loved children and always kept a "stack of children's books in his desk and various denominations of new silver coins in his pocket. . . . Every youngster who came to see him got a shiny piece of silver and a book."[705] When visiting a ward, George would visit the Primary and tell the children of their importance and of Heavenly Father's love for them."[706]

Some of George's duties were not quite as enjoyable, however. One unpleasant situation occurred in January 1947 when George had to say good-bye to a fellow Apostle. Elders Charles A. Callis and Harold B. Lee of the Twelve had been sent to organize a stake in Florida. Two days after the stake was organized, while traveling in a car, Elder Callis passed away.[707] The Lord was already preparing a new Apostle, however, and in a remarkable way.

Henry D. Moyle was a lawyer who served on the Church's General Welfare Committee. He was in New York working on a case and visiting his daughter who lived there. One day his daughter turned to him and inquired, "Who is going to replace Brother Callis in the Council of the Twelve?" When Elder Moyle claimed he didn't know, she replied, "You are." He quickly expressed his doubts, stating, "President Smith told me that I would not be needed at this conference." Just then, a telegram arrived requesting that Elder Moyle call President Smith. During that phone call, Henry D. Moyle was called to be a member of the Quorum of the Twelve.[708]

---

703 Swinton, 21.

704 Ibid., 25.

705 Swinton, 29.

706 Lavern W. Parmley, Interview by Jill C. Mulvay for the James Moyle Oral History Program, Nov. 1974 to July 1976, LDS Archives (Salt Lake City, UT), OH296, 19–20.

707 Gibbons, 327.

708 Pusey, 338–339.

That same year, George also called Matthew Cowley as President of the newly organized Pacific Mission, where he would be responsible for all missionary efforts in Hawaii, the Central Pacific, Samoa, Tonga, Tahiti, New Zealand, and Australia, with headquarters in Salt Lake City. As George issued the call, he gave Elder Cowley an important suggestion: "Never write a sermon. . . . You tell the people what the Lord wants you to tell them while you are standing on your feet."[709]

George's method of issuing calls to such leadership positions was far from routine. For instance, when Elbert R. Curtis called George's office to discuss a problem in the stake over which he presided, Brother Curtis noticed that George did not seem to be listening to what he was saying. In the middle of the conversation, the prophet asked, "How is your health? How is your wife? How are you doing in your business?" Then he simply remarked, "Some of the brethren have been talking about you for the M.I.A." About a month later, Elbert was called as general superintendent of the YMMIA.[710]

As 1947 got underway, George sanctioned the Relief Society's initiation of a campaign to raise funds to construct the society's own office building directly across from the Salt Lake Temple.[711] He also celebrated the centennial of the pioneers' arrival to the Salt Lake Valley. The centennial had commenced on Pioneer Day in 1945, when George had broken ground for the This Is the Place Monument. The next year, in July 1946, George led a party of historians, writers, and personal friends over the pioneer trail from Nauvoo to Salt Lake City.[712]

Under George's direction, the centennial celebration included sports, drama, and dance. Happily, the pioneer celebration that year coincided with the University of Utah's win of the national basketball championship, and the publicity surrounding the championship brought attention to Utah and the Church. A new play, *Promised Valley,* was also presented, along with a Churchwide dance festival.[713] At the traditional

709 Matthew Cowley, "Miracles," *Matthew Cowley Speaks* (Salt Lake City, UT: Deseret Book, 1954), 237.

710 Pusey, 338.

711 Gibbons, 330.

712 Pusey, 330.

713 Gibbons, 329–330.

pioneer parade on the July 24, spectators watched the prophet ride on the back of a police officer's motorcycle, "cheerfully wav[ing] greetings to the crowd."[714]

Having the This Is the Place Monument erected was one of the pinnacles of George's public life. George wanted to recognize other influences besides the Church in Utah's history, so though he had originally conceived the idea for a large pyramid with a nice plaque, it was decided instead to erect "a tower with people on their mounts atop it, signifying the first Latter-day Saints to see the valley, and on the wings of the tower a series of figures representing the early explorers, trappers, and missionaries." This change drove up the cost of the project, but George was happy to patiently see it through despite obstacles.[715]

Weeks before the dedication, George had seeds scattered around the base of the monument each morning to attract seagulls. On the morning of July 24, 1947, dozens of seagulls were circling for their daily handout. The agenda for the service included a Catholic priest, a Protestant bishop, and a Jewish rabbi. State, county, and city officials also attended.[716]

George was driven to the dedication ceremony in his Cadillac, his grandson Tom Elliott serving as chauffeur. It was a hot and dusty day, so they had rolled down the windows. Driving up to the monument, traffic was coming in from different lanes to merge onto the main road. At an inopportune moment, Tom gunned the accelerator and cut off another car. Not knowing who was seated in the passenger seat of the Cadillac, the driver of the other vehicle leaned out the window and started to curse at Tom. About halfway through his diatribe, the driver realized who the passenger was. Turning a deep shade of red, the driver stumbled over an apology: "President Smith could you . . . I realize the language was . . ." George, who pretended not to have heard anything, simply turned his head and said "Hello."[717] He had once again displayed his kindness and forgiving nature.

714 "LDS President Steals Show on Motorbike," *The Salt Lake Tribune*, 25 July, 1947, LDS Archives (Salt Lake City, UT), ms 00279.

715 Gibbons, 147.

716 Ibid.

717 George Albert Smith V (Morris Plains, NJ), Phone Interview by Mary Jane Woodger, 16 Aug. 2007, transcription in possession of Mary Jane Woodger.

At the dedication ceremony for the monument, George stated:

> It was in order that we might know what God's will is toward His children that He gave Joseph Smith, the boy prophet, the latter-day revelation which resulted in the organization of the Church of Jesus Christ of Latter-day Saints. Then some of the very stalwarts of the earth were pricked in their hearts with a desire to know the truth, and the missionaries of the church sought them among the nations, and the pilgrimage to this western world began. The community comforts that we enjoy here are the result of their faith and devotion.
>
> The only way we have of giving convincing evidence of our gratitude is by honoring Him and keeping His commandments.[718]

As the monument was unveiled, the United States Marine Band accompanied a chorus that sang, "Come, Come, Ye Saints."[719] When the day was over, George recorded in his journal that July 24, 1947, was "a great day."[720]

---

718 Richard Neitzel Holzapfel and William W. Slaughter, *Prophets of the Latter Days* (Salt Lake City, UT: Deseret Book, 2003), 112.

719 Pusey, 334.

720 Gibbons, 147.

Chapter 19
SHARING THE GOSPEL

In 1948, George had the singular honor of having a book published. *Sharing the Gospel with Others* would be the only book published under his name besides *The Teachings of George Albert Smith*—a compilation of excerpts from his sermons delivered over forty-five years, edited and published in 1996 by Robert and Susan McIntosh. *Sharing the Gospel with Others* reemphasized the doctrines and principles he had been preaching for more than half a century, including:

- The gospel is our Father's work.
- We are all the children of God.
- Keep on the Lord's side of the line.
- Seek ye first the kingdom of God and His righteousness.
- Love one another.
- There is only one aristocracy that God recognizes, and that is the aristocracy of righteousness.[721]

Just as George received inspiration during his sermons, it was not uncommon for him to receive revelation while he was about his daily work, "showing him in a moment what he should do." And in other instances, answers and inspiration came only after careful analysis and fervent prayer.[722] George said about his experiences with revelation: "If you have something that the Lord asks or expects you to do and you don't know just how to proceed, do your best. Move in the direction

721 *Sharing the Gospel.*

722 Gibbons, 48–49.

that you ought to go; trust the Lord, give him a chance, and he will never fail you."[723]

One issue George adamantly taught was the proper use of the name of the Church. In the 1948 October general conference, George told a story about a sister handing him a paper on which she had written her testimony of the Church of Jesus Christ. She then asked George why many Latter-day Saints did not "pay attention to what the Lord has said about its name. We sometimes call ourselves *Mormons,* not members of the Church of Jesus Christ, and she wanted to know why." This experience had a great bearing on the prophet, as he reminded Latter-day Saints in a session of general conference:

> There is only one Church in all the world that by divine command bears the name of Jesus Christ, our Lord. I am sure we will show our appreciation of that great and wonderful name by respecting it, and not be found calling ourselves Mormons as the world nicknames us. The name Mormon to many people in the world means anything but the gospel of Jesus Christ. In fact they do not know what it means.[724]

After this incident, George asked publishers and others to use the correct, full name of the Church. He pointed out that there was neither a Mormon Church, an LDS Church, nor a Church of the Latter-day Saints.[725]

In addition to his counsel on the proper name of the Church, George continually emphasized proper respect for women. George was the only prophet in the dispensation of the fullness of times to enter into the office as a widower. His marital status may have made him more intent on teaching the men of the Church how to treat their wives. In the 1948 April general conference, he instructed:

> Brethren, be kind to your wives. I hope that there is no man here who has married one of the daughters of God—and He loves them, they are His daughters—who

723 *Sharing the Gospel with Others,* 16.

724 George Albert Smith, CR, Oct. 1948, 167.

725 Emerson R. West, *Profiles of the Presidents,* 3rd ed. rev. (Salt Lake City, UT: Deseret Book, 1974), 56.

> is not willing to do by her as he knows the Lord would have him do. Do not make her just a convenience in the home to do the slavery and to gratify his appetites—that is not what women were given to men, as wives, for—and I want to say to you that it is your duty and your privilege, as men who hold the Priesthood, to honor your wives and your children if you expect them to honor you. Unless you honor them, God will not be pleased with you. Live in such a way, in love and kindness, that peace and prayer and thanksgiving will be in your homes together. Do not let your homes just be a place to hang your hats at night and get your meals and then run off some place else but let your homes be the abiding place of the Spirit of the Lord. . . .
>
> Some men think that because they hold the Priesthood that gives them a special way in which they may conduct themselves in their homes. I want to tell you that you men who hold the Priesthood will never get into the Celestial Kingdom, unless you honor your wives and your families and train them and give them the blessings that you want for yourselves.[726]

George wanted all to understand he was "proud to belong to a Church which was the first to extend the franchise to women." He explained:

> It was the Prophet Joseph Smith who first turned the key for the emancipation of women of this world. . . . It was not a whim of his; it was an inspiration from the Lord. . . . He didn't intend that womankind should be in slavery to man. . . . The Lord has not said that woman should not be her husband's equal in all good things, and in the blessings that would flow to the sexes. And so, my sisters, you have been given not only your franchise in the Church, but you have been given your franchise in the country, in the Union in which you

726 George Albert Smith, CR, April 1948, 183–184.

> live. The Lord has given you these privileges. Your vote counts just as much as the vote of your husband or your brother, and it should be just as intelligently used.[727]

Also in 1948, George became concerned with reopening the missions that had been closed during World War II. In August, missionaries were again allowed into Japan. Germany did not reopen her doors to missionaries until July 3, 1949. An interesting innovation in missionary work was also implemented at this time—airplane travel: "On September 14, 1949, twenty-nine missionaries boarded a chartered airplane and flew to their assignment in New Zealand. When the airplane arrived in New Zealand, twenty-nine returning missionaries boarded the chartered plane and flew back to America." This flight signaled the beginning of the practice of having missionaries flown to their assigned locations,[728] and air travel was later used by all Church missionaries going to distant lands.

After World War II, missions were reactivated or created in North and South America, Europe, Asia, and the islands of the sea. This revival resulted in an increase of the missionary force from 386 in 1945—when the war ended—to almost 3,000 by the end of 1946. And by 1951, this force had nearly doubled to 5,800.[729]

George also believed that mission homes should represent the Church well:

> He sent Ezra Taft Benson to New York to buy a new home for the Eastern States Mission—"a building that would be worthy of the church."
>
> "Where do you want it," Ezra Taft asked, "on Fifth Avenue?"
>
> "Fifth Avenue would be all right," he replied. "We ought to have one of the finest places in New York—if we can afford it."
>
> Ezra Benson found an appropriate building at Fifth Avenue and Seventy-ninth Street opposite Central Park.

727 George Albert Smith, "Vigilant Loyalty to our Standards of Government," *Relief Society Magazine,* vol. XII, no.1, 12 Jan. 1925, 10–11.

728 Bassett, 11–12.

729 George Albert Smith, "Liberty under the Constitution," *Improvement Era,* LIII, Dec. 1950, 963–965.

> The Russian government was trying to buy the home for $135,000. The owner, a French woman, finally sold it to the church for $105,000 because she wanted it to be used, she said, for a good purpose. George later visited this mission home and referred to it as being "very elegant and beautiful" and "well suited to the New York area."[730]

In speaking to missionaries, George wisely counseled them how to invite people of other faiths to hear their message. In a general conference address, he said, "We say to them: Keep all the good that you possess. Keep all the virtues, keep all the truth, keep all the goodness that has ever come into your lives, and then permit us to share . . . the additional light that our Heavenly Father, in his tender mercy, has bestowed upon the children of men in our day."[731] Along with missionary work, George viewed the gospel and the Church as something bigger than its individual members:

> It was the function of the church to bring about this human rejuvenation while at the same time clinging to all the fundamentals of Christ's teachings and resisting all compromise with evil. He saw the church as being bigger, greater, and more important than any of its members, including the general authorities. Men in even high positions might be false to their trust or wrong in their judgments, but this did not in any way alter his faith in the gospel or his devotion to the church as an institution.[732]

As seriously as he took his duties as prophet, George often infused humor into difficult situations. Pusey notes that "he had a habit of easing tension or monotony with a funny story or remark." For instance, one time Bishop Hunt of the Roman Catholic Diocese in Salt Lake City suggested to George "that they jointly issue a statement urging the observance of Good Friday." George pondered

---

730 Pusey, 323.

731 George Albert Smith, CR, Oct. 1927, 49.

732 Pusey, 335.

the implications of such a joint statement and said, "All right, we will be delighted to join you in urging the observance of Good Friday if you will join us in urging the observance of the Lord's day every Sunday." Negotiations halted immediately.[733]

In addition to his sense of humor, George had a sense of calm even in stressful situations. Even with his tendency toward nervousness, other members of Church leadership "almost never saw him lose his composure."[734]

Perhaps in part because of his composed and lighthearted nature, the prophet was very popular. Wherever George spoke, many wanted to shake his hand. Once, on a trip to the Midwest, George "was rushing to catch a train when a mother with four small youngsters stopped him so that her children might have the opportunity of shaking hands with him." He took the time to shake their hands and later received a photo of the incident with a note about his actions that stated, "I am sending you this picture because it is a graphic illustration of the man we believe you are. . . . As busy as you were, in spite of the fact you were being hurried into your car and then to your waiting train, you still took the time to shake the hand of each child in this family."[735]

In response to his great kindness, Church members loved George and returned the affection he gave them. And George loved to be out among the people, busy doing the Lord's work. One such opportunity occurred when he journeyed to Los Angeles in January 1949 to inspect the site chosen for the construction of the Los Angeles Temple. Several days before he left Salt Lake, he was not feeling well, but realizing the importance of the task at hand, he ignored the familiar warning signs. Arriving on a Sunday, he went directly to address the final session of the Los Angeles Stake conference, and on Monday he inspected the temple site.[736]

Two months later George was still in Los Angeles, as he had fallen ill the day after he had inspected the site and had not yet recovered enough to return home. On the morning of March 11, George awoke with a

733 Pusey, 336–337.

734 Pusey, 337–338.

735 D. Arthur Haycock, "A Day with the President," *Improvement Era*, LII, April 1950, 288.

736 Pusey, 344.

start and feared that he was dying. He felt "'terribly warm' inside and 'freezing cold' outside" and was unable to stop shaking. The doctor's diagnosis was that George was experiencing a "nervous reaction" that, thankfully, was not life-threatening.[737]

By the end of March, George traveled home and arrived in good condition. By April 1, he was just well enough to participate in the groundbreaking ceremony for the Primary Children's Hospital,[738] but he stayed in the car until it was time for his part in the ceremony. He then went over to the site, moved the first shovelful of earth, and "spoke with a good deal of freedom and strength." George then went back to the car "so that the little wind which was coming up would not impair [his] health."[739]

Just a couple of days later, general conference began on April 3, 1949, with George as the first speaker. He informed the congregation, "I started praying about two and a half months ago that I might be here, and I am grateful to the Lord that he has heard not only my prayers, but also your prayers, and I take this occasion to thank every one of you for the interest you have had in me and for the kind words that have been written and the prayers that have been offered."[740] By the time the last song began, George had to leave the Tabernacle. Though not strong enough to attend the Sunday afternoon session, he was back to speak at Monday's meeting as well as that night's priesthood meeting.

Much was accomplished during the years President George Albert Smith served as prophet. The Church experienced a growth of 167,703 in membership—and 81,385 of those were converts. The entire Church was in a state of flux, yet no pangs of instability or upset were evident. Much of this could be attributed to George's personality and the image he projected for the Church. More than two hundred chapels were constructed in the immediate postwar period in such places as St. Louis, Montana; Washington, DC; and Berlin, Germany; and new hospitals were built in places such as Logan and Mount Pleasant, Utah.[741]

---

737 Gibbons, 348.

738 Bassett, 17.

739 Gibbons, 339.

740 George Albert Smith, CR, April 1949, 6.

741 Bassett, 273.

George also oversaw a change in leadership at Brigham Young University. Shortly before the 1949 October general conference, BYU President Howard S. McDonald told George "that he had received a lucrative offer to become the president of the Los Angeles State College of Applied Arts and Sciences."[742] George gave his approval for Dr. McDonald to accept the offer and then named a committee to find a new president for BYU. Meanwhile Dr. McDonald recommended as his successor Dr. George Albert Smith Jr., then the senior assistant dean of Harvard University's Graduate School of Business Administration. A group of deans and department heads at BYU also petitioned George to appoint his son as university president. Albert was certainly qualified, but both father and son concluded that the appointment would speak of nepotism, which both abhorred. Instead, the committee recommended Ernest L. Wilkinson, a Washington, DC, lawyer who readily accepted the position. George told Dr. Wilkinson that he should "make BYU 'the greatest educational institution in the world.'"[743]

In addition to making BYU a leader in the collegiate world, in 1946 George prophesied of technological improvements that would advance the kingdom of God on the earth:

> Short-wave broadcasting will continue to improve, and it will not be long until, from this pulpit and other places that will be provided, the servants of the Lord will be able to deliver messages to isolated groups who are so far away they cannot be reached. In that way and other ways, the gospel of Jesus Christ our Lord, the only power of God unto salvation in preparation for the celestial kingdom, will be heard in all parts of the world, and many of you who are here will live to see that day.[744]

Around the same time George made this prophesy, another prophecy was realized. George had warned in the *Church News* on September 8, 1946, that "unless the members of this Church keep the commandments

742 Gibbons, 352–354.

743 Pusey, 348.

744 George Albert Smith, CR, Oct. 1946, 6.

of God and turn to the Lord, the war [they had] just passed through [would] be as nothing compared with what [was] yet to come."[745]

In 1950, when the Cold War turned into an active war in Korea, George knew the conflict was the result of not keeping the commandments. During August and September of 1950, Elder Stephen L Richards was sent to Europe to ensure the safety of the missionaries as tensions grew to the point that it appeared a world war was again a possibility.

During this time, George received an invitation to unveil and dedicate a statue of Brigham Young in the United States Capitol rotunda in Washington, DC. The local Utah committee suggested that George give a *short* speech and dedicatory prayer. They explained to his secretary, Arthur Haycock, that George tended to be long-winded and that they didn't want him to embarrass Utah. Arthur was angry but agreed to present the request to George. George told Arthur to tell the commission to ask someone else. When the committee learned of George's reply, they quickly backpedaled and said he could deliver whatever remarks he liked. At the ceremony on June 1, 1950, George gave a "magnificent talk." Arthur observed, "He didn't ramble; the Lord used him. He knew it and I knew it." The day before the ceremony, as George and Arthur were visiting with President Harry S. Truman, the President "opened his desk drawer in the Oval Office and said, 'Look, President Smith, I've got my Book of Mormon right here.'"[746]

At the end of July, George went to Laguna Beach, California, and rested for a few days before leaving for Hawaii to join in the centennial celebration of the gospel's arrival in the Hawaiian Mission. He was accompanied by his daughters and Elder Henry D. Moyle. In the evening the passengers sat at the captain's table for dinner. During the voyage, George continued his regular diet of wheat, milk, boiled eggs, and bread, but he did make an allowance one evening:

> Looking over the dinner menu one evening, he saw "Roast Capon in Burgundy" and thought he'd try it, since he'd grown fond of chicken dishes while serving

745 George Albert Smith, "The Church with Divine Authority," *Church News, Deseret News,* vol. 5, no. 39, 28 Sept. 1946, 9.

746 Swinton, 37–38.

> on his mission in the Southern States. Emily nudged him, saying, "Papa, you don't want that; it's been cooked in burgundy." President Smith replied, "I don't care if it's been cooked in Australia. I still want it."[747]

Fellow passengers sought George out, "eager to shake his hand and ask questions." But "when one woman asked him if he would explain the mysteries to her, he replied, 'I don't know them; ask Brother Moyle.'"[748]

Hundreds crowded around George and covered him with beautiful floral leis as he disembarked the ship in Hawaii. It was then that he was informed that his colleague George F. Richards had passed away, but because of the distance, George reluctantly decided not to fly home for the funeral.[749] Dressed in a white linen suit for the centennial conference opening on Sunday, August 13, George had never "seen a more attentive or magnificent congregation." He recorded in his journal that as he rose to speak, everyone stood in a "spontaneous expression of good will and fellowship. The Saints listened to every word, leaning forward so as not to miss a word, and with tears streaming down their faces very often, as it was recalled to their minds the blessings they have enjoyed during the past one hundred years that the gospel has been in their beautiful land."[750]

The centennial celebration lasted twelve days. "Between his resting periods and the official functions, George found time to meet with the missionaries, arrange for the calling of additional missionaries from that area, counsel with the local authorities, and visit with Joseph F. Smith, former patriarch to the church." The centennial came to a conclusion with evening services in a new Laie Ward chapel. As he left Honolulu, George was once more serenaded. Hundreds of people came to the wharf to see him off, and his party was so loaded down with leis that George could hardly see over them.[751] On the voyage back home, George went to see the captain of the ship and gave him a copy of the *Improvement Era*.[752] George

747 Swinton, 33.

748 Pusey, 353.

749 Ibid.

750 George Albert Smith, Journal, 13 Aug. 1950, George A. Smith papers, box 70, fld 1.

751 Stubbs, 400–401.

752 Henry D. Moyle, "Conference Address," *Improvement Era*, LIV, June 1951, 454.

always looked for opportunities to share the gospel with those with whom he came in contact. Despite his physical challenges, he lived life to the fullest in serving his Heavenly Father.

Chapter 20
AGAINST THE ODDS

Back in Utah, George prepared for the 1950 October general conference, but his principle concern was to fill the vacancy caused by the death of Elder George F. Richards. As he prayed about the matter, his mind began to focus on Delbert L. Stapley, a prominent Church leader in Phoenix, Arizona.[753] In town for the 1950 October general conference, Elder Stapley had previously received spiritual promptings that he would be called to the Twelve. George issued the call to Elder Stapley in the lobby of the Hotel Utah.[754]

At the conclusion of the conference where Elder Stapley was sustained, George offered the closing remarks, saying, "It will be another six months before we are again brought together in this capacity . . . but in that six months, we do not know what may occur."[755] Could he have known what the future might hold?

As George left the Tabernacle, he felt ill and went home to bed. The following Monday he was back in his office. Three days later, on Thursday, George was at the weekly council meeting in the upper room of the temple, where he ordained Elder Stapley as an Apostle and set him apart as a member of the Quorum of the Twelve.[756] During the meeting George said:

> I have spent practically all my adult life in the ministry, teaching the gospel of Jesus Christ to my Father's sons

753 Gibbons, 363.

754 Ibid.

755 George Albert Smith, CR, Oct. 1950, 159.

756 Gibbons, 365.

> and daughters. I have covered approximately a million miles in that service and wherever I have gone . . . I have found good men and women, men and women who are kind and helpful and generous. I would be an ingrate if after my years of experience I should forget the kindness, love and helpfulness of my Father's other children who do not understand the gospel as I understand it. . . .
>
> I know that in the not-far-distant future I will have to stand in the presence of my God and account for the things I have said and done in my lifetime. . . . If I do not tell the truth then I will be held accountable for that. I realize that and it will be an unfortunate thing for me, because our Heavenly Father has said that a liar has no place in the celestial kingdom. But knowing the seriousness of it, and realizing what it may mean, I leave with you this night the assurance that I have that I know that God lives, I know that Jesus is the Christ. I know that Joseph Smith was the medium in this latter day of restoring the gospel of our Lord and organizing the Church that bears the name of the Redeemer of mankind. I know that, and knowing that and realizing the seriousness of my telling you, that if it were not true, . . . I bear you my witness that these things are true.[757]

The three weeks following general conference continued to be busy. The busier George became the more tired he felt. Then his busyness came to a screeching halt on the evening of October 20. While he was eating dinner, George suddenly fainted. Frightened, his daughter called the doctor, who prescribed the usual treatment—bed rest. George did not improve for some time and did not go back to the office until mid-December.[758]

As the Christmas holidays approached, George's daughters encouraged him to do something different than his usual greeting

757 George Albert Smith, "Sermon at the Washington D.C. Ward," 4 Nov. 1945, cited in Pusey, 329.

758 George Albert Smith, Journal, Oct. 1950, George A. Smith Papers, box 70, book 1.

cards. Instead, they asked him to make a recording. George dictated a message based on Luke's account of the birth of the Savior, and his voice blended with Christmas carols in the background played by Alexander Schreiner on the Tabernacle organ. George was a bit reluctant about giving his gift, afraid it might be considered by some a bit egotistical, but Arthur and the girls loved the idea, and worked hard on it for him.[759]

During the holidays, George was able to attend a few socials, including the annual Christmas party for the Church Office Building employees. As he addressed the employees, little did he know he was giving his last public address.[760]

After the holidays, George was well enough to go to his office and work until January 9. After that, he never returned to his office. His health began to quickly decline. He lost his appetite and frequently had a fever that caused him to perspire heavily. Eventually, George required around-the-clock nursing. By February 3, his condition worsened to the point that he required hospitalization.[761] It was publicly announced that George was just at the hospital for observation and that he was expected to be there for just a few days, but those close to him knew otherwise.[762] While he was in the hospital, his condition seemed to worsen. The next day, February 4, was one of the hardest days George had ever experienced. He dictated the thoughts of his mind to Arthur, with his daughter Edith attending: "Last evening and last night were the hardest for me. I felt like perhaps my time had come. If it has, it's all right; if not I'd appreciate the continuing faith and prayers of the people. Tomorrow is the regular meeting in the temple, and I would like the Brethren to lay the matter before the Lord."[763]

Two hours later, President J. Reuben Clark came, and George told him:

---

759 Pusey, 356.

760 Stubbs, 428.

761 Gibbons, 366.

762 "President Smith Is Hospitalized," *Deseret News*, vol. 334, no. 34, 3 Feb. 1951, LDS Archives (Salt Lake City, UT), ms 00280.

763 Swinton, 41.

> I've had a bad day, and I don't seem to be making any gain. I've been so weak for several days, but I am grateful to be as well as I am. Tomorrow is the meeting in the temple; I want you to take a message to the Brethren. I've lived a long time, and I'm in the midst of difficulty without question, and I seem to be unable to gain my strength. It's been suggested that I go to some other part of the country to try and get my strength, but the headquarters of the Lord's work is here. . . . I have two counselors in charge so that if the president is sick they can carry on. If the president is sick, things will go forward anyhow.[764]

He also wanted to be sure that Arthur knew where his account books and financial papers were located, and he suggested to Arthur, "I would like in the disposing of my funds that those who are most in need will not be overlooked . . . 'I would like to do [the Lord's] will. I would like my family to do the same.'"[765] Getting his affairs in order, George stated, "I am willing to stay or I am willing to go, whatever the Lord says," after which Arthur and President Clark gave him a blessing.[766]

The morning after George received the blessing, he felt better. Despite this improvement, George "realized that he was losing strength. 'Unless the Lord takes a hand,' he said, 'it will not be long before it is over. I am not concerned about passing out just like that,' he added with a snap of his fingers." That day, as Arthur came in to see him with his daughters, George wanted to make sure that a few financial matters were taken care of. He told them that he wanted his hospital bill to be paid from his own resources and not by the Church. He also reminded his daughters that the Cadillac he rode around in belonged to the Church. After three weeks in the hospital he finally convinced the doctors to let him go home.[767]

On February 26, 1951, George did go home. However, he did not rest very well. His "hands and his feet felt funny, as [though] they were

764 Swinton, 42.

765 Gibbons, 366.

766 Swinton, 42–43.

767 Pusey, 357.

semi-paralyzed," and he began to feel very weak.[768] Over the next few days, George realized that he was losing track of time as he would "doze off and on through the day and the night with the shades drawn."[769]

By March, George did not feel he was "making any gain." He seemed to be getting weaker and weaker, though the doctor assured him his heart, lungs, and pulse were in good condition. Again, George stated that his only desire was "to do the work as the Lord would have [him] do it."[770]

A little more than a week later, George again had a very poor night. He experienced pain in both legs that was so severe he could not sleep. His temperature was up again, and he felt very weak and tired.[771]

Arthur continued to bring George his mail from the office, and on March 17, George sent a telegram that was delivered to BYU's basketball team that was then competing in the NIT championship in New York: "From the top of the Rockies, I send you my love and blessing. Many thousands share my pride in your record. I have faith in your abilities. Play clean, play hard, play fair, play to win. God bless you." BYU went on to win the tournament.[772]

Around this time, General Relief Society President Belle S. Spafford stopped by the Smith home but did not go inside. She asked for the nurse to relay to George "the love and concern of the women of the Church for his well-being." She also wanted him to know that they were praying for him. "The nurse kindly asked [Belle] to wait a moment while she conveyed the message. Returning to the door, she said the President wished [her] to come in, as he wanted to talk with her."[773]

The nurse helped George into the living room. George thanked Belle for the constant support he had received from the women of the Church throughout his presidency. He "said he knew that his earth

768 George Albert Smith, Journal, 26 Feb. 1951, George A. Smith papers, box 70, book 1, 909.

769 George Albert Smith, Journal, 28 Feb. 1951, George A. Smith papers, box 70, book 1, 910.

770 George Albert Smith, Journal, 3 March 1951, George A. Smith papers, box 70, book 1, 911.

771 George Albert Smith, Journal, 14 March 1951, George A. Smith papers, box 70, book 1, 913.

772 George Albert Smith, Journal, 17 March 1951, George A. Smith Papers, box 70, book 1, 913.

773 Belle S. Spafford, *Speeches of the Year: BYU Devotional and Ten-Stake Fireside Address* (Provo, Utah: Brigham Young University Press, 1974), 35.

life was nearing its end, that he was unafraid of death because he knew he understood it. One thing he sorrowed over, however, . . . was the fact that he might not be spared long enough to dedicate the Los Angeles Temple. This had been a long-time dream. He said he knew it was just a human and selfish desire," though. George also talked about the importance of overcoming selfishness. Then he went on to bear his testimony about the importance of trusting in the Lord's plan, accepting the "release from earth life with joy," and he asserted that the Church would always stand with a prophet at the helm. His testimony was "a deeply moving experience" for Belle Spafford.[774]

On March 20, George suffered a light stroke that paralyzed his right arm and impaired his speech.[775] It was around this time that Dr. LeRoy Kimball at last diagnosed George's illness as lupus erythematosus, an autoimmune disease that affects all the tissues of the body and produces chronic weakness.[776] Later that day, George suffered a relapse. His son, Albert Jr., was summoned and immediately came from Boston.[777]

The night of March 21, George slept well, but only with the help of medication. The next morning, however, George found it "difficult to talk or understand much that was said to [him] because of the effects of the medicine." The medicine disoriented him, and a few days later he experienced trouble with his left hand going numb, something he'd already experienced with his right hand. The next day, he lost control over most of his bodily functions and had a fever; by March 28, he'd developed a kidney infection. When President Clark stopped by on the last day of March, he was told that there was not much hope for George's recovery.[778]

By the first of April, George had taken a turn for the worse. When Albert Jr. arrived at eight-thirty the next night, joining the rest of the family at George's bedside, George calmly told his family that this was probably the end. He reiterated how grateful he was "for the blessings

774 Spafford, *Speeches of the Year*, 35–36.

775 Gibbons, 367.

776 Daniel Ludlow, "Smith, George Albert," *Encyclopedia of Mormonism*, vol. 1 (Salt Lake City, UT: Deseret Book, 1992), 1327.

777 Gibbons, 367.

778 George Albert Smith, Journal, 21 March to 31 March 1951, George A. Smith Papers, box 70, book 1, 914–917.

[he had] received and for the opportunities which [he had been given] to serve [his] Father in Heaven."[779]

As April 4, 1951, dawned, George recorded his journal's last entry: "Today is my 81st birthday. It dawned clear and beautiful." Most of the day, his daughters, his son, and their families stayed close. Dr. Kimball also remained in constant attendance.[780] President David O. McKay came to the house, laid his hands on George's head, and released him to return to his Father in Heaven.[781] Then Albert leaned over George and asked him, "Father, is there something you'd like to say to the family—something special?" George got a smile on his lips and said, "Yes, only this: I know that my Redeemer liveth; I know that my Redeemer liveth."[782]

President George Albert Smith kept not only his testimony but maintained his concern for others until the end. When Albert and one of the nurses lifted him into a more comfortable position, he said, "Be careful; don't hurt yourself." These were his last words before he "slipped quietly into death."[783] Leaving this world on the day he'd come into it, George Albert Smith had once again shown his unique character.

779 George Albert Smith, Journal, 2 April 1951, George A. Smith papers, box 70, book 1, 918.

780 George Albert Smith, Journal, 3 April and 4 April 1951, George A. Smith papers, box 70, book 1, 918.

781 Bill Kimball, Phone Interview by Mary Jane Woodger, 15 March 2007, Salt Lake City, Utah, notes in possession of Mary Jane Woodger.

782 Robert L. Simpson, "The Powers and Responsibilities of the Priesthood," *BYU Speeches of the Year,* 31 March 1964, 7–8.

783 Gibbons, 368.

Chapter 21

HIS NAME WAS LOVE

President George Albert Smith died at 7:27 PM at 1302 Yale Avenue. As George breathed his last breath, one of his daughters said, "This is the only way father could attend conference."[784]

As soon as his death was announced, many came to George's home to offer their respects. Others showed respect for the prophet by stopping their cars and sitting in silence.[785] As the news spread, accolades and sympathy flooded George's home. President Harry S. Truman sent a telegram that stated, "The death of your father causes me great personal sorrow. He not only was my friend and the grandson of a friend of my grandfather but I looked upon him as one of our country's great moral leaders."[786] Shortly after George's passing, the doorbell of the Smith home rang. George's seven-year-old paperboy stood on the doorstep in tears. The boy said, "I've lost my best friend. Is there anything I can do?"[787] The family decided to ask the paperboy to be one of the pallbearers.[788]

Former BYU President Franklin S. Harris wrote of George, "His leadership, his broad human sympathies and his understanding of the problems of the west, led workers from all parts of the country to rally to his support and to follow his capable leadership." President Harris also noted the uplifting influence George's leadership had

784 David O. McKay, CR, April 1951, 3.

785 "News of Death Bows S. L. In Reverence," *Deseret News*, 5 April 1951, LDS Archives (Salt Lake City, UT), ms 00284.

786 Harry S. Truman to Emily Smith Stewart, 4 April 1951, George A. Smith Papers, box 102, fld 20.

787 George Albert Smith III, as related to Truman G. Madsen, cited in Madsen, 235.

788 Madsen, 235.

had: "In the presence of George Albert Smith, no one ever thought of expressing anything but the highest sentiments of which he was capable. No one would think of telling a low or vulgar story or doing anything that was not on the highest plane."[789] Irene Jones, a blind member of the Church who was undoubtedly familiar with George's work with the blind, said, "Wednesday, April 4, 1951, was a dark day in the lives of the blind, for we feel that we have lost one of the dearest friends we will ever know, one of the greatest humanitarians that ever lived. . . . He is not dead. Such men forever live in the boundless measure of the love they give."[790]

Funeral services were scheduled to be held Saturday morning, April 7, 1951, in the Tabernacle on Temple Square. A session of general conference that had been planned for that time was canceled for the funeral. George's body lay in state on Friday evening and Saturday morning in the foyer of the Church Office Building at 47 East South Temple Street, just a few hundred feet away from where George had been born.[791]

President David O. McKay opened general conference that April announcing the death of the prophet by saying,

> Though his chair is vacant this morning let us hope that the influence of his Christ-like character will pervade every heart and his high ideals be an inspiration to us all. Truly he was a noble soul, happiest when he was making others happy. In his daily life he strove sincerely to apply the teachings of Jesus to "love the Lord thy God with all thy soul, and with all thy mind, and with all thy strength . . . and thy neighbor as thyself."[792]

The funeral was conducted by President David O. McKay, who read tributes from US President Harry S. Truman, New York Governor Thomas E. Dewey, and others.[793] President McKay said that the vast congregations

789 Franklin S. Harris, unpublished manuscript, George A. Smith Papers, box 100.

790 Anderson, 112.

791 "Services Bring Change in Conference Schedule," *Deseret News*, vol. 335, no. 5, 5 April 1951, LDS Archives (Salt Lake City, UT), ms 00379.

792 David O. McKay, CR, April 1951, 3.

793 Pusey, 360.

crowding the different buildings and the thousands listening on the radio were saying to George Albert Smith, "'The love you have shown to your fellow men is reciprocated fourfold.' It is hard for us to express that love, but this is one manifestation of it, for truly the love you have given throughout your life is reciprocated in our hearts for you and we pray for power to emulate your example throughout our lives." President McKay went on to say that George had "lived as nearly as it is humanly possible for a man to live a Christ-like life. He found that the answer to the yearning of the human heart for fullness lies in living outside oneself by love. President George Albert Smith proved the truth of Christ's paradoxical saying, 'He that will lose his life for my sake, shall find it.'"[794]

Elder Matthew Cowley also expressed his love and admiration for President George Albert Smith at the conference:

> The kindest, the most generous, the most appreciative, the most considerate, the most forgiving, the most loving neighbor I have ever known has passed on. . . .
>
> President George Albert Smith had a creed. To those of us who knew him, it is not necessary to read that creed because his life was the creed. All of us who knew him could have written his creed. What an achievement! . . .
>
> To be in his presence was to be healed, if not physically, then indeed spiritually. . . .
>
> Men like this never die. He is an eternal being. God attracts the godly, and I am sure that the shortest journey this man of God ever made in all of his travels has been the journey which he has just taken. God is love. George Albert Smith is love.[795]

As a fitting tribute to the man who saw all as children of God, one of the speakers, nonmember John F. Fitzpatrick, said, "He was a man without guile, a religious man and a spiritual leader, not only in his own Church—in any group. Even alone with him you had a feeling of this man's spirituality."[796]

---

794 David O. McKay, George Albert Smith Funeral, *Deseret News*, vol. 335, no. 11, 11 April 1951, 10.

795 Matthew Cowley, George Albert Smith Funeral, *Church News*, vol. 335, no. 11, 11 April 1951, 12.

796 F. Fitzpatrick, George Albert Smith Funeral, *Church News, Deseret News*, vol. 335, no. 11, 11 April 1951, 13.

The most succinct statement was made by George's First Counselor, President J. Reuben Clark, who said: "It has been properly suggested that his real name was Love. . . . I think no man that we have ever had in the Church had a greater love for humanity than President George Albert Smith. . . . He gave his love to all."[797]

Ten Catholic priests stood on the steps of their church in respect for the deceased leader; "as the funeral cortege passed the Catholic cathedral on Third East in Salt Lake City, the cathedral bells pealed their salute to a great friend."[798] In death, as in life, George was surrounded by family. His body was laid to rest next to Lucy's. Not far away were the graves of his father, John Henry Smith; his grandfather George A. Smith; and his great-grandfather Uncle John Smith, along with the graves of their wives and children.[799]

A few years later, in honor of George's ninetieth birthday, George's son, Albert, dedicated a monument at his father's grave. In the dedicatory prayer, Albert reminisced about his father's life:

> As we reflect on the life of George Albert Smith, we associate immediately with it and with him, many of the virtues, the insights, the principles of life in which he had unflinching faith, and which he exemplified with uncommon success:
>
> His own boundless and timeless love: his belief in the universal need for love, and in its miraculous power.
>
> His unshakeable faith: faith in God, faith in him, faith in the Gospel, in the divine mission of Jesus Christ, faith in the church, faith in the calling and mission of Joseph Smith.
>
> His sensitivity, his humaneness, his compassion.
>
> His unfailing courtesy and good manner.
>
> His broad view of life.
>
> His ability to see the simple basic elements of situations,

797 J. Reuben Clark, George Albert Smith Funeral, *Church News, Deseret News,* vol. 335, no. 11, 11 April 1951, 10.

798 Francis M. Gibbons, *Dynamic Disciples—Prophets of God* (Salt Lake City, UT: Deseret Book, 1996), 195; and George Albert Smith V (Morris Plains, NJ), Phone Interview by Mary Jane Woodger, 16 Aug. 2007, transcription in possession of Mary Jane Woodger.

799 Gibbons, 370.

and to view them in perspective.

His sense of humor, constructive and always in good taste.

His understanding of human nature; its potential strength, and its almost inevitable weakness.

His understanding of Thy nature, Lord, and of Thy purposes.

His curiosity about everything, his pursuit of truth, and his devotion to it. And his belief that all truths wherever or however learned are of equal importance and validity, be they discovered truths or revealed truths.

His humility.

His abhorrence of sham, and of pretense.

His guilelessness.

The pureness of his thoughts and motives.

His love of beauty as seen in Thy creations, and in the creations of man.

His tolerance.

His fairness: his insistence that the rights of others be observed, their viewpoints be respected.

His ability to combine energeticness with patience and with calmness.

His outward serenity: when pressed by personal sorrow, disappointment or perplexity, or when dealing with the fears, anger or conflicts of others.

His conviction that there is goodness and usefulness in all men; and that it is our unavoidable challenge to discover them and to release them—in ourselves and in others.

His willingness to trust and to rely on others in positions to which he had called or assigned them.

His belief that forgiveness and rehabilitation are to be preferred over punishment and ostracism.

His capacity to rejoice, without envy, in the achievements and success of others.

His ever-dependable loyalty: Loyalty to his family, to his friends—whatever their affiliations; to the stranger in distress; to the known and to the unknown neighbor; his

> loyalty to the church as an institution, and to its officers and members individually; his loyalty to Utah, and to America, coupled with his avoidance of provincialism.
>
> His willingness to be imposed on, rather than run the risk of unfairly hurting or injuring another.
>
> His capacity to discipline his body, his mind, and his spirit, to live the way he decided he wanted to live.
>
> And, lastly, his ability to combine in workable balance this wide compass of virtues, outlooks and talents—and still others not mentioned—and to apply them in actual and effective living, to the blessing of all of us, and to Thy Glory.
>
> As spokesman for Emily, Edith and myself, here before his grave, before this company of friends, and before Thee, I express deep gratitude, oh God, that we had the inestimable good fortune to be his children.
>
> And as spokesman for all of us here assembled today—as also for many others whose presence was prevented by limitations of time, or distance, or other circumstances, I say, "We thank Thee for his life, his teaching, his example, and his leadership.[800]

As George's children left the cemetery that day, reflecting on their father's life, they too must have felt that what he had accomplished was beyond all likelihood given his humble beginnings. George Albert Smith is now on the other side of the veil with his beloved Lucy, but here on earth, he has left a legacy of service and love. Indeed, through his example of unselfishness, his exemplary teachings, and his never-failing care for individuals everywhere, the name of George Albert Smith has become synonymous with love.

800 George Albert Smith Jr., "Dedicatory Prayer," 4 April 1960, LDS Archives (Salt Lake City, UT), ms 3379.